I0826844

ISBN: 978-1-7369574-0-0

First Printing—April 2021

FINAL FRONTIERS FOUNDATION
1200 Peachtree Street • Louisville, GA 30434
800-522-4324 • www.finalfrontiers.org

Scriptures are taken from the King James Bible.

To order additional books, contact:
www.TheGreatOmission.com

Printed and Bound in the United States

Great Commission Conundrums

Dispelling Issues that Have Long Hindered Our Fulfillment of Christ's Parting Command

By Jon Nelms
Founder of the Final Frontiers Foundation and
Touch A Life Child Rescue Centers

Endorsements

In a day when there is a dearth of writing by independent fundamental pastors and missionaries on most subjects, finding a book that stimulates and even challenges your thinking is always refreshing. Most notable is a lack of writing on the subject of missions. Yes, you may come across a few booklets here and there, but most would agree that, with the exception of biographies, real missions books in a person's library would be single digit in number.

Jon Nelms has done a service to the church, the body of Christ, with his first book, *The Great Omission*, and now with this book, *Great Commission Conundrums*. I write as one who has experienced 51 years of local church ministry and 40 of those as a senior pastor. I've been privileged to pastor in a foreign country and make multiple missions trips to multiple countries of the world generally for a month or more at a time. For over 20 years and at present, I am in contact with missionaries monthly. Missions has been and still is an important part of my life. For over a decade, I have known Jon Nelms, and his accomplishments in missions are legendary when you consider what one man's vision and burden has accomplished worldwide.

In my opinion, this book should be read by all missionaries, pastors, mission boards, mission committees, teachers of missions in Bible colleges and all who love biblical missions and missionaries. Jon does not write from theory but from practical, firsthand experience on mission fields worldwide. This book poses questions many have considered but few have answered sufficiently—if at all. This book dissects problems of both missionaries and pastors, then supplies suggestions and answers to these conundrums. Quite simply, this book makes you think. What a concept!

You may not agree with all of Jon's conclusions; it's a free country, and you are entitled to your opinion. Jon doesn't ask you to agree, but don't be so high and mighty as to knock a man who has taken the time and effort to put into print a resource that can help all who are involved in missions. I would encourage you to read it more than once, meditate on areas that you may not have contemplated or that you may initially disagree with. Really think about it.

The fact that Jon has been a student of missions most of his saved life oozes from his writings and conversations. I've been with him on the mission field, and I have seen his compassion for reaching people with the gospel, helping national pastors and caring for the poor and starving. He lives among people in a very modest at best room—not in a compound in an upper-class neighborhood in a foreign land surrounded by other American missionaries. I have seen him slandered and taken advantage of by those in whom he invested time, resources, money, knowledge, and housing without complaint or retaliation.

What you will read in these pages has been learned and honed in the "arena of faith." You will be blessed and educated on the needful and practical subject of missions. I believe the cause of Christ will be bettered by this book and God's servants will be bettered by digesting the advice given and implementing many of its concepts.

– Don Ohm, *Retired Pastor*
Lighthouse Baptist Church
San Antonio, Texas
Author, Cool Waters to Thirsty Souls

If the title "Mr. Missions" was given to anyone during the last century, it would go to Jon Nelms. His latest book not only exposes Jon's passion for missions but reveals his tremendous insight on how to make it work biblically. After preaching for 58 years and serving as a missionary for 30 years, I have never read a more challenging book on what biblical missionaries are. I studied missions in two Baptist universities and two Baptist seminaries and never heard an accurate description of biblical missions like this.

If this book is justly exposed in Baptist colleges and seminaries, it will do more to win our world to Christ than any previous book written. I recommend it to pastors, mission classes, missionaries and persons wanting to understand what the Bible says about how to fulfill the Great Commission.

– Dr. M. Dennis Ellis, *Founding Pastor*
Living Grace Ministries, St. Petersburg, Russia
Founder & Director, Open Light Ministries
Professor, Southern Baptist Seminary Extension

Dedication

To those who give, to those who go, and to those who dream of doing so. May your eternity be a delightful reminder of all you did while you could.

And to those who made it possible for me to have this life as a missionary—my parents, siblings, mentors, supporters, friends, and most of all, my most precious family.

A Word of Explanation from the Author

Conundrums are the hurdles in our race to complete the Great Commission. They can make you run slower or trip you, so the race is never finished. Thus, the ideal solution is to remove the hurdles altogether.

A *conundrum* is a "confusing and difficult problem or question," which is often a roadblock to progress until and unless it is confronted and resolved.

Over the centuries, many such puzzling issues have thwarted the Great Commission's fulfillment.

In this book, I hope to address four primary categories, which in my opinion, have done damage to our efforts of fulfilling the Lord's direct mandate.

These *Great Commission Conundrums* are regarding financing, policy, accountability, and philosophy. And while this book primarily addresses their relationship to missionaries and churches (the pastors and leaders thereof), it is also written to apply to individuals and families who consider themselves Great Commission Christians and who want to do their part to see its fulfillment in their lifetime.

– Jon Nelms

Table of Contents

Section Two: Great Commission Conundrums Regarding Policy

Section Three: Great Commission Conundrums Regarding Accountability

Section Four: Great Commission Conundrums Regarding Philosophy

Foreword

I have traveled with Jon Nelms multiple times around the globe, watching and learning missions in action. I observed souls saved and baptized, churches started and preachers/pastors encouraged and educated from his dedication. In the beginning years of Final Frontier Foundation, working with nationals was not popular in America. Yet God is not running a popularity contest; HE chooses the foolish things of the world to confound the wise; and the weak things of the world to confound the things which are mighty.

I took my first missions trip in 1984. Through the years my heart has been stirred as I met the people and saw the dedication of national pastors all around this world. I saw the little that a pastor had in material things and the great need of the gospel. For more than twenty-five years I have traveled abroad preaching, working, observing, encouraging and then reporting back to Tabernacle Baptist Church in Orlando, Florida, where I pastor.

In 1997 because of the work of my ministry in India, I was asked to attend a meeting concerning a national Indian pastor. There I met Jon Nelms by happenstance, but little did we know our meeting was in the providence of God. Our paths crossed again in India in 1999, and we traveled to a few locations together. I marveled at how God had His hand on Jon in his preaching and leadership style, in his efforts to meet the needs of the people and give direction to the pastors.

As you read this book, I pray the Lord will give you "nuggets" that you will want to share with others. Dr. Nelms looks at missions and the challenges from his education and great experiences from all over the world. May you too see the need for the Word of God, the preaching of the gospel, the hungry children, the weak and the base of this world, and may you have a desire to reach them. May your heart be fired not only to "come and see" but to "go and tell."

Those who have had the opportunity to see Bro. Jonny in action, see his heart and love for the souls of men. I pray that you will get a glimpse of his desire as you read and also that your view of missions will be from a godly, global, giving and going perspective.

– Dr. Steve A. Ware, *Pastor*
Tabernacle Baptist Church
Orlando, Florida

PREFACE

IN MY FIRST book, *The Great Omission*, I endeavored to expose what, in my opinion, were the primary causes for the body of Christ to have never fulfilled the Great Commission. I addressed how we had abandoned and ultimately forgotten the definition of the terms *missionary* and *mission field* and had substituted our conceptions for God's plan. Today, most people still think that a missionary is someone who looks like them and goes to preach to those who do not look like them. Or they think a missionary is someone who goes to another place to evangelize other than where they live.

Thus, if someone from the mainland USA goes to Hawaii to pastor a church, he is considered a "missionary"; however, if a Hawaiian minister pastors a church in Hawaii, he is not considered a pastor (unless he is trying to raise support for that purpose. Then he calls himself a *missionary* because churches will support missionaries but not pastors.). The same illogicality is true in other metro areas such as Atlanta, Chicago, Miami, etc. If you want financial support, call yourself a "missionary."

I contended that being a missionary is a calling of God with a specific job requirement. It is not to be a pastor in a foreign land but rather to be a church planter in any land (or area) unexposed or barely exposed to the gospel.

The missionary Paul, our primary biblical example of the position, never ministered in a land that was not under Roman control; thus, he never left his "country" (empire). Although he certainly had to deal with different cultures and even languages in each location, he could always rely on the empire's culture and language as a foundation for his activities and teaching.

The missionary Paul never pastored a church. He may have worn that hat for a short time, but he shared it with Barnabas, Silas, Timothy, Titus, Philemon, Aristarchus, and others—even an occasional Demas. His job was to evangelize and plant the church, train disciples, appoint pastors, and move on to the next target (taking some of his companions with him and leaving others behind as the shepherd/pastor to care for the congregation).

Paul stayed in Corinth several years but was in Thessalonica for only three weeks before moving on. He understood what he was there to do and did it, and then he moved on. The more help he had, the more quickly he could move on. My contention remains that a missionary is a Pauline church planter—not a sedentary or appointed pastor, as per James's example.

I believe we should send out missionaries who fit the calling's biblical pattern and discourage men from going who merely intend to move abroad and pastor an already established congregation. Such men are not missionaries; they are foreign pastors ministering in a foreign land. Theirs is an honorable service to God; it is just not missions. Thus, let that local church pay for its pastor as we do here in America. That, too, is a biblical pattern.

However, an argument arises regarding this pattern: a foreigner who is a "pastor" cannot receive a salary because he has a "missionary" visa and not a "work" visa. Thus, he must receive support from America and not a local congregation. I will address this conundrum in this book.

I wrote *The Great Omission* after having garnered twenty-five years' experience in missions. I could have written it sooner but felt that it would be more difficult for my positions to be dismissed without consideration since I had decades of experience. At that time and even today, the "typical" faith-based missionary (one who has to raise support rather than being a denominational employee with a salary) had a ministry life span of fewer than six years. Consider this fact: a staggering 55 percent of all the missionaries who made it through their first four-year term and returned to the States for "furlough" never returned to their mission field again. Sadly, an even higher percentage never made it to their first furlough, quitting within the first three years of service.

In my mind, having served for twenty-five years at that time, I was somewhat of an expert on the subject, if not an enigma, and was qualified to say many things others wanted to, but were refrained by their connection to a mission board. Some critics suggested that I was "anti-missionary," but the missionaries didn't feel that way. They appreciated that I had exposed the failures of today's missions' methods and had offered a solution.

Since that time, many missionaries have contacted me, saying, "*Before I read your book, I thought I was a missionary, now I realize I am not. I'm just a pastor, and that is not what God called me to be.*" Since that time, most of these have become biblical missionaries, freeing themselves from obligation to a single congregation and reaching out to plant new churches and disciple new converts. The book has been widely used in Bible institutes worldwide and has been translated into Spanish and is currently available in several other languages.

I am encouraged that others in the past grasped the same truth that affected my life and ministry and, by doing so, began earlier mission-movements that have changed the world. Men like the Wesley brothers, Taylor, and Wycliffe are recent examples.

My primary purpose in life since 1986 has been to educate American churches to the works of national missionaries in other lands and to motivate them to help fund these men for a fraction of what it costs to send an individual missionary like me.

When I began this ministry, I am not sure the term "national preacher" had yet been coined. I was called a traitor for seeking to "steal" American money to give to foreign preachers. I could hardly find a single church in America that was supporting a national preacher. But within twenty years, I could scarcely find a church in America that was *not* supporting national preachers. I was not the only one God had awakened to this concept of supporting the nationals. Even Paul did it, and the apostle John endorsed it. Yet the centuries had somehow deluded Europeans and Americans into thinking that only they could be entrusted to carry the gospel to the nations. Was it spiritual pride or a satanic delusion? Whichever, this conundrum is now eradicated from our thoughts.

Recently I was reading about Hudson Taylor, the great missionary of the past century. Why was he great? Because his efforts force-fed us to accept a reality that we had overlooked. In his day and previous to him, missionaries lived and served in coastal cities, rarely venturing inland. Early British and American missionaries, by example, taught that missionaries should target the expatriates living in the coastal seaport towns, and while doing so, reach the nationals as well. Paul somewhat established this practice, not geographically but practically, in that when entering a city, he seemed first to target the Jews and then reach out to the Gentiles.

In modern-day missions, William Carey followed this example. Some would argue he established it. Carey did this ingeniously by use of business, printing, and education of the more impoverished people. He used the tithes of the expatriates to finance it.

Taylor did it radically by abandoning the European lifestyle and dress and taking on himself the appearance of the Chinese coolie (lower class). He moved out of the missionary compound and into a Chinese boarding house, dressed like them, ate like them, learned to talk like them, traveled like them, and even grew a pigtail like them. And for this, he was fired by his mission board. Yet, to this day, no one recalls the name of a single board executive who fired him, but everyone knows the name and fame of Hudson Taylor. He spent his life training the nationals to leave the coast and go into China's interior, where the masses lived. His new organization, which was appropriately called China Inland Mission, was emulated all around the world and is what made him great—not just because of what he did, but what he encouraged and enabled others to do.

Incidentally, Taylor once commented that the biggest mistake he made in his ministry was encouraging young men and women from Britain to join him in his work. He felt they only enlisted for an opportunity to work with him (the great and famous missionary). Generally, within six months in China, they wanted to quit, having wasted all the time and energy spent training them. Typically, within a few months, they felt qualified to tell Taylor everything he was doing wrong and how they, having no experience, would do it. They would then leave him to start their own works that generally failed. Others like James O. Fraser succeeded triumphantly. I borrowed some of his policies of accountability to establish those of Final Frontiers.

I can attest to Taylor's comment as being the greatest mistake I have made as well. But I do thank God for the few that came, remained, and have flourished. I have learned not to attempt to recruit but to allow God to send me those He has chosen to walk beside me and share my yoke.

In reading further, I discovered something amazing. Upon his death, Taylor and the Chinese men he trained, his Timothies, had started 49 churches. From those, no doubt thousands of others have been started. I have even met men in Southeast Asia who trace their spiritual lineage back to Hudson Taylor, who led their great-great-grandfather to Christ. Our men tell stories of entering unmapped, jungle villages that already had the gospel and found that decades earlier, a Chinese evangelist had passed through and converted them. All of this harks back to the work and the legacy of Hudson Taylor.

I am no Hudson Taylor; I couldn't hold a candle to him. However, the preachers we fund have already started over 350,000 churches. The tireless efforts of 28,000+ preachers in our network, documented by our global staff in their quarterly report forms, give evidence to that outreach.

If you are interested in learning more about our ministry and how you can help us support more of these men through our Great Commission Fund, please visit our website at www.FinalFrontiers.world or contact our office at info@finalfrontiers.org or you may reach me directly at jnelms@finalfrontiers.org.

I don't want to rehash my entire ministry philosophy and history here, but I hope to encourage you to dig deeper and perhaps partner with us in this cause.

Now, ten years after writing *The Great Omission* and after 35 years as a missionary, I feel that I have gained the right to address other issues that have hindered the completion of the Great Commission. I call these issues conundrums because a conundrum is a complicated question or issue. Since these issues remain, I want to expose them, analyze them, and expunge them from the ever-shrinking list of topics that keep us from doing what He commissioned us to do. In every generation, we are to go into all the world and preach the gospel to every ethnic group (nation).

The Great Commission is not an option or an opportunity; it is an *obligation* of all devoted disciples to both fulfill and maintain in each generation until our Lord returns. In my teen years, my pastor and mentor was Curtis Hutson, and I was privileged to spend a great deal of time with him and his family and even serve briefly on his staff. Of all the principles he taught me, this one, his version of Edward Everett Hale's famous quote, made the most significant impact: "I am not everybody, but I am somebody. I cannot do everything, but I can so do something, and what I can do I must do, and with God's help, I will."

I hope you will enjoy examining and resolving the following conundrums—just try not to become one!

Introduction

Don't kid yourself. Like any other calling or endeavor in life, missions, though seemingly tranquil on the surface, is riddled with twists and turns, dead ends, and potholes. The farther down the road we get without addressing these problems, the more damage we do to our transport and the less likely we are to reach our intended destination.

Two essential travelers are on this journey—the missionary and the supporting donor. Whether it be a friend, a family member, or a church, both assume they are traveling on the same route and both believe the other is living up to his expectations (though they may have never been clearly defined). I intend to do a deep dive into each of the conundrums as they apply to missionaries and the supporting churches. I must admit that when I say churches, I will, for the most part, be speaking to the pastors who lead the churches. I hope I have also written in a manner making each topic interesting and compelling to the laymen consumed with missions.

Thus, to solve each conundrum of missions so that we all arrive at our destination safely, successfully, and on time, we need in each case to take the following steps:

Explaining the Conundrum

To *explain* means "to make a subject plain, to manifest it, or make it intelligible." Explaining is the act of defining the conundrum. Doing so will answer the question:

- *What is the problem?*

Examining the Conundrum

To *examine* is "to elaborate on the subject in greater detail." Doing this may involve giving its history, background, use, and of course, the logic of both sides of the issue. This step will help us determine:

- *What is the cause(s)?*

Exposing the Conundrum

This process logically and scripturally resolves the various points of the conundrum, thus rendering it from being a conundrum with a debatable or unreachable conclusion to that of being a simple question. The process involved in accomplishing this is to determine:

- *What are the possible solutions?*
- *What is the best solution?*

Eliminating the Conundrum

By employing this term, I hope to present the solution in a manner in which it can be accomplished, applied, or put into use. Saying your destination is at these specific GPS points is one thing, but another is to give instructions on the route to drive, the turns to make, etc. In this final step, I will share my opinions based on experience, while realizing that the readers may also have their own experiences that are more acceptable to their current situation.

In other words, we may all agree on the destination but have differing opinions on the best route to take. This final hurdle of each conundrum involves the consideration of:

- *What steps should be taken to reach the solution?*

As a fellow missionary seeking to help others, I will be happy to hear from the readers any suggestions or solutions they may have for these conundrums. I will also be delighted to hear of any other problems you may want to share or to be addressed in the future.

My understanding of the biblical requirements of a missionary has been shaped over decades. It's not that I invented new requirements but instead became aware of those the Bible had already given us. Over time, I carry less and less baggage from my upbringing and teachings on missions. I no longer accept that we should continue doing things the way we always have. Instead, we should question the norms that have locked us into an unsuccessful pattern of missions for two centuries and return to the original way of doing missions—God's way.

As you read through these conundrums, keep in mind that I have tried to group them in logical sections and that there may be some degree of repetition as a thought, or a principle may relate to more than one subject. I produced the bones of each chapter over five years and now have added the meat. Therefore, you may see patterns or even some replication of principle or philosophy. You may want to read this not as a novel from start to end but as a series of questions and answers. Thus, some topics will overlap.

From time to time, I will make statistical references. Unless otherwise noted, they are from a survey sent to well-known Independent Baptist Mission Boards, of which twenty-three responded and were published online by Missionary Gil Anger around 2010. Gil was an example for all missionaries to emulate, having served God on seven continents and was perhaps the most successful missionary recruiter of our generation.

Gil and I shared a common belief in the nobility of being a missionary, as well as a common concern over what seems to be a diminishing faithfulness and lack of sturdiness in the call. I last saw Gil while in Burma in December 2016 with my wife Nolin and Joshua Martyn, who was influenced by Gil. Meeting his newest missions' partner, sharing a meal and spending a few hours with my last mentor was a blessing. Both his son and his daughter serve as missionaries to this day. He passed away in his homeland of Australia in December 2020, survived by his wife Joy, who was a devoted missionary wife. *See you soon, my friend.*

I have addressed these conundrums, hoping to educate churches, donors, and missionaries on the biblical principles of missions. Whenever necessary, I intend to reprove unbiblical methods, exhort those attempting to be their best for Christ, and encourage those who feel they are lacking. Keep in mind that we all are.

As you get started, remember that I am writing from my perspective as a missionary with thirty-five years of experience, having worked with and counseled thousands of missionaries in eighty-plus countries. I have learned a lot from Him and them that I hope to share with you.

SECTION ONE

Great Commission Conundrums Regarding FINANCING

A mountain village of the Lisu tribe

#1
Is It Ever Legitimate to Drop the Support of a Missionary (American or National)?

Explaining the Conundrum

Churches and even families sometimes feel it necessary to suspend a missionary's support, but they struggle with the decision. As hard as it is for a missionary to get support committed from a church, once achieved, churches are reluctant to suspend that support under any reason. Their missionary support has become "the sacred calf" that dare not be touched—even though they would dismiss their pastor or church staff for the same cause. Is this sound practice?

Examining the Conundrum

Let's get serious. Many pastors are unhappy with some of the missionaries their church supports and would like to curtail their support but feel guilty even thinking of doing so, knowing it will hurt the missionary and offend some of their church members.

Thus, they endure continual ministry inactivity and/or a lack of regular communication with the church for years. Letters that do arrive speak much about illness, family trips, and birthdays but little about souls saved, churches started, and preachers trained. Pastors grapple with the assumption that it is "wrong" to drop a missionary's support, as if he has an inherent right to their funding, even if he is not producing results. Admittedly, if a staff member were not fulfilling his duties after confrontation, he would be quickly and justly dismissed without question, but doing the same to a missionary is a pill too large to swallow.

Before I respond to this conundrum, keep in mind that until a little over a hundred years ago, missionaries were not typically supported as they are today. Most were funded by their board (as many still are), while others worked with their hands to pay their own expenses. Whatever they received was a welcome blessing but not enough to provide a full-time income. Paul, for example, was a tentmaker. Having such a profession allowed him to meet other tentmakers like Aquila and Priscilla, dye merchants like Lydia, and no doubt many other tradesmen and craftsmen, not to mention wholesalers and customers.

When the modern-day missionary emphasis began two centuries ago, the first missionaries emulated his pattern. William Carey owned businesses and factories. Missionary friends of Adoniram Judson served as translators and government liaisons. Moravian missionaries sold themselves as slaves, allowing them to live and work on the sugar cane plantations of the Caribbean, giving them access to the slaves living there. They also started what became the largest shipping company in the world.

In the past five or ten decades, we missionaries have gone from *hoping* churches will support us to *expecting* them to do so. Churches, in some circles, now gain recognition over the volume of their missionary support. What "their" missionaries are doing or what they have accomplished is far less important than how many they support. Many churches exaggerate their missionary fervor's appearance by giving a smaller amount of support to a higher number of missionaries. And, of course, we missionaries are happy for any amount of support you give us.

Most Missionaries Will Admit to These Two Points:

1) It is hard to get a church to support you. Typically, a missionary will only get support from about 30 to 50 percent of the churches

he visits, so he has to present his ministry to several hundred churches to raise enough support to meet the board-recommended $5,000 to $8,000 monthly support. For your information, most churches will pledge (but not necessarily give) between $50 and $400 monthly to support a missionary family, and it will be one of the 50 to 100 churches that support that family. By contrast, our Final Frontiers national preachers receive between $25 and $200 for full support; any additional funding must come by teaching their church members to take care of their pastors and preachers.

2) It is rare for a church to drop a missionary's support once they begin it. (Hallelujah!) However, this policy is changing now as more pastors demand reports from those they fund and drop support if they don't hear from the missionary. Still, most pastors realize how hard it is for a missionary on the field to replace lost support and that the missionary will have to wait until furlough to return home to acquire more, so they are hesitant to drop him until his feet are on his home soil.

Exposing the Conundrum

Perhaps I am in a unique position to address this subject in that while pastoring, I supported missionaries and was at times faced with this problem. Now, and for the past thirty-five years, I have received support as a missionary, serving as the leader of Final Frontiers. As such, I certainly understand both the caution and concern in dropping the support of a servant of God. For that reason, we have established policies that, on the one hand, safeguard their support, while on the other, demands the cessation of it.

Over the years, we have dropped more than a thousand national preachers for various reasons. The most common reasons other than death was that they no longer needed our help. For others, it was because of a change in ministry (we only support biblical missionaries = church planters). For others, it was a change in life (too old or too sick, etc.) or sometimes, though rarely, a change in doctrine. However, most were defunded because they refused or were inconsistent in reporting their activities to their sponsor. Our unmovable standard is "No report, no support," and its enforcement works well.

I realize that no church is under obligation to support me or any other missionary, yet each church is under a biblical mandate to do its part to fulfill the Great Commission. Thus, logically, every church's responsibility is to give while, at the same time, realizing they are stewards of God's money and will be held accountable for how it was utilized. Stewardship may be a noun, but steward is a verb, requiring action.

Some churches wrongly feel it is their job to give, and then it is between God and the missionary how the funds are used. I respectfully disagree. If you buy a hamburger and the server gives you raw meat or no bun, you don't eat it; you confront the manager and get a proper replacement or a refund.

Giving is giving, but stewardship is administration. Let me explain. Stewardship is not simply spending money; instead, it uses it wisely and with accountability, clearly demonstrating that it accomplished the desired and expected results. (And if they were not, an explanation is required detailing why not.) Stewardship then is a coin with two sides. One side is the giving, and the other is the administration of the gift with proper accountability.

Good stewardship demands the giver verify that the Lord's money, which was given is used for the Lord's causes, for which it was given. Though the giving may benefit the giver with God's blessings and heavenly rewards, the real purpose of the giving is not to receive a blessing but to multiply, expand, and enhance *the steward's efforts*—not simply to benefit the receiver. Thus, the giver should give wisely, prudently, and with the expectation and evidence of results. He should seek to invest God's funding into ministries and ministers that are the most productive (and accountable) for the kingdom, not those who have the best personality, the prettiest wife, or the cutest, most well-behaved children. And it is certainly not for those who have the best "tear-jerking" story to tell at every church they visit.

As a ministry, we support those who had produced abundant spiritual fruit without significant help before we came along. I believed that if a man accomplishes great works for God because it is in his heart to do so, he will accomplish much, much more with a little funding.

Now back to the "contract." There are written contracts and verbal contracts, but every contract, like every coin, has two sides (except the contract/covenant/testament God made with us where Christ does the work, and we receive His finished work as a free gift of grace). In short, the two sides of any contract are: I will do this, and you will do this.

Contracts have reasonable expectations from both sides. The missionary expects the church to give as pledged and on time as committed. If that becomes impossible, he should at least be informed as much in advance as possible. If the church's offerings are too low, they should not abandon promised support. It would be better for the church to seek out and put aside some unnecessary fluff in the budget than to abandon the servant of God doing God's work, whom the church has committed to support. Nothing says you will support the missionary except your word, and that should be enough. With your mouth, you made a commitment that is as valid as your obligation to pay your staff, your utility bill, and your church mortgage. You willingly committed, now fulfill it, or at least ask his permission to break the contract.

On the flip side, the church (should, must, better) expect a certain amount of productivity or commitment from the missionary. If he is not fulfilling his side of the deal, then he, not you, has already canceled the contract.

From time to time, we hear from a concerned sponsor because they have not received any reports from the national preacher being supported. When I look into it, we often find that the sponsor has not only failed to fulfill their monthly commitment but has not given in a year or more. The missionary or national preacher should not be obligated to report to someone who is not supporting them. Still, they should be required to report to anyone and everyone who is. And as a missionary, may I point out that I have seen my family's prayer cards and letters displayed on many church walls that do not support us now and some that never have. The members think they do, but the pastor knows they don't. That duplicity isn't ethical.

Supporters should expect and demand more than just a letter, an email, or a Facebook entry. They should want some meat on the bones of the report. Let me be brutally candid about this: if a missionary is sending you a report and habitually does not mention leading someone to Christ, discipling a new convert, training a young man for ministry, or starting a church, then there is likely only one reason—he hasn't been doing it. I recommend you drop his support.

You are supporting him with the reasonable expectation that performance and results are expected. If there are none, then he is either sadly incapable or incredibly lazy. You have to determine what you expect from the missionary as each field is different, and some produce fruit slower than others. As a supporting church, you should let the missionary know when his support will begin and exactly what you expect from him. If he does not fulfill your support requirement, you are wrong to continue giving it to him. You are encouraging laziness and indifference, and it will metastasize to other missionaries. (Frankly, it already has.)

The bottom line is that you should treat him as you treat any other person serving in your church. If your music director fails to lead the singing, organize specials, etc., you replace him. If your youth pastor never has activities, the youth group does not grow, and he never visits, you replace him. Likewise, if you have a missionary who is not doing what you expect a missionary to do, replace him, and don't feel guilty about it. Remember, you are a steward; your calling is not to support him; it is to support missions. By continuing his support, you have failed in your calling. Keep that up too long, and maybe the Lord will be replacing you with a better steward.

A final thought: the first missionaries we read of were Paul and Barnabas. Their hard work and success drew many a new convert to them. In fact, we have no idea how many. We do know was that it was enough that, in a very short period of time, they had "turned the world upside down." Paul declared that he was moving to Spain because, in the entire region of Greece/Turkey, there was no place where the gospel had not already been preached (either by Paul or one of his disciples or one of his disciple's disciples). As a missionary (church planter), Paul needed to move on because where Christ is named, you need a *pastor.* Where Christ is unknown and unnamed, you need a *missionary.*

One of Paul's first assistants was a young man named John Mark, the nephew of Barnabas. After spending time with him in ministry, Paul determined that he would no longer work with John Mark. Though Demas later abandoned Paul for the world's pleasures, Paul dismissed John Mark (dropped his support because Paul personally financed the men serving with him) because he was considered unworthy. He was too young, too homesick, and his work was negatively affected by his loneliness and inabilities.

Barnabas was not a "full-time" missionary; he spent much time at home and visiting Asia's established churches. He was what Ephesians chapter four would call an *apostle* and a *prophet*. He was better suited in personality and calling to deal with a young John Mark's inadequacy and to mold him into what Paul would later call a "useful" minister whom he was desirous of having as an assistant.

Missions is not a USO performance. It is a deliberate invasion deep into hostile, enemy territory. As a missionary, Paul did not have time or resources to spend on a ministry infant. He had a job to do and a limited time in which to get it done. His laying aside John Mark caused a breach in his relationship with Barnabas, but it also resulted in the potential of taking the gospel to twice as many regions simultaneously.

Paul "dropped" John Mark for a time so that he could receive more training from Barnabas and live to serve with him another day. Dropping a missionary could be just the impetus that a young (or old) man needs to awaken him up to his calling.

Eliminating the Conundrum

Suggestions for Missionaries:

How to Keep From Being Dropped by a Supporting Church

- Fully explain to the churches not what you hope to do but what you have already been doing. An abundance of young, inexperienced missionaries say they will go plant a church in another land but have never planted one in their own land, culture, or country. That progression is not logical. Nobody wants a heart surgeon who plans to do well or a pilot who intends to be successful; we want experienced veterans. So too, if you are going to call yourself a missionary (church planter) when you have never qualified as one, you are misleading and deceiving yourself and the churches from which you ask for support. If that is you, then be honest about it. Tell them where you are going, who you will work with, and how that veteran has agreed to help you become a successful, lifelong missionary, and what you have already done to prepare.

- Have substance in the letters to your supporters—both churches and families. The letter's purpose is not simply to make a mandatory connection but to help the pastor encourage his members in giving to and going as missionaries. You are his partner; help him out. Show the churches how you are making progress in your journey as a missionary, so they will know they are good stewards by supporting you.

- Talk a little about family; after all, your supporters love you but remember they have fellow members in their church who have forgotten you or never met you. They don't care if your cat died, if you're taking a family vacation or if the fuel price has gone up. Tell them what YOU are accomplishing because of THEIR support.

- Don't promote the work of national pastors or other missionaries as if it is your work. Be sure to "give honor to whom honor is due." It's a small world, and you don't want to become known as one who exaggerates your efforts. Many national pastors think missionaries are foreign preachers who come to visit with a camera, take pictures of their converts, their baptisms, their facilities, their schools, and then return to America, using the pictures to raise support for themselves. They resent that the support is not shared with them because their works were photographed. Why do you suppose missionaries have that reputation? Because it's true.

- Remember, if you don't take the time to report, those who have committed to support you have no reason to take the time to write you a check. You are in a contract with every church that supports you. Live up to the terms and expectations of the contract. In the past, doing so required missionaries to write and post letters. Now all you have to do is type a Facebook post, attach a picture or video and send it off to everyone, all at once, free. If you can't do that at least every quarter, you are either lazy, ignorant of the need, or an absolute waste of good support.

Suggestions for Churches:

How Can You Keep From Having to Drop the Support of a Missionary?

- Do not commit 100 percent of the pledged mission support as some members will fail you, and others will lose their jobs or move away. Better to commit to 70 percent, and if you have funds left at the end of the year, you can use them to help with a special mission project, send members or staff on a mission trip, or have an emergency buffer for the next year.

- Determine what you expect of a missionary, put it on paper, have the missionary sign it, and give him a copy. If he wavers in the expectations, use it to remind him. If he does not heed the reminder, then he has broken the contract. Drop his support with a clear conscience. He knew his responsibility, and (hopefully) you gave him a fair warning and perhaps a chance to improve.

- Make a distinction between foreign missions and home-based ministries like prisons, tract ministries, anti-abortion, and other worthy and needy causes that you want to help. Remember that simply because a need is worthy of support does not mean it is *missions.* Otherwise, why not pay your utility bill from your missions' account? Remember that biblically, *missions* means "taking the gospel to those where Christ is unknown and planting churches, training pastors, and moving on to repeat the process." In making this distinction, you could perhaps classify them as *foreign missions* and *outreach ministries*. That being done, determine what percentage of your giving will go to missions and what percentage will go to outreach ministries. In this way, you will not accidentally tip too far in either direction. Many, if not most American churches, give over half of their "missions funds" to causes in the USA, i.e., children's homes, Bible colleges, legal services, pastors' fellowships, Christian schools, etc., all of which are worthy and needy *ministries* but are **not** *missions*. Good intentions will not fulfill the Great Commission.

- Have fail-safe protocols such as "No report, no support." Watch for patterns of failing results in their activity while recognizing that some fields are more challenging than others. If you see patterns develop, i.e., no souls saved, no converts baptized or being discipled and/or no new house churches begun, then you have to ask yourself (and the missionary), "What is he doing?" (Even in Middle Eastern lands, our men produce fruit.) The reality is, if you have to drop their support, it is because they left you no other choice. They dropped themselves.

We know that you get what you go after. You receive what you ask and seek for. A missionary who is not producing "fruit that remains" is not yet equipped to be a missionary. He may need more training and a better understanding of his calling. He may be a John Mark who needs a Barnabas. Help him but don't continue supporting a non-producing branch of the vine.

- Any changes you make to your policies should be forwarded to those you support so they can adapt, examine their compliance capabilities, and have an opportunity to strengthen their relationship with your church rather than losing it.

#2
Is the Purpose of Giving to Missions to Support the Messenger or the Message?

Explaining the Conundrum

A dear friend, who is one of the most missions-minded pastors I have ever known, recently shared a story with me. He stated that he had to drop a missionary in a particular country because he was leaving. He wanted to know if we had anyone serving there so he could transfer the support to that missionary. He additionally stated that he was supporting that missionary family only because they were serving in that particular country. It seems that he had a particular burden for that particular land and the peoples that inhabit it. In this case, their intention had not been to support the messenger (missionary) but was instead to fund the proclamation of the message in that country. And as the missionary was now removing his ministry from that land, my friend wanted to end their support relationship.

Examining the Conundrum

Many missionaries have confessed that after serving on a field for some time, they begin to feel a burden to move elsewhere. When they inform their supporting churches of their intention, a percentage of them drop their support. They hear statements like, "If you don't know where God wants you, then we don't want to support you." As you can imagine, this reaction is very frustrating to the man seeking to follow God's will. It is also financially crippling at a time when he needs extra funding to finance the move.

Churches with this mentality presume that God never redirects a missionary to another ministry or country. They are wrong. The irony of this reasoning is that the pastors of supporting churches who drop a missionary for moving fields have often pastored in several different churches and even in several states. They would undoubtedly claim that God directed their moves. Why should a missionary changing his field be any different? If moving is acceptable for a pastor, it should be acceptable for a missionary. This is especially true when you consider that most "missionaries" are not truly missionaries (church planters) but are pastors in a foreign land.

In that situation, the problem for that particular church was that the missionary had not produced any national fruit to take over his ministry, or at least he did not indicate that he had. If so, the church could have transferred their support to his "Timothy." Instead, I had to recommend a national missionary living there who was doing an outstanding work and could benefit from their support. In this way, they were able to continue their outreach in that land.

In my mind, the missionary should have been dropped long before his intended move since he was not fulfilling the very purpose of his call. He had not planted a single church, nor had he won, discipled, and trained a single national for the ministry.

Exposing the Conundrum

I have long believed that God's calling is more to a people than to a country. Country borders change over time, but tribes (people groups) generally do not. For example, Prussia no longer exists, but its people do; only now they live in what is known as Poland, Russia, Lithuania, Denmark, Belgium, the Czech Republic, and Germany. As a result, they may now speak various languages, whereas before, they primarily spoke what has become an extinct Baltic language. But they are still the same "people"—no matter what language they speak.

Statistically, as of around 2015, an existing language reportedly goes extinct every two weeks. For example, the Busuu language has only eight living speakers. In addition to their native tongue, 96 percent of the world's population speak one of the four most common languages: English, Mandarin Chinese, Hindi, and Spanish.

Consider how short-sighted and damaging this reasoning can be. Suppose a missionary to the Cherokee Indians living in Georgia in 1820 decided to move to Tennessee, Alabama, or North Carolina to reach the Cherokees living there. His support would have been terminated due to his "moving fields." Let's suppose he decided to risk his support, leaving the Cherokee churches he had established in Georgia in the hands of faithful men and moved to North Carolina. He left his field, but soon he has a new problem. From 1836 to 1839, nearly all of the Cherokees were rounded up and forcefully relocated to Oklahoma in a trek now called the Trail of Tears.

Now the missionary was presented with another problem: does he move with them and continue his calling, or does he stay in North Carolina and retain his remaining support? His location had changed several times, as did the tribe's, yet they were the same people that they always been. They had the same blood, same language, culture, dress, diet, and traditions, only with a different and constantly changing location.

So the question that begs an answer is, are we to support the *messenger* (the missionary) or the *message* (the gospel)? The answer is simple—yes. This conundrum can be looked at in at least two ways, so now we are back to the two-sided coin.

Heads—A Biblical Perspective

Accepting that a missionary is not a pastor serving in another land but is instead a church planter and a discipler of church planters, logically he will not, cannot, and perhaps should not stay in one place long-term. He must move on as surely as a bird must fly or a fish must swim. Moving is in his nature. However, keep in mind that with today's good roads, modern vehicles, and instant communications, a missionary can more easily base his operations from one place and still reach out to multiple locations—much like the spokes of a wheel reaching out from the center.

Paul never stayed anywhere more than a few years and, in some places, like Thessalonica, he stayed for only three weeks. His stated purpose as a church planter was to plant the church and appoint elders who could then mature the saints into duplicating that pattern. This strategy freed him to move on and start again. (In Ephesians chapter four, he used the term *apostle*, from which we get the English word, "missionary.") His church planting process would then be solidified and accelerated by traveling "prophets." These were preachers who were teachers and exhorters. Next would follow "evangelists," who were men and ladies who were gifted in soul winning. Philip, probably a Hellenic believer of the Jerusalem Church, was called an "evangelist," as were his daughters. Finally, the congregations could multiply by the ministry of "pastors and teachers" who cared for the sheep, matured the new believers, and developed more recruits for the same "offices" already mentioned. Why? Was it so that congregations could grow to become "megachurches" and build massive structures on ever-expanding campuses? No, but rather so the gospel could spread into every corner of the globe, and each new congregation would have the support of prophets, evangelists, and pastors to help them plant and mature even more churches. By this method, they would fulfill the Great Commission.

As a missionary, Paul did not spend his time in one place. When his job was finished, he moved on. He and his disciples were so successful with this pattern that there was no place left in Greece and Asia Minor for him to plant new churches (Romans 15:23, 24). Thus, he announced his plans to go to Spain and start over.

What? Paul was not saying there were no established churches where he could preach. He was stating that no villages were left to evangelize and plant a new church. They (his disciples and their disciples, etc.) had covered the subcontinent and "turned it upside down" (Acts 17:6). Thus, to continue his church-planting calling, he was compelled to move farther out. Why? Because his rule was that he did not "build upon any other man's foundation" (Romans 15:20, 21) In other words, he did not plant churches where others had already been before him. He went where the gospel was un-preached and unknown and started churches. He did not follow others; they followed him. He was not the evangelist, the prophet, or the pastor; he was the missionary.

Of course, Paul did take the opportunity to visit other established churches like those in Antioch, Damascus, Jerusalem, and Rome, none of which he had started. He went there not to plant but to encourage and strengthen the Body (as a prophet). Thus, we see that a missionary can wear multiple hats as long as they are temporary, but his primary purpose is church planting.

But what about moving to another country?

In a sense, every time Paul moved, he was moving to another country. In reality, they were more separate "cultures" than "countries" since they were all under the supervision and administration of the Roman Empire. Everywhere he went, the people had their own culture, language, gods, foods, etc., but they were also familiar with and subservient to the Roman language, culture, gods, and customs. He was always both a foreigner and a "homeboy." Practically speaking, he may never have had to learn a different language to minister because the empire had two common languages—Greek and Latin. In most regions, locals were allowed to keep their mother tongue while not in other regions.

Thus, from a biblical perspective, a missionary moving to another field is not wrong; to the contrary, it should be a common practice, though multiple fields could all be in the same "country." For example, in Thailand, a missionary can minister to the Thai in Bangkok, the

Burmese speakers on the western border, the Laotian and Cambodians on the eastern border, and the Malay on the southern tip, or one of several dozen different tribes in the north—all while living receiving support as a missionary to Thailand.

I have been a missionary for well over thirty years. Some churches refer to me as a missionary to Thailand; others classify me as a missionary to Honduras, others say the Middle East, and still others India. I can tell when a church began their support by how they designate me. Our quarterly magazine, the *Progress Report*, clearly reveals that I am based out of the USA and plant churches worldwide, encouraging the established churches and planting new ones. To my knowledge, no church has ever dropped my support because I was someplace other than where they thought I was or should be. The fact is, the purpose of the *Progress Report* is to make my location known as well as my labors and purpose. When at home, I do not lounge until it's time to get on a plane. I work long and hard, as we are all supported to do.

Tails—A Practical Perspective

Sometimes a person or church has a particular burden or even calling to personally take the responsibility to reach a specific people group or cover a specific region with the gospel. If you desire to reach a tribal group living on a specific island and supported a missionary precisely because he can/will evangelize that tribe, it would make sense to drop his support if he decided to move elsewhere. You were not supporting *him* as much as you were supporting *them*. It's very logical.

This was the situation with my pastor friend that I mentioned in the opening paragraphs of this conundrum. His church has a burden to reach Honduras. His church supported an American man working with us there who eventually left to do other ministries. The funds they gave monthly were not intended for the missionary/messenger's benefit but rather for preaching the message to those people. So, it made perfect sense to give the funds to another messenger in Honduras.

When I was in the fifth grade, I couldn't pronounce "s" correctly, so my parents hired a tutor to help me. Rather than saying "s" with the front of my mouth, I let it slip out on both sides at the back of my mouth. My tutor taught me to practice by repeatedly saying, "My sister Susie likes strawberry ice cream" and "Sam picks up seashells by the seashore." The exercise was a brilliant success as I have since been able to pronounce the formerly elusive "s" correctly. That tutor moved on to help other children with speech problems. I cannot remember any discussion of my parents continuing to pay her after her job was done.

Two years later, however, I was struggling with math. When seeking a tutor to help me, they did not continue paying the speech tutor; they hired a tutor who specialized in math. Locking the speech tutor into a lifetime contract would have been ridiculous as her job was already done. Likewise, simply because her title was "tutor," hiring her to help me in math would have been equally silly. Having skill in one subject does not mean skill in all subjects. Speech and math, though both educational subjects, are as different as pastoring and church planting. For the minister to be proficient in both is highly unlikely. As with a tutor, pay him for what he can do—not for what he cannot.

At one time, Paul was called to go to Macedonia. It is feasible that someone having the same burden could have supported him until his purpose there was complete, then support those he left behind to finish the task. Macedonia was not a city but a region of Greece with many villages yet to be reached. Paul left the region because his missionary purpose was to knock over the first domino and move on, letting the others fall by his converts' efforts.

Some churches get upset about this concept because occasionally, the missionary informs his supporters about a change of fields while still in language school, even though he has not yet visited the country of his calling. They feel, therefore, that he is uncertain of the will of God.

Having been a missionary in Central America, I know that most missionaries attend language school in Mexico or Costa Rica. Costa

Rica has the highest standard of living of all the Central American countries. The climate is more temperate, the people are often blue-eyed and blond-haired, and English is commonly spoken. Besides that, the culture is nearer to that in the USA than any other country in the region because more than 70,000 "ex-pats" (mostly retirees) live in Costa Rica. The country caters to them and entire subdivisions are designed for Americans. Store signs and street signs are in English; the cost of living is lower, medical care is excellent, the infrastructure is superb, the crime rate is low, and the government is not as corrupt as those in other Central American countries. As a result, missionaries fall in love with Costa Rica. The wife makes friends, the kids learn their way around, and soon their advertised call to Honduras, Nicaragua, El Salvador, or Guatemala gives way to the allure of a new call to Costa Rica.

Basically, Central Americans are all the same people, so does it matter to which country the missionary goes? No, probably not. However, for a church to doubt a missionary's discernment and calling when he presents himself to churches on the pretext of having an overwhelming, all-encompassing, life-changing burden for one place, then quickly moves on to another is not strange. On the contrary, had his call been presented as being to the "people" of Central America, rather than to a specific geographic location, there would have been no problem.

Eliminating the Conundrum

A Helpful Conclusion for Those Who Sponsor:

We commonly have sponsors who drop the national preacher's support they have been funding in our ministry for one reason or another. Often, we initiate it by informing them that the preacher they had been supporting is no longer serving, has passed away, etc. Some sponsors end their support at that time, and we never hear from them again. That is because, from their perspective, they were supporting that particular preacher, the *messenger*. Over the years, they had developed a relationship with him and his family, and now that he has passed on, they feel no impetus to continue support. Others in that situation (and this is far more common), ask us to assign them another preacher. Usually, they don't care who he is or where he is because, from their perspective, they are primarily supporting the proclamation of the message. The messenger is not the issue; the issue is the message that he is declaring. Whenever possible, our policy is to try to assign them another preacher (messenger) from within the same accountability group of preachers and the same region or country, so the group is not weakened or shorthanded.

In summary, the two perspectives are not competitive; rather, they are virtually the same. In the book of Romans, Paul pointed out the following:

1. The pagan cannot believe in Christ if they have not heard His good news *(the message)* (Romans 10:14).
2. They cannot hear the message if someone does not take it to them *(the messenger)* (Romans 10:14).
3. That particular "someone" *(messenger/missionary with the message)* cannot go unless he is sent (financially enabled by the sponsor) (Romans 10:15).

So then, whatever your perspective is—you play a vital part.

Suggestions for Missionaries:

- Churches are more inclined to continue their support if you have been proven worthy of it. Remind them of what you accomplished with their support, the fruit you produced that will remain behind to carry on, and why you feel it necessary to leave. If not, this is just an opportunity for them to jettison dead weight. Many churches struggle with meeting their missionary budget each month and cannot turn a blind eye to a legitimate reason to drop a missionary who is not meeting their expectations.

- Give the churches some notice rather than just springing it on them. Remember they are "partnering" with you. They should know what their "partner" is considering and why. Paul had a reason for where and when he moved. Often it was because relatives were living there of his converts living here.

- Please realize that the intent of their support may have been for your field's evangelization more than for your needs; so don't take it personally. Be gracious and understanding. Your attitude could go a long way in persuading them to continue your support on the next field you target.

Suggestions for Churches:

- In each support scenario, determine if you intend to fund the message or the messenger who is bearing the message. Whatever your choice, and it could be different for different missionaries, inform the missionary upfront. This will settle whether you feel it necessary to drop support if a missionary decides to move to another field and will not come as a surprise to him.

- If you decide to support the message, then look for someone there to take the place of the messenger. In most cases, we would have a national preacher in the land, or the mission board that the missionary served with may have another who could benefit from your help. Certainly, the missionary himself should be able to recommend you to other men who are serving there.

- Consider that nearly the entire Muslim world, where you probably support no missionaries, has gone without the message because the messengers had to leave. Look at the absence of Christianity that has resulted! Final Frontiers now has messengers living in almost every Islamic North African and Middle Eastern nation closed to missionaries. You could help one of them.

- Keep an open mind about missionaries moving around. A dedicated, biblical missionary will always be conquering new territories for Christ. And consider this, if Paul had remained where he started, he would have been the assistant pastor to Barnabas and would have only been known as the first missionary to Cyprus. (Barnabas was from there, so it was his home.) Aren't you glad he moved from place to place? Why then should missionaries today do otherwise? Remember, those who move are missionaries; those who remain stationary are pastors serving in foreign lands.

#3
What Is the Biblical Example for Dispersing Missions' Funds, and Were They Used for More than Just Supporting Missionaries?

Explaining the Conundrum

I suppose another way of framing the question is, "On what should we or should we not spend our missions' dollars"? Missions giving is primarily considered to be for the support of missionaries. But is using mission funding for needs or causes other than personal or ministry support legitimate?

Assuming your answer is affirmative, you now have to determine your budget and the budgeted items. I cannot help you with the first, but I can give some counsel on the second. To be more specific, you have two options. The first is to decide if you only want your missions' money going to purely missions' efforts, i.e., church planters, church planting, evangelizing, and training new preachers and pastors. The second is to decide if you want some of it to go to other causes that may or may not have anything to do with what I call biblical missions, i.e., orphanages, feeding centers, clinics, schools, rescue missions, anti-abortion clinics, etc. Keep in mind that these ministry needs, and ministry programs also need to be funded and often assist in what I call "pure" missions.

My intention is not to persuade you to take funds away from these various ministry causes so you can give them to missionaries. Instead, my intention is to keep you from taking the funds that you intended for missionary support and diverting them to non-missionary causes. Almost every church I have consulted regarding their missions' program has faced this dilemma because most churches consider any monetary gift that leaves their physical address to be classified as "missions." So then, how can this problem be resolved?

To me, the solution is easy. Have two separate budgets; designate one for missions and the other for ministry. All these various ministries need funding and should be considered. I have found that if we don't intentionally give missions funding to pure mission items, then "missions" becomes nothing more than a catchword that we use to define our support of anything that is not listed in the church's operational budget. Mission budgets often and unintentionally become slush funds used to cover unfunded or underfunded projects. For example, if you can't afford the high summer utilities, take it from missions. If you can't pay the pastor this week, take it from missions. Suppose the church bus needs new tires; take it from missions, etc.

If we define missions scripturally as church planting, we will see the necessity to fund it carefully and specifically. Otherwise, the budget is in danger of becoming a well-meaning, unintended slush fund.

I have heard of churches using their missions fund to build a basketball court. The reasoning is *this will help us reach the youth of the area, which, after all, is our mission field.* Wrong! The local youth are not *missions*; they are *ministry*. In His Great Commission, Jesus included Jerusalem as a mission field—until Pentecost. When the Holy Spirit came, the gospel was preached, and the entire city was evangelized in a single day. It was no longer a mission field; it was now a ministry field. House churches were everywhere, meeting daily, and great assemblies met outside the temple compound. Pastors were shepherding their flocks, and preparations were being made to take the gospel worldwide. Sure, people were still being converted, but the city as a whole had already been "reached" with the gospel.

May I make an observation here? When Jesus gave the Great Commission, He told them to preach in Jerusalem, Judaea, Samaria, and the uttermost parts of the earth. He skipped over the Galilee region, a separate geopolitical region, recognized and administrated by Rome. Why would He command them to preach in Jerusalem and then intentionally skip over Galilee? I can only submit an opinion. If you study the Gospels, you will see that Jesus did very little of His preaching in Jerusalem, though He did some in nearby communities like Bethany; yet He performed most of His miracles and teachings in Galilee. (Some say over 80%.) Most of His post-resurrection appearances were in the Galilee. He had already saturated Jerusalem with the knowledge of who He was and what His message was. They didn't need to be told what they already knew. They needed only to be confronted with the choice of accepting or rejecting Him. But the rest of the world still needed to hear that same gospel; thus, the mandate to go.

Suppose you accept that biblically, a missionary is a church planter, and a mission field is a region where Christ is unnamed and unknown. In that case, it is an admission of absolute failure when we call our neighborhood or city a mission field. So, let your funds collected and designated for missions be used for missionary support and activity, and use the funds designated for ministry needs for their particular purposes. If you read on, you will find an example of Paul's doing precisely that.

EXAMINING THE CONUNDRUM

Let's first establish a foundation regarding giving. David's greatest desire was to build a permanent temple for God so that He could live among them in a befitting manner. God may have been satisfied with an old tent (the word for "tabernacle") but David, living in what was luxury to him, felt despondent that God should have less than he enjoyed; less than His glory was worthy of. However, due to his sins, he was not allowed to construct the temple, so in his mind, he did the next best thing. He began gathering and storing the materials needed so that his son Solomon could build it.

To make this a nationwide enterprise, allowing everyone to participate, he gathered his leaders before him and declared what he was personally going to give, thereby accomplishing two goals. First, it showed his dedication to God and that his love for Him was more significant than his love of wealth, demonstrating that it was not right for him to have so much and God to have so little. Secondly, it served as an example for the leaders to follow personally, display publicly, and used as a motivating example for their local citizens to emulate (I Chronicles 22).

David anticipated that some would seek excuses for not participating. He reminded them their offering was not a loss of "their" wealth; it was returning of a portion of "His" wealth, with which he had both blessed them and over which He had appointed them as stewards. Listen to his words as he prayed:

> I Chronicles 29:14, *"But who am I, and what is my people, that we should be able to offer so willingly after this sort? for all things come of thee, and of thine own have we given thee."*

David did not infer but rather stated emphatically that "all" we give to God came from God, so in effect, when we give, we are not giving to Him; instead, we are "giving back" to Him. Logically then, if we do not give, we are withholding from God what is His. That is embezzlement and theft, and don't expect to get away with it.

Technically, we are not owners of our wealth or possessions but rather the stewards of God's. He allows us to keep a portion of His wealth for our maintenance and blessing, but the rest is for His work. If we keep too much for ourselves, then He may take back what He has given us. If we properly manage His funds and use them according to His pattern, then He, in turn, blesses us, giving us more to manage (Matthew 25:14-29).

Exposing the Conundrum

The best way to put this puzzle to bed is to look at passages of Scripture that directly refer to it.

Biblical Examples of Funds Used for Missionary Support:

First, in Romans 15:24, Paul wrote to the church in Rome, which he did not start and had not yet visited, though members of his own family attended there. He said he planned to visit them while on his way to do missionary work in Spain and asked them to help him on his way.

Second, in Philippians 4:16-18, he praised them for sending help to him over and over, whenever he was in need and acknowledged that they would share in his heavenly rewards for what he accomplished with their help.

Third, in III John, we find the apostle somewhat concerned and perhaps perturbed. He wrote this letter after being reunited with some traveling preachers who reported what they encountered at the hands of the church leaders, to whom he had referred them.

The first was Gaius, whom he called a "dear friend." He commended him for his testimony and persistence in faith and example. (We cannot be confident this man was a pastor/elder; if not, he was perhaps a prominent layman in the local house church.)

In the first half of the letter, he praises Gaius for taking care of these traveling preachers, men who had received no support or help from the unconverted Gentiles to whom they had been proclaiming the gospel. These men were, without a doubt, missionaries. We do not know their race or nationality, but it is apparent that they were not a part of this particular church body. John stated that these traveling preachers/missionaries were strangers to this local congregation (v. 5) though they came bearing his regards.

In the last half of the letter, John refers to a second man, a pastor named Diotrephes. Regardless of what good he may have done in life and ministry, his name is forever infamous because of his actions against these preachers. Was he an adulterer? A drunkard? A scandalous criminal? Not at all. His sin was that he was puffed up with pride (v. 9), unwilling to humble himself under the apostle's teaching. He spoke against John's ministry, person and authority and refused to receive these brothers whom John had both sent and recommended. To add to his infamy, John concludes his condemnation with the fact that Diotrephes not only refused to support them personally, but he also forbade the members of his church to help them. He even warned that if anyone disobeyed him by helping these traveling preachers, he would expel that man/family from the congregation. This expulsion was going a step too far.

This pastor obviously had a problem with the apostle John, but it seemed to carry over toward anyone affiliated with John. It was not enough for him not to give "his" money to help these men, but he insisted that his church members not give "theirs" as well.

John began his conclusion with two points. Having plans to pass by their town, he stated that he would personally confront this pastor and put him in his place (v. 10). Then he admonished Gaius and the others to continue to do as they had been doing, reminding them that they should *"follow not that which is evil, but that which is good. He that doeth good is of God: but he that doeth evil hath not seen God"* (v. 11).

Though a pastor, this man had strayed far away from the teachings of God and had become "evil." Later in Acts 20, in his farewell address to Ephesian elders, he reminded them that they are to help the weak, and *"it is more blessed to give than to receive."* Obviously by context, helping involves more than sympathetic words. Sympathy may console, talking may comfort, but giving alleviates the need.

I can recall many occasions when I first started this work of supporting national missionaries. Well-meaning pastors would sometimes rebuke me, saying that I was a traitor, an enemy of missionaries (which I still hear to this day though I am a missionary), and that "American money belongs to American missionaries." The first two judgments I ignored. But with the third, I always agreed but reminded them that *"the earth is the Lord's and the fullness thereof,"* meaning all that it is, is His—not America's. And so, my viewpoint was and still is that whatever is yours belongs to you; spend it as you will, but whatever is His belongs to His servants, doing His work, regardless of race or citizenship.

I was always troubled to hear a pastor or mission board director make such improper and unbiblical comments. However, it was worse when taken a step farther by telling his church members not to support a national missionary. Afterward, he would call other pastors to warn them of my "evil actions," saying I was "trying to destroy American missionaries" by funding national missionaries.

After 35 years of teaching the value and validity of supporting national preachers, I thought this hostile attitude toward them (and me) had ceased. Still, a few months ago, I was speaking with a young missionary at a conference. He mentioned a mutual acquaintance—a man who has been kind to me when in my presence. He said that when my name was mentioned (as it often is in missionary circles, referencing my efforts to raise support for national preachers), he said, "Jon Nelms just goes around stealing money from missionaries."

I know that most missionaries do not feel that way about me or Final Frontiers. They appreciate our efforts to support the national preachers, and many refer men to me whom they know to be needy and worthy of support. However, there are still those out there who feel threatened that a national preacher would get a share of the limited missions funding available rather than it going to them.

My issue is not race or citizenship; it is credibility. I am opposed to any missionary, red, yellow, black, or white if he is lazy and unproductive. I wouldn't give $50 to any preacher who is like that—American or national. For that reason, we carefully monitor the quarterly reports of the men we support so that if need be, we can cut them off. But the reality is, if you support a national who is lazy and unproductive (and many are), then you have wasted $50 a month of God's money. However, when you support an American who is likewise unworthy, you waste $5,000 to $12,000 a month. This is why I make a crusade of helping churches understand that they are stewards of God's missions' money and will be held accountable for any waste—national or American. I would never say that all missionaries are that way. I only suggest that you make sure the ones your church supports are not among them.

A Biblical Example of Funds Used for Other Causes:

Let me say that the following passages are not doctrines but rather are examples that are logical, credible, and accountable. If followed, the possibility of fraud and deceit is limited. Furthermore, it may surprise you to learn that the purpose of this particular gift was not for missionary support but for what some call *social work* and what I call *ministry.*

The closing verses of Acts chapter 11 and II Corinthians chapter 8 are complimenting passages. Years earlier, various prophets had warned that a famine was coming to Jerusalem. Paul, who was emotionally touched by their upcoming tragedy, began asking the Gentile churches to take up offerings to send to them. We don't know why this was such a great concern to Paul. Perhaps it was motivated by his lifelong regret for having formerly persecuted the believers living there.

We read this passage as if Paul requested it on Saturday, collected it on Sunday, and left for Jerusalem with the offering on Monday. Nothing could be further from the truth. It was a full ten years later that the famine finally hit, and when it did, Paul began to go from church to church collecting their decade-old, pledged gifts. Some, namely Macedonia, collected more than planned, while others, namely Corinth, failed to collect much at all, despite having pledged. He praised some and rebuked others; then he outlined their success or failure and the logical steps he would take to collect and disperse their funds. That's what I want to bring to your attention by looking specifically at Acts 11:27-30.

How the Funds Were Collected and Dispersed:

- There was a *motivation* for their giving (a famine).
- There were the *means* of their giving (each according to his ability).
- There were the *messengers* of their giving (Paul and Barnabas were to receive, collect and deliver their gifts).
- There was the *method* of distribution (the gifts were to be dispersed by the church leaders in the targeted area).

When I first stumbled across this principle more than twenty years ago, I realized I had unintentionally copied it; and that we were soliciting, collecting, and dispersing funds precisely as Paul had. Over the decades, I have been surprised to see that many of our ministry protocols have been established intentionally and unintentionally according to actual biblical examples. Let me explain.

- ***Motivation.*** You give willingly because of a need (whether for a preacher, a child, Bibles, PowerPack, project, etc.)

- ***Means.*** I expect that most give according to their ability or desire, but if not, at least they give.

- ***Messengers.*** Your funds are sent to us directly or sometimes given through your church. We process them to the budget item or project for which they were intended. Next, a receipt is sent to the donor. For accountability purposes, our administration is overseen by our executive board, with annual accountability given to them, the IRS, and all donors and finally published online for all to see.

- ***Method.*** We send the funds to national pastors who oversee the use and distribution of the funds according to the need or project for which they were given, requiring they, in turn, provide a report for their administration to us, which we then forward to the donors.

This is done because of American pastors, who are eager to see *God's money* used to support *God's servants,* whoever and wherever they are. Thank God that our pulpits in America have few like Diotrephes and many like Gaius.

Give attention to the method that Paul used to distribute the funds; he did not give them to the people, the families, etc. Instead, he gave them to the pastors to distribute. Why? Logic implies that Paul did not know the individual families. He did not know which one needed how much and could have been misled or manipulated by someone with a tear-jerking story. The pastors, on the other hand, knew them. They lived with them. As shepherds, they knew where they lived and their needs; thus, they were best suited to handle the distribution after Paul handled the delivery.

We use this same principle in dispersing funds for preachers, orphans, widows, etc.

Eliminating the Conundrum

Suggestions for Missionaries:

- Remember that Paul did not only ask people to give; he told them why he was asking, what he was asking for, how they could provide the funds, and how he would distribute the funds. Missionaries often make the mistake of being too vague with their request. They think that because it is a supporting church, they don't need to give details. But they do! First, giving details is part of the accountability process, and secondly, it promotes the need by touching the heart. People give for what moves them. We raise millions of dollars a year, but it is all for specific preachers, people, projects, or purposes. And the funds only come because we have carefully and honestly elaborated on the need before asking for their help. It is also because, after thirty-five years, we have developed a reputation for honesty and transparency that does not come overnight or by happenstance.

Suggestions for Churches:

- Establish a policy in your church about how and for what the missions' funds will be dispersed. It may be helpful to set up both a mission budget and a ministry budget. If this is too complicated, then study your current giving to determine how much of your missions' funding is going to missions. I think most pastors will be surprised to find that 30 to 70 percent of their "missions" dollars are diverted to social and ministry causes in their state, city, and neighborhood. This may be a good testimony in your town, but is it what you wanted to accomplish with your missions giving? If so, keep up the good work, and if not, make the necessary changes.
- Sometimes churches are not aware that their people give outside the church because they are not in agreement with how they use their funds. When people are unhappy, they tend to "vote with their feet," but usually, long before that happens, they have "voted with their finances." The wise pastor understands that it is not his place to control his people but to lead them.

Suggestions for Families:

I add this category this time because it applies to the passages we have studied.

- The families brought their gifts to be collected by the church, who then appointed Paul to deliver them to the pastors abroad, who then distributed them to the families in need. In short, the process went from families with financial ability in one area to families without financial ability in another area. Everything else was a part of the process that made the objective possible. Make sure that you have a purpose for your giving and that it is managed as you expected.

#4
Who Establishes the Support Levels for the Missionaries in Each Country, and Why Do Novice Missionaries Make as Much as Veteran Missionaries?

Explaining the Conundrum

This two-part conundrum will probably surprise most of you, and by *most*, I mean anyone who is not a missionary. Even missionaries tend to take these questions as absolute and dare not seek an answer. They are as fixed as the law of gravity and, thus, are seldom questioned. We don't jump off tall buildings, and we don't ask questions like these, as either could bring us to a swift and definite end.

I combine the two questions because they overlap, and I ask these questions because I have nothing to lose. I don't have a mission board to answer to—just a board of directors of the ministry I founded in 1986. They, like me, tend to ask hard questions in the hope of finding answers. Failure sometimes comes from seeking answers to well-established practices and questions, but so do successes.

Someone once got tired of walking and made a wheel. Naysayers must have mocked him and asked, "What are you going to do with that thing?" That question made him think, "I don't know, but it was so much fun, I think I'll make a second one." When his friends saw him making a second wheel, they must have rightly surmised, "If one wheel is a failure, then two wheels is a double failure." The humble inventor eventually figured out that he could move without walking by joining the two with an axle and putting a platform on it, or so he thought. It worked great going downhill but not so great going uphill. That's probably when the word "push" was invented. Then a brainstorm persuaded him to attach a horse and now he had a cart that revolutionized transportation. His necessity to push soon became the horse's mandate to pull, and all he had to do was sit and enjoy the ride.

This plan worked well for thousands of years until a few years back, someone without a horse, or disgusted with the cost of feeding them and the mess they left in the streets, invented an engine. And the rest is (more recent) history.

It is true that failures sometimes come from asking well-established questions, but so do successes. So, let's take a risk and ask.

Examining the Conundrum

These are good questions asked by many pastors and laypeople, so I decided to research and see what I could learn. First, I wanted to separate the financing of denominational missionaries from that of faith missionaries. The following points list some differences in the two types given in the most general of terms.

A *denominational missionary* is one who the denomination's mission division hires. He is an employee who receives a salary and various compensations. He does not have to go on deputation, raise support, or answer to individual churches. Generally, once hired, he is quickly sent to his field of service to do whatever his denomination tells him to do. His calling is determined by them—not necessarily by the Lord's direction. He may want to plant churches but is assigned to run a youth camp. Financially, he is well taken care of and provided with lodgings, vehicles, insurance, household servants, etc. Typically, he will be given a furlough every fifth year and return to America where he is NOT required or expected to speak in churches. He is to rest for the year and then return to the field or move on to his new assignment.

A *faith missionary* must raise his support and generally does not receive the perks of the denominational missionary. He is his own boss and can-do whatever ministry he feels led by Christ to do, wherever that may take him. His support is dependent on the faithfulness of those who pledged it. When he returns home for furlough, there is no rest at all. He and his family travel from one supporting church to another, giving updates on their work and trying to squeeze in new churches to gain additional support. The initial raising of support can take from one to five years. Usually, if not raised by that time, the missionary assumes he misunderstood God's will and resigns his title and serves as a pastor or faithful church member.

I want to begin by addressing the denominational missionary's situation if for no other reason, to make the reader more informed and make the faith missionary a little jealous. None of us want to give up our autonomy, yet the thought of having immediate, full support with perks, and having no deputation, no financial stress, no wearing two or more hats since they work with teams—each man having his own job and a year off with pay every five years—is very tempting. So, let me begin with examining the denominational missionary and then spend the bulk of my time in my world, that of the faith missionary.

Online at thenest.com, I found an article by Dana Severson entitled "The Average Missionary Salary." The photo caption accompanying it stated: "The average salary for missionaries is relatively low." Here's a breakdown of what I discovered, all stats being relevant to 2012. As you continue, note that the article addresses missionaries who are sent by an organization (they are employees), as opposed to "faith missionaries" (those who have to raise their support).

Supported denominational missionary couples received on average $121,000 a year, but the Bureau of Labor Statistics stated that the average salary was a low $30,650. That's because, due to additional other subsidies, the "salary" was only equal to 47 percent of the "income." So, what else is included in the non-salary income? Are you ready?

- $6,050 per couple if living in areas where the cost of living is higher than in the USA. What? Well, keep in mind that among Baptists, about 20 percent of our missionaries (over 570 of them) live in Europe, where things are likely more expensive. There are 112 missionary couples who live in the United Kingdom alone and 104 in Canada. There are 68 missionary families in Japan; I can't imagine how expensive that must be. Then, of course, there are 77 in Australia and 29 in New Zealand. *(I would have thought they already had the gospel, but since most churches and people define a missionary as being a pastor preaching anywhere other than at home, it makes sense to call them missionaries.)*
- $10,000 housing subsidies are necessary since many career missionaries maintain a house in the USA while living overseas.
- $8,500 per couple was allocated for travel expenses.
- $10,890 was an allotment to cover medical expenses.
- $8,470 per year was designated for administrative expenses (presumedly, this is for the mission board that handles their accounts).
- $8,470 for other incidentals (?)
- $7,260 for pensions
- $4,840 for taxes

I want to ask the question here that I think all missionaries, if honest, would ask, "Where do I sign up for this job?"

Thinking that this report must be an exaggeration, I looked further. That's when I found an EFCA article by Daryl Anderson of *ReachGlobal* (year unknown), stating that "The average cost to support a missionary family from North America is $10,338 per month." (That's $124,056 annually.) It continued, "However, support needs range from a low of $4,000 a month ($48,00 annually) up to $16,000" ($192,000 annually) depending on family size, location, start-up costs, etc.

Well, that makes sense, I guess. The nebulous "start-up costs" were defined as travel and vehicle purchase, maintenance, and relocation—you know, the same kind of expenses that the ordinary person who buys a car, takes a trip, or moves to another location has to incur. And I forgot, it also includes the cost of a computer. These are all needed and legitimate expenses. Still, you have to seriously question the need for such funding when you realize missionaries don't have to ship their belongings since furniture and appliances can be purchased anywhere. And as for travel, you can sometimes fly from Atlanta to Budapest, Beirut, Tokyo, Paris, Rome, London, or Manila, cheaper than you can fly from Atlanta to Seattle.

As I read further, I saw the list contained a line item that I found particularly curious entitled, "Readiness Evaluation and Pre-Field Training." The title alone seems to imply that you may not pass muster, and if not, then what happens to all the support you raised and the years it took to raise it? Shouldn't your readiness be determined, and your training be finished BEFORE you set out to raise support? No corporate executive would hire a man and give him a title and a considerable salary, hoping that he performs well. That's why internships were invented. Corporate headhunters seek experienced men with a resume. So, why do we treat God's work in this way?

Organizational and denominational missionaries earn far more than your typical "faith" missionary. Still, in fairness to them, I have heard that some graciously share their salaries with poorer missionaries who lack support. And since I am assuming that most of the readers will be involved in faith missions, let me approach the issues from that viewpoint.

Exposing the Conundrum

When I was younger, I learned that mission boards set the support amount based on what country the missionary was called to, and their determination is made based on the pay scale of a certain level of the US Embassy staff in that country. This is why someone going to France is required to raise more funding than someone going to Jamaica. Frankly, you would have to survey each faith mission board to learn how they determine support levels. Wisely, all either recommend or require the missionary to be debt-free before departing.

Most missionaries never mention the amount of funding they are trying to raise; they are taught to refer to percentages rather than to amounts. That way, they don't have to answer those embarrassing questions like, "Why do you need so much?" When asked amounts rather than percentages, potential-supporting-pastors often comment, "That's nearly twice what I make!" To be honest, we missionaries are embarrassed about the amount we are trying to raise. Most of us will make more as a missionary than we ever did in the pastorate or business. Few will take a pay cut. This becomes incredibly embarrassing when we realize that we will likely be making more than the president of the country in which we will live—if it's a developing nation. You quickly learn why it is better to talk in terms of percentages rather than amounts when someone like me comes along, reminding churches that the average national preacher in the land where the missionary is going earns only one-tenth or one one-hundredth of what the average missionary earns.

By the way, this is one reason why some mission boards have branded me as being "anti-missionary." Why is exposing the truth considered "anti" and hiding the truth "pro?" I have known some missionaries, whom I feel were worthy of $20,000 a month because I knew how productive they were and that they would use the funds to expand their ministry—not for personal gratification.

Some reading this book will immediately determine that missionaries make too much, and in many cases, they would be correct. To be fair, you need to understand, however, that missionaries are like you. Wherever we live, we want the best circumstances we can have for our family, including a good education, health care, comfort, etc. And logically, if all we have to do is ask for it, with no proof of success required to show that we are worthy of the sum, then why not ask? And if churches will give it, why not take it? The problem is, we have come to expect and demand the things that previous generations considered luxuries as necessities. And that applies to those pastors and laypeople living in America as well.

I do not think that a missionary should be poor or expected to live in poverty. If a pastor can have a house and a car, why can't a missionary? However, one crucial consideration is that the pastor's members, not the missionary's converts, are the ones paying for the missionary's car. But that's another conundrum that I will address later, so I will leave it alone for now.

I have known a few missionaries who intentionally lived like the poor. I have no problem with that mindset because they later realize that all the people are not poor. From experience, I have learned that if you do this, the poor people, knowing you are from a wealthy land, will think you are crazy for living in a slum or a dangerous area when you could live elsewhere. They may respect you sooner or later, but initially, they will think you are crazy, a loser, or mentally deranged. On the other hand, the rich will shun you because of where you live, how poorly you dress, etc. Paul addressed this when he said he had become all things to all men. I would recommend living in a middle-class surrounding so you can reach down to the poor and up to the rich, being accepted and respected by both.

God help the man who, for lack of finances, will not go where God leads him or do what God tells him to do. God bless the missionaries who use "their support" to help the low-income families in their churches, build schools and church facilities, pay medical bills for others, and save for the travel expenses of the mandatory furlough every four to five years. Consider, if a small missionary family of five has to pay $1500 round-trip airplane tickets for each family member every five years. That need would require an extra $1500 a year—an extra

$125 of monthly support to be raised and set aside for airline tickets. This amount does not include the travel and lodging costs they will incur once they arrive, and remember, during their year on furlough, they still have to pay rent on their house in the foreign land and the required utilities. The bills add up.

I don't care how much a missionary makes. I only care about how much he accomplishes. I have known some salesmen who were worthy of a million-dollar salary and others who weren't worth a thousand. It's not the size of the family, the location on the planet, or the missionary's oratorical skills that should determine how much he earns; it is his worth. And frankly, such worth cannot be determined by his age, intellect, or prior home-based ministry status. It can only be determined by how productive he is once he gets on the field. This is another reason to require lengthy internships in the field before being classified or supported as a missionary.

Few men are productive in their first term. During this time, they are getting acclimated to the weather, culture, and language, and until this is accomplished, they are the blind trying to lead the seeing. By the end of their second or third year, however, you should have an idea about the man's value. That is why I recommend the first term be spent, not just with a veteran missionary, but with veteran national pastors.

In the American culture, being a veteran merely means having spent time at some task. I don't see it that way. I have met many men who have been on the field for thirty years and have never discipled a single convert, never produced a single preacher, and never started a single church. By veteran, I mean a man who has accomplished what he was sent to accomplish. He was not sent to just pastor old sheep but to birth new lambs, plant churches, train men for the ministry and work himself out of a job continually so that he has to move elsewhere and start over.

We need to remember that since a novice missionary will likely become like the missionary who mentored him, he needs to be discipled by someone who has himself excelled. The Bible says that we produce after our own kind. That principle applies to birds, animals, and missionaries.

This brings me to the next part of the conundrum—why do novice missionaries make as much and sometimes more than veteran missionaries?

The answer? That's the way it has always been done. Is it right? No. Is it fair? No. Is it productive? No. It just is. But I argue that it should not be and doesn't have to be.

I am only one man, but I have an opinion, having served as a youth pastor, an assistant pastor, an associate pastor, and a senior pastor for twelve years before becoming a missionary. When moving necessitated my joining the staff at a different church, I didn't make as much as the other staff who had been there for years before I arrived. Later, as a young, inexperienced pastor, I did not earn as much as the pastors of larger churches nor as much as the older pastors of small churches nor did I expect to. Why should I? But when it comes to missions, we give every missionary the same amount. Why is that?

Probably because the churches are not *hiring* us, they are *helping* us. Missionary—let that sink in for a moment. The church has the right to give whatever they want to whoever they want. It is up to God to lead them otherwise. My point in bringing it up is simply as an issue of stewardship. How so?

Statistically, we know that as much as 43 percent of the "missionaries" who start on deputation will never finish it. In a month, six months, two years or more, they will determine it was not God's will and throw in the towel. I respect such men. In my mind, they wanted to serve the Lord and mistook a burden for a call (we have all done that), and once they realized it, they swallowed their pride, admitted their error, and started serving again as a layman in their home church or as a pastor. They undoubtedly learned a lot on the journey, and the churches they visited were hopefully blessed and encouraged by their presentations. However, the problem is that collectively, literally MILLIONS of missions' dollars were wasted in their years of discovery.

Frankly, of those who do make it to the field, another 75 percent quit and go home in the first three years. But that's another story for another time.

The solution in my mind is that the family and the home church send the missionary candidate to the field first for three to six months, so he sees what life will be like, experiencing the weather, the food, the language, the culture, and the difficulty of life in that land. Send him, his wife and family. Immerse them in the experience. Many will come home after only a few weeks when the thrill wears off, so it won't have cost or wasted that much. But if a family makes it through, at least you have an idea that he can make it for the long term. (I say "family" because usually the wife is the one who cannot adapt to the missionary life.)

Then let him begin his deputation with a little experience under his belt—not just a two-week "survey trip." I also recommend they stay on their own in a less-than-adequate environment, so they get the full experience. If they spend their time in a missionary's home, the mall, and coffee shops, they might as well have stayed home. This experience should be their "boot camp," proving their ability to adapt, adjust and achieve.

If the volume in numbers of missionaries supported is not your goal, I encourage churches to invest more heavily in men who have proven themselves for one term, two, or more. These men are not going to quit; they have proven there is no risk in the funds invested in them. Like consider supporting the national preachers; they already know the culture, the customs, the language, and the people. They have already gone through the heavy winds of ministry and even the storm's eye and come out the other side victoriously. They are veterans with experience and success under their belts, with the churches they have started, the preachers they have trained, and the schools they have founded while still having the energy to do more. Why waste his time with another year-long furlough? Keep him on the field doing what he does best. Give him a raise in his support.

Doesn't that sound at least a little bit logical?

Now, I realize that some churches simply want to see how many men they can support in how many places. If that's what you're all about, then go for it. God gets the glory either way. My suggestion is only given so that what you give will impact more lives. I'm all about numbers. Final Friends now has over 28,000 preachers in our network. However, not some, not most, but every man we support is a church planter. Every man we support had already proven himself with years of ministry. He had trained men for the ministry and had personally started at least two churches before we even began to consider him for support. I love the idea of quantity, but I adore the value of quality.

Some will think I am writing this book so that I can get more support. You have wrongly judged me. We have over seven thousand subscribers on our mailing list, and very few "support" my family and me. However, thousands support our preachers, children, etc. (This is because in over 35 years as a missionary, I have never done deputation.) Of those who support me, most are friends, not churches, so my logic doesn't apply to them; thus, it does not benefit me.

I share said all this because I have both a forum to say it and the respect of pastors, churches, and laypeople to listen. I'm trying to help you consider possible improvements for your mission program so that collectively, we can all do more to advance the preaching of the gospel to places where it has never been preached before.

Eliminating the Conundrum

Suggestions for Missionaries Regarding Acquiring Support:

- Remember that no church owes you support; they chose to give it because they believe in your intention to perform mighty exploits for God. Don't let them down. And remember, they are not supporting you until they are supporting you. The late John R. Rice used to say,

"Talk is cheap; it takes money to buy whiskey." I have often wondered why he used that expression and how he knew, but it was comical to hear him say it. The point is, don't count on promises for support. Remember Proverbs 13:12 says, *"Hope deferred maketh the heart sick: but when the desire cometh, it is a tree of life."* Often when a church affirms support, they are expressing an intention and not stating a promise.

Suggestions for Churches:

When you tell a missionary, you are going to support him, do it. To do otherwise is to lie. Let him know the following:

1) How much you will give
2) How often you will give it
3) When you will begin his support

In this way, he can make his budget and not be concerned that you have forgotten him.

Suggestions for Missionaries Regarding Maintaining Support:

- Don't fail to report your progress and your difficulties regularly. Be honest.

1) Share a testimony of a convert, not just a statistic,
2) Include photos.
3) Share the reasons behind your prayer requests.

Information is vital. If you cannot take the time every three months to write a letter, then why do you expect your supporting churches should take the time every month to write you a check?

- When told you will be taken on for support, show proper gratitude but remember that what you expect to happen tomorrow may take close to a year to be fulfilled. Why? Because churches work on a yearly budget, even when using Faith Promise. Perhaps their "new year" starts in January, and you are at their church in March. When the pastor says, "We are going to support you," that probably means the support will start next January. This means you won't get your first check until February, unless they pay quarterly, in which case it won't arrive until April—over a year later!

- This being the case, it is perfectly acceptable for you to ask the pastor when the support will begin. Put that date on your calendar, and a few months before that date, send the pastor a gentle note, letting him know how much you are looking forward to their support coming and what a benefit it will be for your family and ministry. Maybe even share with him how you will be using his support. By doing this, he is not simply a supporter of your ministry; he is a partner with your ministry.

Suggestions for Churches:

- Remember that you are his partner in ministry—not his silent partner. You are an investor who needs to be kept informed of his progress and setbacks. Read the letters and hold the missionary accountable to perform as expected. If he does not, reevaluate his support with him. Maybe you can help him improve but keep in mind if he is not yet a mature minister, he should be back home becoming one—not on the field, hoping to become one while setting an improper example for others.

- Let the missionary know what you expect from him. Do you want a letter monthly or quarterly? Can he send it by email or just give you a link to his Facebook postings? Is there something that he or his wife or family can do to help you boost mission giving and participation? Try not to condemn the missionary for not answering questions that you never asked.

- Pastors, please avoid questionaries. They can be a legitimate tool, but most missionaries have 80-to-100 supporting churches. If each one requires a unique questionnaire, then you have crippled his ministry. Imagine if each member of your church required that from you—and now having done so, "do unto others as you would have them do unto you."

- New pastors, please don't be so eager to undo what the church voted to do under your predecessor. It is common for a new pastor to want to wipe the missionary slate clean, keeping only those who went to his school or are from his favorite board. Just because you have never heard of some of these men does not mean they are not worthy. They have probably not heard of you either. We say that we believe in the local church's autonomy, but often a new pastor disregards the decisions prayed over, made, and adopted by the church before he arrived. That is not biblical, and it's not even logical. From time to time, I get a letter or even a phone call from a new pastor wanting to introduce himself and get to know me. That is a blessing and accomplishes what the pastor needed to make him feel comfortable with the missionaries his new church has been supporting. Later, if you begin to have questions or doubts, as a pastor, you have the right and the requirement to investigate and come to a decision about that missionary's support.

#5
Is It Wrong for a Missionary to Be a "Tentmaker," Having Other Sources of Income and Still Receive Support?

Explaining the Conundrum

Tentmaking is a growing trend that has perhaps risen from requirement and necessity and may become the next major shift in missionary work and funding. And while it has generally been discouraged over the past decades, the tide is beginning to turn. And why not, when you consider that the first missionary of the New Testament was self-employed as a tent-maker, in addition to being a preacher and a church planter.

In addition to Paul, we know that Luke, who was not an apostle or preacher but a layman, a doctor, and a prolific writer, also traveled and ministered with Paul. Should we, or better yet, could we possibly assert that Luke never plied his trade in all those years? Should we assume that he only treated Paul and the team but never used his skills on others, saved or unsaved, to help raise funding? Logically, if Paul used his tentmaking to finance his ministry, including the support of his team (Acts 20:34), why should we assume that Luke rejected that model?

So then, if there is a scriptural basis for "tentmaking," as well as multiple examples, why is it discouraged? I shall now address that conundrum, both positively and negatively.

Examining the Conundrum

Suppose you lived during the days of Paul. Would you have financially supported him? Of course, you would say "yes," but would you?

If you believe that a missionary should not have outside income, you could not have supported Paul the tentmaker, Peter, James, and John the fishermen, or even Jude, the son of James, a hired farmhand.

No one can deny that Paul was not only a missionary; he was also a model, serving as our example for what a missionary is and does—or at least is supposed to be and do. And no one who has ever spent a few moments in the book of Acts can deny that Paul worked making tent fabrics, though we are not sure if he was involved in the dying, the selling of fabric and related tentmaking materials, or in the actual production of tents. And it doesn't matter.

I find it interesting that when Paul went to the military town of Philippi, he and his partner took a walk down to the river to pray and came upon some women who had gathered there. Among them was a woman named Lydia, who though a Gentile, worshipped according to the Jewish faith. She was a foreigner from Asia Minor (Acts 16:12-15), so what was she doing there?

Lydia was from the city of Thyatira (recorded in the Revelation as one of the seven churches of Asia), a place devoted to the worship of Apollo the sun-god, whom they called Tyrannus, indicating that he was the patron god of their city and region. A large contingent of Jews was living there, and she had evidently converted to Judaism, having learned the Jewish faith either from Jewish missionaries or their converted Gentile counterparts. By trade, Lydia was a purple dye seller, which would have been a profitable business in that day. Purple was a color distinguishing high rank; thus, her clients would likely have included landowners, politicians, and the wealthy, local elite.

Purple dye was made by boiling the sea snails that had been harvested on the Tyrian coast (by land, 700 miles to the southeast). These snails were boiled for days by the thousands in large vats made of lead. Even though this process produced a horrible stench, purple but a highly sought-after dye. Lydia was perhaps an importer of Tyrian snails, overseeing her own production facility, or she imported the dye already produced and, acting as a middleman (or woman), made her living by selling the dye. Being a dye importer is more likely and would have allowed her to eventually expand her trade from her home in Asia westward to Greece (Philippi), where she met Paul, who would have likely purchased dyes from her for his tents. The fact that the Bible refers to her as a "seller of purple" dye does not imply that Lydia did not trade in other colors. But unlike the other dye merchants, Lydia had a business contact enabling her to stock the rare and expensive purple dye; thus, she was known as "the seller of purple."

Feasibly, before speaking to her at the riverside, Paul may have already heard of Lydia, noticed her in the market, or even met her. When Paul met and proclaimed Christ to her from the Old Testament, she became the first authenticated convert in Europe, and she immediately offered her house to Paul as a place to live and establish a church.

Was Lydia financially able to fully support Paul and his team? That we do not know, but what we do know is that Paul remained there to establish a church before moving on, and as in Corinth, there is no reason to suspect that he interrupted his tentmaking business to do the work of the ministry. In fact, we find that the reason Paul met Aquila and Priscilla was that they, like him, were tentmakers. They also invited Paul to live with them (Acts 18:1-14). In turn, they not only discipled others (Apollos, for example) after the manner in which Paul had discipled them, but they also traveled with Paul on some of his journeys (Acts 18:21).

Furthermore, when Paul spoke to the Ephesian church elders (Acts 20:32-35) who came to visit him in Miletus, he made it a point to remind them of two things. During his three years in Ephesus, he had provided for his own needs, not asking help from them and that he had worked manually to provide for all the men who were with him—his

Timothies. He did not have to say how he provided these needs without their assistance; they all knew he was a tentmaker by trade.

So, we see that Paul was able to be a successful missionary while also working manually to finance himself and his ministry. His ministry's results came from his business contacts and comrades, not going door to door or even street preaching. (I am merely making a point, not attempting to demean other methods that I also use.)

I am not a scholar, but I have long heard that it was a custom among the Jews for a boy to be apprenticed by another man in his trade, having already learned his father's trade, so that he would always have a second career to fall back on. Since Paul was a trained theologian, perhaps in his youth, he had apprenticed as a tentmaker, giving him the knowledge and experience he needed to provide for himself.

Without question, other passages indicate that there is no problem with a missionary's working to support himself, his family, his associates, and his ministry. Some would suggest that since Paul worked, he did not receive support from churches. That supposition is not correct. In II Corinthians 11:7-9, he wrote,

> *"Have I committed an offense in abasing myself that ye might be exalted because I have preached to you the gospel of God freely? I robbed other churches, taking wages of them, to do you service. And when I was present with you and wanted* [lacked financially], *I was chargeable [the debtor] to no man: for that which was lacking to me the brethren which came from Macedonia supplied: and in all things I have kept myself from being burdensome unto you, and so will I keep* [continue] *myself."*

In this passage Paul mentions support from other churches as being his "wages" or salary. And when he suffered needs, God sent representatives from the church in Macedonia with a love offering for him. With all this biblical evidence, why do some still say it is wrong for a missionary to work if he receives support from churches back home?

Exposing the Conundrum

The simple answer is because we often build our doctrines on assumptions rather than on God's written Word. Once a respected preacher says something, it becomes doctrine and is embraced as doctrine until someday, someone exposes that "said doctrine" has no biblical basis. (Usually, the whistle-blower is branded as a heretic.) Let me share a few examples:

"Cleanliness is next to godliness."

"Everything rises and falls on leadership."

"If you don't stand for something, you'll fall for anything."

And my all-time favorite: "Your walk talks and your talk talks, but your walk talks louder than your talk talks."

These sayings may be correct, but they are not in the Bible.

Other assumptions have shaped our Western understanding of Scripture and that of the countries that imitate us. For instance, the teaching that the wise men (only three of them out of the scores that historical records record and identify by nationality or name) were present at the birth of Christ. The Bible does not say that; in fact, it says they saw the star, then researched the meaning (probably from the writings of Daniel), and then set out on a journey to find the babe. This process took a year or more. That is why Herod ordered not *all* the young boys killed, but all those under two years of age.

Then in other cases, we build doctrines based on our American culture. I have heard preachers say, "If your church building does not have a steeple, then it is not a church." I have also heard preachers say, "If the soul winner was not using a King James Version of the Bible [which I use] when he witnessed to you, then you are not saved." (If this were true, then no one came to Christ before AD 1611).

One of the most significant misunderstandings caused by our American culture is that a church is a building instead of a congregation.

We often have people question the number of new churches our team starts until I point out that they are house churches. Suddenly, our large numbers become acceptable when the naysayers realize no property was purchased, no facility, pews, PA systems, or offering plates were involved. Sadly, most "new churches" started in America are, in reality, new corporations comprised not of newly saved and baptized believers, but of relocated, disgruntled church members. And by the way, while I am ranting, let me say that the church building is not "God's house"; the individual believers are. When we continually say the building is God's house, mature believers may know what we mean, but children and new converts do not. For them, our words become doctrine.

Here's another example. At some point, someone suggested (preached or taught) that it was wrong for a missionary to be anything other than a full-time preacher, unencumbered with a manual work schedule. They even say that having an outside job is evidence of his lack of faith. That sounds spiritual and is undoubtedly desirable, but it is not a biblical requirement. After all, nearly half the pastors in America today also work another job.

Historically, in the first few centuries, very few pastors served full time. Most all churches met in small homes, markets, shops, or under trees. Thus, their congregations typically would not have been large enough to support a full-time pastor—just as they are not today in developing nations where they often meet in homes. Historically, the first building erected as a designated place of worship (a "church") was not built until the third century AD. So, we can say with certainty that neither Jesus, Paul, Peter, Stephen, James, John, Philip, Nathaniel, Matthew, Thomas, Barnabas, Silas, Timothy, Titus, Apollos, Clement, Ignatius, nor Polycarp ever preached in what we would call a church building. Never. Not even once.

But still, some feel it is wrong or inadvisable for a missionary to be a tentmaker. What are the reasons for their belief?

Argument:

A productive missionary will eventually need to spend all his time in ministry for oversight purposes. After all, how can he keep up with church programs and train pastors and students if he is working elsewhere full time?

Rebuttal:

Perhaps he should allow the men he has won to Christ, discipled and trained, to handle the administration while he busies himself producing more of them. It worked for Paul, and no one would argue that he was not a productive missionary.

Argument:

You can't plant a church while working a full-time job.

Rebuttal:

Thousands of examples worldwide rise in opposition to that theory. Even in America, most men who plant churches also work for a living. Some continue outside work after the church is large and flourishing because of the opportunity it gives them to relate to their members who work long hours and are yet expected to give time to church functions. It also provides the opportunity to meet and talk (evangelize) with employees, clients, and even competitors. Pastor Robert York of First Baptist Church, Streetsboro, Ohio, is an excellent example.

Historically, the Moravian missionaries to the Caribbean serve as an example. When they were forbidden to enter the sugarcane plantations to evangelize the slaves, they sold themselves as slaves, allowing them to live with the slaves and reach them for Christ. They worked daily in the hot, equatorial sun but were free to evangelize and plant churches at night. By doing this, they became "all things to all men."

I might add here that my father, as a layman, started three churches. He was saved as a young man. A lady in town gave a weekly Bible story in my mother's second-grade class. One day after the story, as the children were dismissed, my mother approached her with questions and was led to Christ. Later that day, she waited at home for my dad to arrive from work and told him what had transpired. My dad was so taken by the message that he called this lady to their home to learn more, and that evening, she led my dad to Christ. They were soon baptized and got involved in a local Baptist church. Feeling that it was the right thing to do, my dad quit smoking and drinking alcohol and began to tell others about Jesus.

At that time, he was rising in the ranks of his local Masonic Lodge. Often in the evenings, he would drive to other small towns to help the men organize a lodge for their community. Shortly after his conversion, while on his way to do just that, an inner voice spoke to him and said, "Now that you are a Christian, you should give your efforts to starting churches—not lodges."

That night, he made a U-turn on the highway and went home. He never attended another lodge meeting in his life, but he did plant three churches with the help of several friends, and having done so, found men to pastor them. He started three churches while working a full-time job with the Southern Bell Telephone Company and was also actively serving in his local church. Three of the four sons he and my mom raised became first pastors and then missionaries. Our oldest brother Ben is not an official "minister"; he works for a living. My dad, by the way, was finally ordained as a pastor at the age of 71. Less than a half year later, when barely 72 years old, he died of a brain tumor.

You can work a full-time job and still plant churches and disciple converts.

Argument:

It is illegal for missionaries to work since they are on a missionary status and do not have a work permit.

Rebuttal:

True, but it doesn't have to be. The preferable method is to acquire a legal resident's status in the country, which is a simple process. It will also cost less than airline flights in and out of the country to satisfy the requirements of temporary visas.

It is true that missionaries usually enter and live with a missionary visa, but that status is not a requirement. It is also why missionaries are not allowed in so many countries, and their number is increasing. Some suggest you go under the disguise of being a businessman. Still, when your ministry activity is discovered, you will likely be permanently evicted, and the general supposition is that all missionaries (Christians) are dishonest.

Several years ago, all the missionaries in Morocco were expelled and given between 24 and 48 hours to leave the country. (Imagine how difficult it would be to pack your belongings, close bank accounts, sell items like cars, and then lose rental deposits or mortgages on your house given such a short time to vacate.) The reason given was that most of these missionaries were involved in children's ministries and were supposedly doing only social work. The Moroccan government determined they were using their humanitarian work as a cover for their evangelistic purposes and expelled them. Those who have "remained" live in one of two autonomous cities on the Mediterranean coast, which are territories of Spain, called Melilla and Ceuta. Technically they are not in Morocco but can still go in and out.

The best way around these hurdles is to go on a work visa if you can, and if you can't, go there to live, get a residency—not a visa and start a business. In most cases, this solves all the problems. Governments don't want an American taking a job from one of their citizens. Still, they know that if you start a business, you will eventually, if not automatically, be hiring their citizens and providing new jobs. Many missionaries are English teachers and are paid by a host-school. They probably also need a bit of extra support. Every day they have direct communication with dozens of students and the opportunity to visit with their parents and siblings.

In the mid-1980s, as I was making plans to move to Thailand, I was contacted by three different private schools in Bangkok and offered a position as an English teacher for conversational English. As a result of my negotiations, I would be allowed to use any "textbook" I wanted, including the Bible. They each offered me a sizable apartment for my family, a car, a driver, a maid, and a salary equal to three times what they were paying their Thai teachers. I would have five to seven hour-long classes a day, where I would have thirty or more students from wealthy families sitting at my feet, learning to speak English with a Southern accent. I was free to meet their parents, take the students to the park, or have any contact with them I wanted. What a ministry opportunity!

At that time, the doors to China were wide open, offering the same opportunity, and hundreds took advantage of it. Still, the same opportunity abounds in many other countries. Also, or as a solo enterprise from your own home, you could teach or tutor English to the millions who want to learn it.

You don't have to be a specialist or an expert. You merely have to have a trade (tentmaking) that will provide for your needs. Are you a mechanic here? Be a mechanic there. Are you a barber here? Be a barber there. Are you a teacher, a banker, a landscaper, a musician, an accountant, a handyman, or a nurse here? Then be one there. And each day, you can invite your new converts for a discipleship lunch or an evangelistic meal with their family and yours. All the while you are developing friendships and amazing them with your answer to the continuous question, "Why are you here when you could stay in America and make so much more money?" The answer? That your love for their people brought you there with a message from God. The message is that He demonstrated His love for mankind by sending His Son to be sacrificed for our sins.

Argument:

A tentmaking missionary will spend too much time on his business and not have time for ministry.

REBUTTAL:

I can see that happening, and I have seen it happen. It even happened to me for a time. But if your heart is right with the Lord, it won't take long to realize you have misplaced your priorities and find your way home. But I would ask you, how much time is too much time? We expect bi-vocational pastors (and laypeople) in America to work forty hours a week and then preach or teach, go on visitation, etc. If we can do that here, why can't a missionary do it there?

I have seen many missionaries hard at work, spending enormous amounts of time in their home office, developing a Bible institute curriculum. At the same time, you can find thousands of them online, already prepared and doctrinally sound. Is that not a waste of time?

Most missionaries choose to raise support by going on deputation rather than working as a tentmaker; how much time is he wasting in his two, three, four, or more years of deputation?

Finally, we have to ask why we tend to separate work from ministry? Do you think that while Paul made tents, he was not also discipling his workers, witnessing to customers, etc.? We tend to think that the missionary's "work" is only preaching. That is why most church members think their pastor only works on Sundays and Wednesday nights. They don't understand all that is involved in ministry. In my experience, mixing with the public every day, all day, gives far more ministry opportunities than being cloistered in your office writing Bible institute lessons.

ARGUMENT:

The Bible says a double-minded man is unstable in all his ways.

REBUTTAL:

Yes, it does. Let's suppose when James wrote those words that he was referring to missionaries working secular jobs. If we are going to strain at that gnat, let's swallow the rest of the camel. He also said that pure, undefiled religion is taking care of widows and orphans. Are we doing that? The truth is, that is not at all what he was referring to when he mentioned being double-minded. Again, let's not build doctrines on assumptions.

Before I move on, allow me to give you two words that will help you understand why I believe a missionary can be (though not necessarily should be) a tentmaker and yet be a successful missionary at the same time. Those two words are *occupation* and *avocation*. An *occupation* is a job you do that puts food on the table and pays the bill. An *avocation* is what you do in the non-working hours that brings you joy and fulfillment. In short, your occupation is what you *do to live*, and your avocation is what you *live to do*.

Paul's occupation, when necessary, was to be a tentmaker. His avocation at all times was to be a proclaimer of the gospel, a discipler of converts, and a planter of new churches (congregations).

On a Personal Note:

I have been in missionary work for 35 years, and during that time, I have lived for significant periods in many countries and have been a resident of Honduras for twenty-three years. Does tentmaking work? Absolutely. Even now, our Touch a Life ministry is registered as a Honduran corporation, and we have many people working with us. We help them create their own sub-contracting business of running a feeding center. We provide them all they need to do it properly (facilities, tables, chairs, stoves, ovens, cooking utensils, pots, pans, plates, bowls, weekly food, and even the light bills). Our training and provision give them an income for their families and church members and provides a community service. As such, can you imagine how well "Brother Jon and Sister Nolin" are respected and received in those communities? No one in our region does not know who we are, what we do, and where we live (while in country). Since we are both read and known by all men, we must publicly live exemplary lives of service, sacrifice, hospitality, and example for God's glory and the benefit of mankind.

Because of our service, I have met the last five Presidents of Honduras and had private meetings with three of them. I have met several Congressional Presidents (their Speaker of the House equivalent who is third in line for the presidency). The last man who had that position was once an employee of mine. Unfortunately, he passed away two years ago. Our name and ministry have become so well known that I was approached to run for Congress several years ago. I would have, but for the law that only natural-born Hondurans can hold public office. That would have been the ultimate tentmaking position! That being said, I do feel a missionary should have the ability to serve full-time; but the lack thereof should not be an excuse to keep him from going.

Critics often say the national pastors only work because of the money we give them. Still, when an American missionary says to you, "We are at 'x' percent of our support now, and as soon as we get the other 'x' percent, we will be leaving," he is actually saying that without enough support, he will not go.

You've probably heard that from every missionary presentation at your church. But when was the last time you heard a prepared man say, "God called us, and though we have little or no support, I can swing a hammer there as well as I can here, so we're leaving in a month, with or without support"? Believe it or not, I have met some who have done just that.

So, if someday you hear a missionary say that—and then follow through, I recommend supporting him. He may just be the next Paul.

Eliminating the Conundrum

Suggestions for Missionaries:

- Never hide your plans from your supporting churches. If being a tentmaker is part of your "business plan," then make it known to your supporting churches. *"Provide things honest in the sight of all men"* (Romans 12:17).

- I have known couples who heard the call in a church service, and within weeks they were on the field. In some places, that is possible—but not in all. Do your homework, find out legally what you can and cannot do. You may have to travel there and hire an attorney to learn this, but if you have a trade that you can do elsewhere, you will likely be allowed to move there and start a business. Probably they will require you to provide evidence that you can take care of your own financial needs and not become a burden to their economy. If you are retired, it is much easier, and you don't have to be 65 or older to get a retiree's visa, which will also allow you to work. If you collect Social Security, your benefits may be enough to meet their guaranteed income demands.

- Make sure that you are led by God and not by your own emotions or desires. You might get away with that if others are supporting you, but if you are dependent on yourself, times will be challenging, and if you are there on anything less than a call from God, you will not last. Burdens may fade and change, but a call is permanent.

- Make sure you don't dedicate too much time to the business. You want to grow and succeed but remember your purpose is to plant churches. I have known several missionaries who were church planters that eventually got their eyes off the ministry and on the money. Demas was the first such missionary that we know of. Don't be a Demas.

- If your trade involves startup costs, you may want to consider asking churches to help you with that rather than ongoing support. They may also consider supporting you for the first year or two while your business grows. To me, this is wise and admirable. Their contractual support could also help you verify that you have sufficient financial backing to support you in the foreign land.

- Be realistic about what business you want to do, and don't do anything you are not familiar with. (That's experience speaking.) I once knew a trailblazing tentmaker who wanted to raise funds to open an automatic car wash in a particular country. I thought he had a great idea but not a great plan. If memory serves me correctly, he needed an amount that today would be equal to over $100,000, just to purchase and ship the equipment overseas. Next, he would have to buy or rent land in a congested, urban area and build a car wash facility. I advised him against that particular plan but was not able to convince him. His thought was that since there were none in that city, and all the car washing was done by hand, he would be guaranteed a great business. I had two concerns: 1) The amount of money he needed to raise just to get started, and 2) If people are sitting in their cars as they go through the automatic car wash, when would he have the opportunity to evangelize them? In the end, unable to raise even a significant fraction of what was needed, he went the traditional route and started deputation.

- Finally, get a work visa if you must and realize that missionary visas are fast becoming a thing of the past. My recommendation is to apply for residency. Once that is approved, you will have all the rights of a citizen, except for voting. And you won't have the expense and time drain to leave the country every three months, six months, or every few years to satisfy the country's visa demands. You will be living in your legal and adopted home and have the right to stay and have your own business(es).

Suggestions for Churches:

- Don't discount the validity of a man patterning his ministry after the apostle Paul. Sure, Demas failed, but Paul didn't. You've supported other men who never made it to the field. So, check out his plan and see if it is doable. If you feel it is, then give him a chance.

- If you know a brother in this position, you may want to help him get started. I would suggest that you have him meet with businesspeople in your church and let them determine if he will succeed or fail, based on their knowledge and experience. If possible, help him get additional training and experience in his chosen field, even a certificate or diploma. I have long said, "If you can cut hair here, you can cut hair anywhere." However, there is a difference between being an actual barber with skill and experience and cutting your son's hair with a salad bowl and your $20 generic clippers in the garage (as my dad did for his four sons, saving a lot of money).

- What about James and Peter? Good question, but now we're talking apples and oranges because they weren't primarily missionaries. James pastored in Jerusalem, and Peter, while I'm sure he planted some churches, is not known for that in the Scripture. In Acts, Peter is presented as an evangelist, a visiting preacher, an elder in the Jerusalem church, and a "prophet" speaking to established churches—Jewish and Gentile alike. He had a general calling to "go" but a specific calling to feed the sheep. Christ told all His apostles to go, and Peter did, but three times He commissioned Peter, "Feed my sheep."

- There are always trends in missions; some last, others don't. Let's be supportive of any method that helps to accomplish the Great Commission. Allow me to borrow from the poet, Alfred, Lord Tennyson: "It's better to have tried and failed than to live life wondering what would've happened if I had tried [tentmaking]."

- A church once dropped my support because I was doing secular work on the side. I found that interesting because the church pastor had his own side business with which he had made a fortune, and his church members were aware. At first, I bristled over the contradiction but eventually realized that they were not casting judgment on me; they simply had a policy that they did not support men working as tentmakers. So, pastors, you have the right to determine your missionary support policies. Just make them known so the men you support will not accidentally breach your policies.

- Whether you agree or disagree with the tentmaking concept, churches should be aware that this is a growing trend among missionaries, especially those targeting and entering closed countries. Consider what policies you plan to guide you, so when confronted, you'll be prepared.

A Few Final Thoughts in Defense of the Tentmakers:

Tentmaking provides extra funds for the missionary family, whether it is full-time or part-time. Maybe they raise chickens, have a garden, own a little grocery market, a barbershop or a beauty salon, an ice cream truck, a used clothing shop, drive a taxi, teach in a school, or tutor. Any of these avenues can help alleviate their increasing expenses without returning to America to ask for help from more churches or asking your church to give more. And if you still think it will take too much of their time, consider this: it can keep them from having to go on furlough to raise more support. That alone saves them one year out of every five being away from their ministry, plus all the additional travel expenses involved. If successful, it will not drastically take away from ministry time; rather, it will increase it.

No one can say that it will not take some time away from ministry, but if a man can get on the field in a few months as a tentmaker, that will save him two to five years of deputation time, where he is doing no ministry at all. Keep in mind, too, that 43 percent of all missionaries who start on deputation never finish it. They give up and stay home. Deputation can also be a waste of time, keeping a man from all ministry.

Another consideration is that you will be able to drop their support entirely at some time because the missionary will no longer need it. This then frees up your support to help other missionaries.

One final advantage is that this concept will intrigue businesspeople in your church and lead them to get more involved in missions, perhaps even taking trips to visit the missionaries or serve them as consultants or suppliers. That will help them, help the missionary, and help your missions' budget.

SECTION TWO

Great Commission Conundrums Regarding POLICY

Cambodian orphans with a Bible and hymn book

#6
If We Expect the National Churches to Support Their Own National Pastors, Why Don't We Expect Them to Support their Missionary Pastors Who Serve for Years or Even Decades as Pastors of National Churches?

Explaining the Conundrum

The short answer is ignorance or bias—and both are inexcusable. Now, let's take a not-so-short look at this conundrum.

Human nature seems to demand that we live by double standards. Nowhere is this more obvious than in the political sphere, where lies from the opposing candidate are shameless and must be exposed. But lies from our own candidates are excusable and must be justified.

For some reason, most people have always seemed to believe that missions funding is for *the messenger's support* rather than for spreading *the message* (see Conundrum #2). We have long lived with the idea that we should support our missionaries (most of whom are pastoring churches, not planting them), while the pastors whom they produce should not be helped at all since they are nationals. Some would say that is logical; I would say it is illogical and based on either ignorance or bias.

EXAMINING THE CONUNDRUM

Ignorance

Most of us have just never thought about this before, and so we continue to do missions the way we have always done it as if there is no other way. Change, it seems, is treated like a dirty, four-letter word, that for some reason, happens to have six letters.

In 1986 when I began this journey of persuading churches that supporting national preachers is viable, logical, and biblical, the most common pushback I received was, "That's not the way it has always been done." I was quick to point out that we don't do anything the way it has always been done. We don't warm or cool ourselves the way it has always been done. We don't cook the way it has always been done. And we don't transport ourselves the way it has always been done.

Go to any church, and you will find cars, not buggies. Enter, and you'll find electric lights, not kerosene lanterns. The bathrooms are inside with running water, not outside with a *Sears and Roebuck* or *Montgomery Ward* catalog. Central heat has replaced wood stoves, and air conditioning has replaced the ever-present, funeral-home-sponsored, handheld fans with the giant tongue-depressor handle. (If you can remember those, you are blessed with long life and a sharp memory.)

Think about it: when we get hungry, we take a little frozen cardboard box out of a big metal box and put it in a little counter-top box, press a few buttons, and in three minutes, we have a hot meal. My grandmother never cooked that way; she would probably have called that witchcraft.

Early man wrote on papyrus, then millennia later on vellum (skins), then parchment, and finally on paper. I'm not even doing that. I'm writing on nothing, arranging imaginary ones and zeros that don't actually exist but yet somehow form what appears to be words on a glass screen. It has never been done that way before or even imagined.

Truthfully, we don't do anything the way it has always been done—except for God's work, and that is inexcusable. Jesus Himself gave us the mandate to evangelize the world, baptize, and teach God's precepts, thereby expanding His prophetic kingdom worldwide. Today, most of our churches still ignorantly and intentionally relegate that glorious, earth-shaking task to eighteenth-century methods.

Bias

Again, thinking back to 1986, the second pushback I received against supporting national preachers was that "the nationals are not Americans and therefore cannot be trusted." Who can't be trusted—them or us? I wondered if they had forgotten about Jim Bakker, the *American* preacher who was incarcerated for using ministry funds to cover his sins; and Jimmy Swaggart, the *American* evangelist, who was knee-deep in sin and disgrace. Having been in church all of my life, I could give you a long list of "American" preachers and pastors who had fallen in sin, and unfortunately, the list continues to grow. I can remember in the early 1990s talking with some friends about the repeated news of pastors falling into adultery. It seemed so common at that time that I remarked, "They all have, and we all probably will," which brought unintended chuckles from a few of my friends. Fortunately, my disappointment-based sarcasm was not a prophetic utterance.

My point is that sin emanates from the heart of man, which is "deceitful above all things and desperately wicked" and has nothing to do with the color of a person's skin or his nationality. Our five senses should bring all we encounter to the praise of God; instead, they lead us to crave the desires of man's ever-evil heart. Here in our hearts, greed, envy, and lust rule supreme, unless hindered by the Spirit of God. Whether your eyes are black or blue, your hair brown or blonde, or your skin dusty or fair makes no difference; all men are sinners, and we are *all nationals* of one country or another.

Did you realize that our ancestors were all named for the pigment of their skin? Noah was not a racist, but he was the father of all current races. He named his sons based on their skin pigmentation. *Shem* means "dusty" (dust from the soil, somewhat beige in appearance); *Japheth* means "fair" (like sandy soil, not light, not dark); and it is believed that *Ham* means "black" (as in black, fertile soil). He named his three sons after three shades of soil. That should not surprise us since we are all made of dust, "and to dust, we shall all return" (except for the rapture participants, Enoch, Elijah, and hopefully us). Take the time to study the Table of Nations. You will discover that the primary regions where these brothers' descendants migrated are still mostly inhabited by people of that particular skin color.

The Scripture reveals no difference in the three brothers regarding their separate intellects, abilities, talents, personalities, or behaviors; all we know is that they had a different skin color, somehow, and for some reason, yet unknown to us. Race is not based on skin color but on people groups. There are many different black, white, and beige races, and they can each be traced back to a particular brother—all of whom had the same father, Noah, and presumably the same mother. Thus, there is only one race—the human race.

Every little boy thinks his dad is the strongest, his mom is the prettiest, his bicycle is the fastest, and his muscles are the biggest…and his little brother is the dumbest. We can't all be right, and thus, conflicts with those who disagree with us are born. As believers, we are all brothers and sisters, and none of us should be spiritually childish but mature. And since we consider ourselves to be mature believers, we should be aware that we are in a spiritual battle worldwide. As such, we should be eager to help any brother on the front lines who needs care, encouragement, supplies, or financing for his reinforcements as he pushes back the Enemy, gaining ground for our King.

Exposing the Conundrum

I asked the conundrum this way, including both the national pastors and foreign missionaries (who typically pastor national churches) because to do less would be an unfair double standard. It's a goose and gander sort of thing.

When I first began supporting national preachers in 1986, before the concept caught on, many American pastors would ask me why the national pastors can't or don't support their own pastors. My reply was that they should do so, and, in most cases, they do, even if only partially. Yet in America, thousands of pastors are not paid full time and many others not even part-time. Internationally, in many cases, the congregation is too small, Christianity is too new, and jobs are too scarce to provide a salary from which to tithe. Some would say that if the church has ten families and each tithed, then the pastor would have a salary equal to his church members' average income. True. Now here's my question: how's that working out in your church? Pastors are like missionaries and church members; some get less than they deserve, some get more than they deserve, but none are getting what they think they deserve—or need!

In many societies, the people live by bartering, especially if you get out of the capital city where so many missionaries tend to live and move out to the rural areas. I have seen many offerings of rice, eggs, and vegetables around the world in rural churches. The people were farmers with no cash crop, yet they faithfully gave 10 percent of their harvest for their offering. While the pastor had rice and eggs to eat, you can't wear an egg, and you can't walk on eggs. Cash is needed to provide for such needs.

In some cases, the congregation is up to 70 percent unemployed (or higher). The pastor uses their offerings to care for the hungry and the widows, the orphans and the abused, and has nothing left for himself. Others, feeling that the tithe is for the Lord's work, use it to purchase tracts or Bibles to give away or buy a bus ticket to travel to the next village to evangelize. They go, hoping God will lead some family to give them food while there. These men work in the fields and forest to earn a living for their families. They are not sitting in a clergyman's office, expecting a salary; like Paul, they work with their hands to earn food for their children. Where is the crime in helping such a man, a brother in Christ who is doing what we cannot do in a place that we dare not go? Where is the biblical mandate not to share our wealth to help a servant of God in need? The apostle John, in his third letter, commanded us to do exactly that.

Consider that at least a third of the world (in 2020) still lives on less than $2 a day. And many of them live on less than $1 a day. In some countries, food accounts for up to 70 percent of their earnings. Much of the world goes to bed having had less than 500 calories that day. They have no cash to tithe from, only a little produce. The pastors live off that produce, selling what they cannot eat. Logically, when the rice harvest is in, giving offerings of rice is possible. But there are two points to consider:

1) Everyone has rice to sell at that time, so the price drops, and the pastor's wife can get very little for her supply.
2) What happens when the rice season is past, and once again, there is nothing left to give?

Again, going back to the conundrum as worded, another comment/complaint I would often receive was, "If you give them (the national preachers) money, you'll ruin them." I countered that they are not children who need to be supervised by more educated, and allegedly, more spiritually advanced American Christians; they are veteran preachers serving God when I was still wetting my diapers. *Why is it,* I wondered, *if I give a national preacher $35 a month to help him care for his family, it will ruin him; but if I give a missionary $7,000 a month, he won't be affected? Is this ignorance or bias or both?*

We need to understand that if a man is a traditional missionary, meaning one who takes a church, not plants a church, and is sedentary in that church year after year, decade after decade, he is not fulfilling the biblical mandate or job description of a missionary. He is, however, fulfilling the job classification of a pastor. I say bravo for him. But if he is doing *a pastor's job*, why is he being supported as *a missionary?* Previously, many people felt that a pastor should only be supported by his congregation, using that reasoning to justify not giving support to national preachers, knowing that the missionaries they support are also pastoring local churches. They continue to give to them, allowing them to receive incomes that likely exceed their national congregation's combined income. Is this ignorance or bias or both?

In other conundrums, I have written about the excuses given by many regarding why churches continue to support "missionaries" who are actually "pastors." I don't want to spend time beating that horse again. My point is equality, that if we can support an American as the pastor of a Mexican church, why then is it wrong to support a Mexican who is the pastor of a Mexican church? And if it makes you feel better, exchange Mexican for Pakistani, Brazilian, Kenyan, Ukrainian, or whatever country you prefer.

I have seen many strange things in my life when it comes to missions. In 1977 when I was 21 and on a church planting team in White Plains, New York, barely anyone wanted to help us. Still, when several friends doing the same in Brooklyn and Queens joined mission boards, printed "prayer cards," and presented themselves as "missionaries" to New York City, churches stood in line to support them.

I worked long hours in the secular world and did ministry at night. I walked when my car broke down and sometimes ate from dumpsters behind restaurants. I don't know how well they succeeded, but our church continues reaching the area and supports missions 44 years later. Why were we successful? We knew that if we were going to eat, we had to work. We had to depend on God and ourselves, and we had to teach the people their responsibility to care for their pastors. Without that pressure, it is easy to get lazy.

Another difficulty for many missionaries is that it isn't easy to teach tithing to new converts who may earn 1/100th of what you make, and they know their tithe will not be used to support you. What is their motivation to give? What pattern have they learned to follow once you retire? Typically, they try to get another missionary or a national pastor without paying him a salary; after all, the missionary never received one.

Another lesson I learned during that time was that a sister church with the same doctrine would go to no ends to raise funds for their ministry but not give a dime to help us in ours. We were both Baptists and from the same "camp," but there was no inclination to help us do what we were both called to do: reach New York. Why was that?

The American mind would say that mindset is normal, righteous, and just, but what does the heavenly mind say? We arrogantly say that God would undoubtedly bless his ministry if the poor pastor knew what he was doing. But even Paul said he had been through times of abounding and abasing. Was God only blessing him in the times of abundance? Did he only know what he was doing when he was abounding?

I wonder if the successful pastor has any responsibility to help teach his unsuccessful counterpart, or is it every pastor for himself? I have been in and served in many large, prosperous, and thriving churches in my life. What is one thing they all had in common? Their congregations were not new converts. The overwhelming bulk of their membership were families who came from other churches.

A few years ago, I sat with a friend who is on the staff of a megachurch. At the beginning of the service, he leaned over and told me that at least 75 percent of their members present that night were not originally from that area. They had moved there to attend Bible college and had never left. The successful and gifted pastors of that church did not build their colossal congregation. It was built by unknown and supposedly insignificant pastors (and parents) from all over the country who had sent the best they had there to train. The megachurch has benefited from their labor, attendance, and tithe. (And for those of you who think you know my history well enough to know where I am talking about, don't be judgmental; you only think you know.)

This happens on a smaller scale in many cities across America. You don't have to be a megachurch to benefit from floating members. In the past, we built churches by soul winning; now we build them by relocating members. When approached for membership by a family from a sister church, my pastor first enquires why they want to join with us. If he detects any problem, he encourages them to make peace and resolve the conflicting issues with their current church before joining us. I think that is 100 percent admirable and honoring to God. My pastor understands that his job is not to build a "bigger barn" but to feed and care for whatever sheep are in his flock. If they are fed well and healthy, they will produce more sheep. If a lamb from another flock gets mingled in with our flock, he doesn't brand it; instead, he helps, if possible, to restore it to its shepherd.

We highlight our mission policies by abusing and shaming national preachers and forbidding them support. When we say that we cannot afford or refuse to help one of "those" national preachers with a mere dollar or two a day, we expose our bias. Because at the same time, we send one of "us" through four years of Bible college, three to four years of deputation, several years of language school, and internship—and all this while being aware that over 85 percent of the missionaries we send will never serve a second term. We look at our mission programs, pat ourselves on the back for a job well done, and extol our good stewardship for funding missionaries who are really pastors while ignoring that the cost of funding just one of "us" could have support 75 to 100 national pastors. I ask again: is this ignorance or bias or both?

The wonderful truth is that many missionaries share their support with the men they have trained and with others they have met who need financial assistance. In doing so, they genuinely teach biblical principles to the national churches, who are aware that their pastor could not survive without the missionary's help. These missionaries are examples of the believer. They should be commended and held as an example for others to emulate.

We should expect and teach the national churches to give obediently, no matter how little they have. But we should also be willing to step in and help them until they no longer need our help. Simple follow-up and accountability will efficiently resolve any possible issues that may arise.

In 1992 we began supporting national preachers in Vietnam and eventually became the second-largest ministry in the country, supporting over 130 men. Several years later, we began helping a group in Cambodia and eventually supported, I think, around 84 preachers. I loved these guys and was proud to help them.

About six to seven years ago, we received a letter from the group in Vietnam and then a similar letter from the group in Cambodia several months later. Though they didn't know each other and spoke different languages, both letters said basically the same thing; it went something like this...

> *Dear Final Frontiers,*
>
> *We want to thank you for all the help you have given us over the years. That help has bought us time to reach our people, establish churches, and train them to tithe. Now our economy is growing, and our people have employment and can support their own pastors. For that reason, we are writing to tell you that we no longer need your assistance and ask that you would transfer our support to other preachers around the world who still need your help.*

You can decide for yourself if the double-standard regarding support is from the standpoint of ignorance or bias. Realize, however, that I am attempting to make two points:

1) I am not suggesting that we stop supporting missionaries.

2) I am not suggesting that we start supporting nationals at the same level the missionaries receive.

We should think about what we are doing, why we are doing it, and how we are doing it — or worse, not doing it. Then we should make the appropriate adjustments to the glory of God and for the advancement of His kingdom.

For us at Final Frontiers, this is all a moot point. First, we don't support American missionaries, and if we did, they would be missionaries (church planters) and not pastors. Many missionaries help us or affiliate with us, allowing us to support their men who need help, and in turn, they provide us with the necessary accountability.

Second, we don't support national preachers simply because they are pastors. Our policy is that we support only church planters (biblical missionaries). The church planter may be a pastor, an evangelist, a traveling preacher, or even a qualified layman. Still, to qualify for support, he must have already started at least two churches without any support and trained at least one man for the ministry. Also, to maintain support, he must be "actively and consistently involved in church planting and discipleship." We partner with these men. They do the work, and we collect and send their support. They compile reports for their sponsors and return them to us. We record and then forward them to the sponsors for accountability. They have their part to play, you have yours, and we have ours: one body doing God's work, God's way with neither ignorance nor bias.

Eliminating the Conundrum

Suggestions for Missionaries:

- Follow Paul's example of supporting the men who are your Timothies. He declared in Acts 20 that with his own hands, he worked to provide for his needs and those of the men who traveled and served with him. If this was not meant as an example for others to follow, why did he do it? The most crucial issue for supporting nationals is accountability, but if they are working with you, you have absolute accountability both from them and for their supporters.

- Many missionaries feel bad about the disparity between their "wealth" and the "poverty" of the national preachers. Sharing your support would be a blessing to them. I am not suggesting an equal amount, as you have expenses they do not have, but to relieve their lack would be a great blessing and endear you to both them and the local churches. What a testimony for you to have!

- Remember that if your ministry is only pastoring a church, you are not a biblical missionary; instead, you are a national church's foreign pastor. If that is what God called you to be, then be it. But if our calling was missions, then be a missionary. Take some of your people and evangelize an unreached area and plant a house church. Nourish it. Send your men back to have weekly Bible study times and watch as the plant matures into an active church. Then repeat the process again and again until the Lord returns, training each new church to do the same. Need help? Give me a call.

Suggestions for Churches:

- Hopefully, "missionaries" who are only pastoring and not planting churches was not the intent of your missions' program. But if it was, you might now want to consider adjusting your missions' program for both missionary support and a ministry fund for all other ministry personnel and projects. Hold each man in each category accountable for fulfilling what you are funding him to do.

- Understand this. When a missionary only serves as a pastor for an extended period, he does several things:

1) He teaches by his example that missionaries are pastors, so if the missionary is not out planting churches, why should they?

2) He tends to absorb the local church's bills, paying the utilities, the water bill, painting the auditorium, buying the musical instruments, adding on the fellowship hall, etc. Over the years, the church depends on him to do it all without a salary from them. When he leaves, they will first expect the new national pastor to do the same, but of course, he cannot. Often, the church will disband or do without the needs and improvements. They were not taught their responsibility to start churches, and they never practiced tithing because he generously took care of everything for them.

3) There are occasions when a missionary does stay in one church for decades and is successful because he does plant other churches. He remains at one, culturally because that is the American way, but from it, he reaches out to plant more, taking his people with him and allowing them to pastor those new churches. This highly successful pattern teaches the national pastors that they have a responsibility while pastoring one flock to create other flocks for other shepherds to pastor.

#7 WHY DO AMERICAN CHURCHES SEND SO MANY MISSIONARIES TO A FEW COUNTRIES AND SO FEW OR NONE TO OTHERS?

EXPLAINING THE CONUNDRUM

WHAT IF THE Great Commission was the *Mediocre Commission* that did not command but only suggested that we go into "part of the world, concentrating on a few desirable spots, while avoiding dangerous and inhospitable places, and preach the gospel to those who gather week after week in our facilities? Based on what American churches are doing and accomplishing with their mission programs, that seems to be the course we have taken. Will our Master not hold us accountable?

Most American churches have a hallway in a predominate area of their facility, where they display the prayer cards of missionaries they support and a recent, quarterly letter from them. When I go to a church to speak, since I am a fellow missionary, I try to read every letter posted, which sometimes requires a fair bit of time. In thirty-five years of speaking in hundreds of churches as a missionary, I have read many thousands of letters. As you might suppose, I have noticed a pattern that has never failed to occur and is rarely confronted.

At any given church, on any given Sunday, almost every letter will mention some or all of these components:

- Personal needs, usually for items like new tires, auto repairs, braces for teeth, etc., that should have provided for in their monthly budget based on their monthly support
- Plans for upcoming furloughs or new ministries, such as a Bible institute.
- Projects for which help is needed, such as a church bus, a new building, etc.
- Family information, like birthdays, vacations, a new addition to the family, how the kids are doing in school, etc., because the letter is being sent to all of their sponsors. Some recipients know them only on paper, and others know them personally and have a great interest in the family.

At the same time, other vital components are almost always excluded from the letters. Based on my vast experience in personally examining the quarterly letters, I will list these areas and estimate how often they are mentioned.

- Perhaps 15 percent will mention having led a soul to Christ in the previous three months.
- At best, 5 percent will mention discipling a new convert or training a man for ministry in the past quarter.
- Possibly 1 percent will mention starting a new church/ mission station/home Bible study/house church (whatever you want to call it).

I hear you. Some of you are saying, "Jon, there you go again being negative about missionaries." I understand it may appear that way, but you have judged me wrongly. My motivation is twofold. First, I hope to make churches aware that they seemingly have no accountability or concern for the missionaries they support. (If they did, why would they permit such ministry failures year after year?) Second, I want to encourage missionaries to grow the 15%, 5%, and 1% to higher numbers. As they do, I guarantee that their supporting churches will notice it and cement their support for a lifetime.

When my doctor told me that I had stage 2 to stage 3 liver disease and chronic kidney failure, he was not critical of me personally; rather, he was warning and motivating me to take the necessary steps to slow and even halt the progression. (I did. I have already lost 65 pounds and feel great.) If you feel I am speaking critically of missionaries, you are wrong. I am pointing out the spiritual disease that allows them to continue a fruitless ministry year after year while having no shame of publicizing it in their quarterly letters.

Thirdly, the missionary wall tells me that most churches load up missionary support on some countries and have no part in reaching other countries, continents, and entire blocks of people. This is the conundrum at hand. No one can deny the truth that has created and perpetuated this concern, so we should take a closer look to see why we do it and how we can correct it.

EXAMINING THE CONUNDRUM

Some logical, practical, and spiritual issues have caused and perpetuate this conundrum. Let's examine them one at a time.

The Logical

Our Exposure. As humans, we are burdened for, drawn to, and influenced by what we are the most exposed to.

I was born in Augusta, Georgia, just two hours away from the city of Athens, home of the University of Georgia and the exalted and glorious Georgia Bulldogs (pronounced *Bull Dauwggs*). So, for what football team do you think I cheer? In truth, I never attended the school, my dad never went there, and my mom only attended for a few years to earn a master of education degree.

For the most part, I grew up in Atlanta, just ten miles away from the campus of the infamous Georgia Tech and the world-famous hot-dogs at *The Varsity*. Due to proximity, one would think the Yellow Jackets would have my allegiance, but no. The simple fact is if you live anywhere in Georgia, and if you have an IQ higher than a stump, you are a Bulldogs fan. (If you're a lowly engineering student, you may be permitted to consider yourself, with understandable shame, a "Yellow Jackets" fan). The reality is if you're from Georgia, and there's nothing wrong with you, it's just logical to be a Bulldogs fan, and more than that, it's cultural and somewhat required. (My apologies to Pastor Charles Blackstock and the other twelve Yellow Jacket fans. You can't help that you were exposed to the wrong team but rejoice—there is mercy and forgiveness.)

By the same token, as I was growing up in the sixties, most of the missionaries who came to our church were seemingly focusing on going to Mexico. Why was that? At that time, most churches would give a missionary about $25 in monthly support, and most missionaries only needed about $300 to $500 monthly; thus, they did not have to raise support from many churches to have their "full support" (12 to 20 churches). In those days, southern missionaries primarily raised support in southern churches and northern missionaries in northern churches. Since Mexico borders the illustrious state of Texas, our southern missionaries had more geographic *exposure* to Mexico than any other country. This reality made travel to and from Mexico, both during deputation and furlough, easily accessible. Back then most missionaries were seemingly going to either Mexico, Brazil, Germany, or the Philippines, so we were mostly *exposed* to Mexico, Brazil, Germany, and the Philippines.

You can see the impact of *exposure* on the migratory patterns of missionaries. In the past century, after World War II, missionaries primarily went to the Philippines and Germany. However, Japan was mostly overlooked, probably because of their aggressive and unprovoked attack against the United States at Pearl Harbor, as well as the news of their infamous death marches in Southeast Asia. Japan suffered from a lack of burden by most missionaries as well as our churches. Our troops were not exposed to them as a people to the degree they were to the Filipinos, Germans, etc. As a country, we were resentful and unexposed and therefore not burdened for the Japanese. This attitude was demonstrated by the comparatively few missionaries who went there to win them to Christ.

In contrast, the Philippines received the bulk of missionaries due to those returning having served there in the war. (Once again, the influence of *exposure.*) Fifty years later, the national pastors trained by American missionaries have effectively evangelized their homeland. For decades, they have insisted they no longer need missionaries; they need only resources to help them continue to reach their people more effectively.

After World War II, General Douglas MacArthur asked for missionaries to go to Japan and the Philippines. Missionaries answered his call to the Philippines, and as a result, they benefit from high exposure to the gospel. In contrast, businesspeople, not missionaries, went to Japan. As a result, they enjoy their status as one of the world's major financial centers with little exposure to Christ and Christianity.

After the Korean War, exposure once again created a considerable migration of missionaries to South Korea. As a result, it is now, per capita, the most "Christian" country on the Earth. The five largest churches in the world are in Seoul, Korea, as are 20,000 other churches.

Vietnam is different. Because that was a war that we were not allowed to win, the outcome negatively affected Christianity's spread. The Communist Party, which still controls the country, would not allow missionaries to enter. There was and still is a burden in the hearts of some who have found a way in, but nearly fifty years later, the permission to go is still lacking.

At one time Final Frontiers was the second largest mission in

Vietnam. At one time, we had over 140 preachers supported there—not to mention the thousands of young men in training. I know from experience that the Vietnamese church planters who were supported received their aid primarily from American veterans of the Vietnamese war. Having served there, they had developed a burden to reach the Vietnamese people for Christ *(exposure).*

Since few to no missionaries were going there, they supported Vietnamese church planters through our ministry. Incidentally, at their request, we now barely support any Vietnamese preachers. Groups totaling over 220 preachers in Vietnam and Cambodia wrote to us thanking us for all the support, declaring that it gave them time to win their people, disciple them, and teach them to tithe. This level of spiritual maturity, coupled with their growing economies, prompted them to inform us that they no longer needed our support and asked us to transfer it to preachers in other lands who still needed our help. (So much for the opinion of those who say the nationals are only in this for the money.)

This same "burden by exposure" is now benefitting the Middle East. Tens of thousands of veterans have a desire to see the land of the Bible evangelized. Since missionaries cannot go there, so veterans help by supporting the national church planters who live (and die) there. They also fund our Bible Smugglers ministry that takes tens of thousands of Bibles each year throughout the world's Islamic-controlled regions.

As you see, missionaries often tend to go to those places to which they have been exposed. This is logical, for as Lamentations 3:51 states, *"Mine eye affecteth mine heart...."* Thus, if we want missionaries to have a burden for other places, we need to expose them to other places, other cultures, and other peoples. It's just that simple. It's also a good reason for families and churches to send their youth on mission trips to mission fields instead of New York City, New Orleans, and New Mexico.

The Practical

As already stated, we often send missionaries where our soldiers have preceded them. Britain, France, Germany, and Holland have all done the same. Historically, to our shame, Protestant missionaries tend to follow their country's armies while Catholic missionaries tend to precede them. Regardless, one point remains constant: we can only send missionaries if they feel called to go, and for whatever reason, ours usually seems to be called after the fighting has stopped.

If that observation is offensive, then let me prove my point. In how many of the 59 Muslim countries does your church support a missionary? Probably none. And if your church is not supporting a missionary to the Muslim world through Final Frontiers, you are probably not supporting one at all. And yet, our commission was to "go into ALL the world." So why is that? Going there is not practical because of their laws, restrictions, bias, and safety issues. Those who do go must be a business professional or a student—not as a missionary or preacher. And by the way, we don't have to send the national preachers; they are already there. And in those few Muslim lands where a missionary can go, though cloaked under a different professional title, he must live in a non-Muslim community and is strictly forbidden from witnessing to Muslims.

Another example of this reality occurred in Russia. When the Berlin Wall fell in 1989, our long-suppressed burden to win our former enemies to Christ caused an overwhelming number of families to go to Russia as missionaries. Praise God for that. Since Final Frontiers was already serving behind the Iron Curtain, this sudden and colossal influx of missionaries caused me to wonder why God had not called others there before the wall fell. Coincidently, now that Communism is back in the driver's seat again, it causes me to wonder why today, probably 95 percent of those who went to Russia have left.

The truth is, we never find an instance in the Bible when the preachers pulled out because of persecution or the existence of a hostile government. Suppose Paul had vacated every empire-oppressed place he went, he would have had nowhere to go. Today, we rarely find an instance when missionaries remain after a hostile government has taken over or enter a land that a hostile government already controls. Why?

Perhaps the answer is that it is no longer practical to serve there. The schools are no longer open to missionary visits, missionary visas are no longer processed, and churches are closed or driven underground. The government is confiscating land from unregistered churches, and most radio and television ministries are now either hindered or removed.

Other lands, free lands, have removed or restricted the missionary inflow by changing their visa laws. In the past, a missionary could go for a four-year term and easily renew his visa. Now some countries, like Panama, have adopted what is called "the European Model." Let me explain what that is. When a missionary visa expires, the missionary family must leave the country, not for a day or week but for the equivalent time that he was there. If the expired visa was for four years, then they must leave for four years.

Also, to be allowed back in as a missionary, they must verify that they returned to their nation of origin while waiting for their elusive renewal visa. (Of course, becoming a permanent resident of that country would forgo all the bother and expense, but mission boards do not generally teach the missionary to do that. Also, entering as a businessman and having either a work visa or a residency would also alleviate this problem.)

This inconvenience and interruption of ministry have had a practical effect on where missionaries will choose to serve in the future. For example, why go to Panama and be hindered when you can go next door to Costa Rica and serve without hindrance?

The result is that missionaries will eventually leave Panama and be unable to return. In the meantime, as of 2010, over 25,000 Muslims were living in Panama, and their numbers are growing. As we leave, they come. This is because they don't enter as Muslim "missionaries" but as businesspeople who buy homes, start businesses, sink roots, build mosques, finance education for the poor and casually convert them. Since American and Western Christians will never leave our comfortable homes and follow that pattern, it is essential for the missionaries to duplicate themselves faithfully and actively so that the national preachers can carry on without their lead or presence. And since we can give the Panamanians our gospel, our missionaries, our culture, our music, our buildings, and our dress styles, why can't we and why shouldn't we give them funding to reach their own?

The Spiritual

God calls where God calls, but we do not always understand His calling.

As I grow older and more experienced, I am less likely to believe that God calls us so much to a place as He does to a people. And of course, we generally find those people at a place. The man from Macedonia urged Paul to come to a place (Macedonia) but for what purpose? It was to "help us," and who were the "us?" Paul's call was not the *place* but the *people* of Macedonia. In Paul's vision, he saw a *man* of Macedonia—not a *map* of Macedonia.

God miraculously translated the evangelist Philip to the desert because an Ethiopian eunuch hungry for the truth was there, who needed someone to explain God's Word to him so that he could, in turn, explain it to his people living in Ethiopia. History tells us that he did so quite effectively.

God sent Jonah to the people of Nineveh, but to find them, he had to go to the place where they were located and concentrated. Jonah wasn't sent to preach to the buildings but to the people. Nineveh was the capital of the Assyrian Empire that was ruling the region at that time. Mosul, a city in today's news, is modern-day Nineveh (a suburb, really). Perhaps God is preparing another Jonah for another citywide act of repentance there even now.

Missionaries, you should ask God to show you the people He has chosen for you to conquer and saturate with the knowledge of His glory and grace. Find them wherever they are and go to them, especially if numbers of them already live in your city, state, or nearby. Then teach your converts to do the same so that you can move on to the next people or region, where the people are still waiting to hear the good news. If you are a missionary, that's what God created you to do. You were not commissioned to be the shepherd of a flock; you were meant to turn goats into sheep, to start flocks, and train shepherds to care for them so you can move on and create more flocks. You have a highly specialized calling. A pastor, by nature of his call and duties, must be a spiritual general practitioner, but a missionary is not a missionary unless he is a church-planting, pastor-training specialist. So, get busy starting some new flocks because the grass will always be greener on the other side for you and me. Enjoy it!

Exposing the Conundrum

Missions Is at a Critical Point.

Around 2010 Missionary Gil Anger presented a questionnaire to many Independent Baptist mission agencies. Of them, twenty-three responded. Their answers, along with data from the *Reaching Beyond Borders* website, reveal a startling vista of our present-day missions outreach.

What is the current number of missionaries?

In 1950 approximately 100,000 Protestant and evangelical missionaries from America served worldwide.

- Since then, an average of 1,000 missionaries are lost each year due to death, retirement, or career change.
- These 1,000 experienced missionaries are being replaced by an average of only 50 inexperienced missionaries per year.

As of 2012, only 29,000 missionaries were serving on the field; of those, about 5,000 were Independent Baptists.

- Of those, 2,628 (53%) served overseas (as pastors, preachers, teachers, children's workers, mechanics, secretaries, etc.)
- 2,372 (47%) served in the United States in various ministry or support positions (such as printers, staff members, evangelists, groundskeepers, etc.)

My first book, *The Great Omission*, was written primarily to expose and discuss this issue of calling everyone a missionary (rather than making a distinction between missions and ministry) and gave meaningful and easily attainable ways to remedy it. Many churches have adopted the policies I addressed and have seen their worldwide outreach grow and their missions giving increase substantially. That is because people give more when they know what they are giving to and for.

Where Are Most Missionaries Serving Today?

There are 195 countries in existence today, but a staggering 30 percent (about 1,500 missionary families) are, for some reason, serving in only five of these countries:

- 253 are in Brazil.
- 206 are in Mexico.
- 112 are in the United Kingdom (England, Scotland, Wales, and Northern Ireland).
- 118 are in the Philippines.
- 104 are in Canada.

What about the other 190 countries? Are we to believe that the same God who commissioned (commanded) us to go into ALL the world has somehow forgotten about the other 190 lands?

It takes only a glance at the five favored countries to see that at least 30 percent of all missionaries are pursuing those who have already heard the gospel or have unobstructed access to hearing it. Why is that? Why do we continue to send men to lands that have the gospel and ignore lands that do not?

I know that some would say that despite their access to the gospel, all have not heard. That is true, and they need to be evangelized as well. That being the case, why is it that missionaries tend to clump together in the capital city or another primary city of their country rather than spreading out to reach the unevangelized areas? In Honduras, for example, probably 80 percent or better of the missionaries live and minister in the capital city Tegucigalpa or San Pedro Sula, the commercial capital on the north coast; yet thousands of towns and villages still have no gospel outreach.

Why is that? Who is teaching our missionaries to ignore the outlying masses in favor of reaching the already reached? Have we learned nothing from Hudson Taylor, David Livingstone, and other missionary legends? What part of the Great Commission makes this attitude and practice acceptable, and why do our churches support it? Would they support a man to start a new church half a mile from their own? I doubt it. Then why support men to pastor a church on top of a church in other lands? Our Lord was a 1%'er. He left the 99 to go after the one lost sheep. Why do we do the opposite? I'm sincerely asking because I don't know.

Livingstone wrote, *"If you have men who will only come if they know there is a good road, I don't want them. I want men who will come if there is no road at all."*

While doing a demographic study on Thailand in 1986 with the expectation of moving there, I learned that 80 percent of all the missionaries lived in the northern city of Chiangmai. At that time, it had a population of only a half million people. Bangkok, the capital, had over 8 million officially and 13 million unofficially and had only a handful of missionaries. Why is this? Every missionary I asked gave me the same answer: "The temperature is so much cooler here than in Bangkok." The truth is, denominational missionaries (salaried employees) go where their headquarters are or where they are told to go, and faith missionaries tend to follow their trail.

I know some would say, "Our churches support those going to already plowed and planted mission fields because we do not know any missionaries in closed or restricted lands, so how can we support them?" The answer is simple, Final Frontiers and a host of other good ministries do know these men; we have found them, vetted them, and have the ability to hold them accountable to you and your church. Contact us. We can immediately give you a preacher to partner with who is already serving without financial support and help you fill in those enormous blank spots on your missionary map.

What About the Next Generation of Missionaries?

If you continue to read, you will probably begin to be discouraged. But hang in there because there is a cure to this mission-disease. Again, my intention is not to be critical of missionaries who are so willing and eager to serve, but for the sake of the patient (world missions), I'm going to tell you what the MRI and x-rays reveal.

I remember sitting in an office with a liver specialist at Atlanta's Piedmont Hospital in the fall of 2015. His answers, interrupted by my questions, went something like this. "Mr. Nelms, you have liver disease, and it's serious… You are at stage 2 and bordering on stage 3… If we don't get this issue under control, we will have to place you on a transplant list, and with your blood type (AB negative), the expectation for a donor is not very good… As it is, you have probably three years left to live, maybe five… Do what I have recommended, and you have a chance… Go home and put your house in order."

This was, of course, devastating news. But in telling me the truth about my condition, the doctor was not being critical of me; he was merely informing me of the problem, the solution, and the probable outcome. In reality, he did me a great favor by informing me what my problems were, explaining the cause and cure, and teaching me to take steps to remedy the problem. I am happy to say that I immediately began implementing his suggestions (he told me to lose 10 percent of my weight, and so far, I have lost 20 percent and am still going). Three years passed, and I was still here, then five years passed, and I remain strong and healthy—praise the Lord.

Now, I am in the position to play doctor and tell churches what their mission problems are and how to fix them. Read carefully because we do not know how many years we have left to fulfill the Great Commission.

As a church member, when you listen to the missionaries who visit your church to share their ministry with you, some are indeed boring, but others who touch your heart, ignite a desire to help them. But in doing so, what/who are you really helping? Consider the following statistics.

- 43 percent of those currently on deputation will quit before reaching their goal of having enough support to leave for their field and began their first term (usually four years).
- 75 percent of those who make it to the field will quit within their first three years of service.
- 55 percent of those who make it to through the first term and begin their furlough (their fifth year as a missionary) will not return to the mission field. Most will remain in America, serving on a church staff or as faithful lay families.

These symptoms of our mission disease have been covered in-depth in my book, *The Great Omission*, so I don't want to dwell on them here. (The symptoms, disease, and cure will be examined in greater detail in a book I am writing for churches on how to make and maintain a missions' policy, so for now, let me make these few observations.)

To become a doctor, you must have a certain amount of education, starting with a bachelor's degree, then four years in medical school, and three year in residency, then you earn your title of "Doctor." Even then more continual education is required on an annual basis to maintain a license to practice medicine.

Another reality is that nurses, as essential and underrated as they are, are not doctors. My dad died of a brain tumor in 1995. About ten years later, I too became the host for a benign tumor. The medicines I took both shrunk the tumor and prohibited it from growing. I had great nurses throughout the discovery and treatment but had surgery been necessary; I would have preferred a doctor's skill over a nurse's tender care.

If you want to be a pilot, you undergo ground school and chalk up hundreds of hours of flight experience, both with and without a certified pilot overseeing you. The time and expense involved are tremendous, and that is why many pilots received their training and certification in the military. Still, being a pilot is not enough; you must be certified for every type of plane you fly. A pilot certified only for a single propeller, Cessna 180, cannot fly a 747 or even a small, single-engine jet, and certainly not a helicopter! Get my point?

I have flown around 2 million miles in my missionary travels. I quickly learned that flight attendants have personality and charm. They speedily deliver pillows, blankets, and hot meals. They are masters of crowd management, security, and patience. But though they are valued employees of the same airline as the pilots, they are not pilots. If they insisted on flying the plane, two things would happen; first, there would be havoc in the cabin, and second, the plane would crash on takeoff.

So, what does this have to do with missionaries?

Most church members think all the missionaries who give presentations at their church are, in fact, missionaries. The reality is that most of them have never gotten any closer to the mission field than you have. At best, they have spent two weeks there on a survey trip, living with a missionary family, observing their work. They are inexperienced, don't know the language, culture, or customs, have never started a church, and have never trained a man for the ministry. Many have no plans to be mentored by an experienced missionary when they get there.

That being the case, why do we call them *missionaries?* Well, the pastor calls them a missionary because that's what the missionary calls himself. But why would he claim that title if he has never spent time on the field or done the work of a missionary? It is our culture, our tradition—not Scripture. His board-certified him as a missionary and told him he was now a missionary. Presto, he was! But why did they do that? Because that's the way it's always been done—at least for the past fifty-plus years.

Did you know that most board members of mission organizations have never served a day as a missionary? They have no experience in making mission-related judgments and don't even know biblically what a missionary is. They think he is a preacher or a pastor who leaves his country to go somewhere else to preach or pastor. That's like saying a professional baseball player is someone who plays baseball in other towns and makes a lot of money. In that case, every member of the Google, Apple, and Microsoft corporate teams are professional baseball players. (Maybe that explains the constant crashes and updates.)

Why are these inexperienced, unknowledgeable men on the board, and why are they allowed to assign the title of missionary to a man who has little to no understanding and no experience? Because "that's the way it has always been done." And frankly, when congregations continue to support novice preachers with no experience, who are at best pretending to be a missionary, it makes them guilty. Please stop it.

Is There Hope for the Future?

If you look only on the surface, you may think there is not. Consider that less than 1 percent of Bible college students today are studying to become a missionary. Still, there is hope because the cure is not quantity; it is quality. Let me explain.

As Americans, we always think in numbers—the more, the better (unless we're talking about pandemics or taxes). Yet, look at our Lord's example. He started with only a handful of disciples (actual daily followers, not just churchgoers), and He grew their number to twelve, then to seventy, then to one hundred twenty. Then He started whittling them down, seeking quality over quantity. Finally, though He had a host of followers, His leadership group, when He departed the earth, was down to eleven. What a failure, right? Yeah, if you're an American. Fifty days later, however, there were more followers than you could count, and since then, there have been billions.

You see, as Americans, we want to know how many trees we have in our orchard when the important thing is not the number of the trees but the amount of fruit each one produces. We like to take the unproductive tree, put a hammock under it and enjoy the shade, giving it a new purpose. Our Lord says to cut it down and replace it with a productive, fruit-bearing tree. If your goal is relaxation and shade, this is a great plan. But if your goal is the Lord's goal, the preaching of the gospel to every people group and every person, then you and your tree are wasting real-estate.

We do the same with our unproductive missionaries. We enjoy the shade they provide by giving us just one more number on our missionary list. We rest in the shade and comfort that we are dutifully supporting a missionary, but by biblical principle, we should cut his support and give it to a productive missionary.

As I see it, the hope is teaching in our churches and colleges what a missionary is supposed to be and insisting that our missionary dollars fund only those qualified and proven. He is not a gardener, a pilot, a printer, a teacher, a pastor, a children's worker, or a legal scholar. He is a church-planting, pastor-training machine that moves from place to place, appointing pastors he trained to take what he produced and grow it to maturity and multiplication.

If our schools would do that, it will take only a decade to turn the tide around. If our churches would support such men, then the next generation would know what they are expected to do to gain and maintain support. In less than a generation, we can turn the world upside down again.

I faced the same challenges in 1986 when no one had heard of or considered supporting a national preacher. It is said that I started the first Baptist ministry in America solely dedicated to that purpose, and now, hundreds of others in many denominations do the same. It took less than a generation for churches to return to the protocols of missions found in the book of Acts, expecting trained national men to do the work rather than depending on reinforcements from "Jerusalem," and supporting them as well as the foreign missionary in doing so. I believe in less than a generation; we can reclaim the biblical definition of what a missionary is supposed to be and demand him to meet his job description to get and keep his support.

Eliminating the Conundrum

Suggestions for Missionaries:

- Don't look to see where others are going so you can join them; go where no one has gone before. Remember, Paul did not build on foundations laid by others; he cleared the land and poured his own foundation and those who followed built on it. Foundations are the missionary's job; construction is the pastor's task.

- Work with a team, so you have strength and fellowship. Who gets the title or who gets to preach is not important. Share. Every team has more than one player (except tennis and chess). Even the golfer depends on the wisdom of the caddy who knows the course. Barnabas had his Paul. That's right, reread Acts. It was not Paul and Barnabas; it was Barnabas and Paul. When they could no longer work together, they both built new teams and continued their calling.

- Don't pattern your ministry after contemporary patterns; follow the book of Acts in every detail. The sooner you can let a capable, solid, doctrinally based church leader preach, the better. Without Timothy, Philemon, Titus, Aristarchus, and others, Paul would have had an incredibly limited ministry and would probably be unknown today. Sharing the ministry grows the ministry. Keeping it for yourself will kill it.

- When you send your quarterly missionary letter to your sponsors, tell them what you are doing—not how you feel. Show the fruit that you are producing—not your dreams for what you plan to produce.

- When you decide where to go, realize there is a difference between a burden and a call. If God calls you to Mexico, then go, but realize that there are more than just Mexicans living there. Seventeen million indigenous Indians live in Mexico in 78 different tribes with their own languages, customs, and traditions. Anyone can go to Mexico; make yourself stand out by targeting a specific people/tribe rather than a place. Educate yourself and your potential donors about the need for them to be reached. By the way, Brazil has 188 people groups, and the Philippines has 100. You don't have to limit yourself to Mexico City, São Paulo, or Manila.

- Remember that we are here to help you. You can be better, and you can do better. Sometimes you simply need someone who is not lost in the forest to come in and point out the path to the fertile fields. Give us a call.

Suggestions for Churches:

- Again, let me say that the professions I mentioned earlier, which are support functions for missionaries, are noble and worthy of support. Paul certainly appreciated Luke. It is just that we have gotten off balance, and now the majority of those we support as "missionaries" are not church planters; they are not even preachers. They perform ministry services and should be helped—but not at the expense of supporting missionaries with our designated mission support. Again, consider having a *missions budget* and a *ministry budget (or sub-budget)* and don't fund one out of the other.

- Look at where you are and are not supporting missionaries. Is your outreach out of balance? If so, you can easily make changes. The imbalance may not be resolved overnight, but you can begin some new policies such as:
    - Support one national preacher for every two, five, or ten Americans supported.
    - The next time a missionary is dropped, the opening will be replaced with a national.
    - Rather than add more missionaries going to the same countries, start supporting missionaries going to places previously not reached.

Make your goal not how many you can support but to plug the holes in your outreach. Target the untargeted.

- Look at productivity. Assign a staff member to make a spreadsheet of all your missionaries. Go back for the past two years, five years, or whatever you want. Record the following in those quarters or years:
    - How many souls did they report leading to Christ?
    - How many baptisms did they have?
    - How many new works did they start or help to start?
    - How many men are they training for leadership or for ministry?
        - Add any other qualifications that you feel necessary.

With a glance, you will be able to see which missionaries are productive and which are not. Your purpose is to verify they are doing what you are supporting them to do. Then ask yourself (and them), if they are not—then why not? I recommend once you have compiled this information, update it every quarter as the new letters arrive.

- Don't judge a missionary by the size of his work, but by the number of his works. Is he pastoring a single church, or is he starting new churches?

- Remember that every field is not as productive as others, so don't use that as an excuse for poor performance. If the field is entirely unproductive, it may be time to shake the dust off and move on.

- Pastors, as the primary steward of the church's funds and to accomplish your part of the Great Commission, develop a policy using strategic analysis to determine who, where, and how to best utilize your giving. If every church is watering the same spot of ground, you won't nourish the field; you'll eventually produce a mudhole surrounded by a desert.

#8
Does the Bible Allow Women to Serve as Missionaries? If Not, Why Do We Support Them?

Explaining the Conundrum

When I received this email from a lifelong friend in 2016, I gave the response in this chapter:

"Hey, I'm writing a lesson for an online homeschool class, and it's on women in missions. What's your take? I think of women missionaries as teaching women and children and doing things like that—children and women's ministries. But maybe that's not technically what being a missionary is. Is it supposed to be strictly church planting, or is it sharing the gospel? Is it biblical for women to be "missionaries"? Or does that depend on the definition that is used? They don't want any of that in the lesson, I'm sure, but I read something online and am now wondering. I know it's not biblical for women to preach, but I never even think of women doing that when I think of women missionaries.

"The main point they want the focus on is how being a woman missionary today is different from, say, when the China Inland Missions was founded."

The Word of God is absolute and unchanging. But in every age, our understanding of Scripture is affected by culture. This is why believers on one continent differ from those on another. If we had all lived in biblical times, spoke the languages, and understood the cultures, our understanding would be more uniform. But alas, we are who we are. Thus, we must study God's Word in context and let it say what it says.

I know that some of you will automatically disagree with me and have already determined that I am about to teach heresy. I commend your concern and caution. However, such a premature determination is a judgmental act that our Lord condemned in Matthew chapter seven. To judge is to put yourself in place of God who alone can read the hearts of man. Satan judged himself superior to God and look where that got him.

My purpose is to address this conundrum that has been often presented based on my understanding of Scripture and experience. As you read, be patient, give me time as a prosecutor to present my entire case; then, as a jury, draw your conclusion. I believe you will find that we are in full agreement.

Regarding this conundrum, and after much consideration before stepping into this minefield, this was my response:

Examining the Conundrum

Sharing the gospel is not missions; it is evangelizing, and we should all do that.

Missionary work is church planting, which would, of course, include witnessing, pastoring for a time, and discipleship, leaving the church in capable hands and then moving on to repeat the process over and over, as Paul did. Every man who worked with Paul was not a missionary. He was training them to fulfill God's specific calling in their lives.

As he progressed, Paul took some men and women with him

and left others behind so as not to slow him down in his process of continual church planting; that is one reason why he traveled with an entourage.

As disciples and team members, some, like Philemon, would stay where they were living. Others, like John Mark, would move on with him. (Yes, the same Mark who later rejoined the team at Paul's request because under the tutelage of Barnabas and, some say, Peter, he had become profitable in the ministry). Sometimes, as Paul moved on, one who had stayed behind, like Timothy, was later summoned to leave where he was and rejoin him in another location. Then there were those like Titus, who was sent to another location to start more churches and care for the region's earlier established works. Finally, at least one stayed almost exclusively with Paul, not as a preacher, but to fulfill his purpose, Luke, the doctor, author, and historian.

Like Mr. and Mrs. Aquila and Priscilla, laypeople also trained by Paul traveled with him on and off, discipling converts and training pastors.

Why then is this an issue?

Throughout the ages, for a woman to pastor a church has never been permissible. The qualifications for a pastor and a deacon alone show that females are excluded, not being the "husband of one wife." However, just because one is a preacher does not mean he is a pastor. That common interpretation is highly incorrect. Do you assume your pastor is a pastor because he preaches? Preaching is probably less than 10 percent of his ministry. He is a shepherd and on-call 24/7/365, but he only preaches for several hours a week. Evangelists preach, but they are not pastors. Laymen can preach and yet not be a pastor.

Preach is a verb; *pastor*, as a title or a position, is a noun. The act of preaching is a scriptural admonition and has nothing to do with an outline, a pulpit, or a title. If we believe the Great Commission was given to us *all*, we must acknowledge that we are *all* told to "preach the gospel" worldwide. Doing this is obediently evangelizing.

EXPOSING THE CONUNDRUM

I think it is logical that women can be involved in church planting. Biblically, they are not excluded from any service, except that of being a deacon or a pastor. Philip was an evangelist, and Philip's daughters were also designated as *evangelists* by the early church and by the Holy Spirit's inspiration. An *evangelist* is the third of God's four gifts mentioned in Ephesians 4 that He gave/gives to His called-out assemblies (the church). A careful reading shows that these gifts from God were given to the church for its maturity and expansion. They probably would not take a leadership role as the new church would still be being "pastored" by the founding missionary, but they were always there to help and teach—but not just to teach the women and children.

Remember that Apollos, who was one of the greatest theological orators of all times and wrested devotion from the followers of both Peter and Paul, was discipled by Aquila and his wife Priscilla. God's Spirit, through Paul's effort, business plan, and writings, went to great lengths to mention that fact in the Scripture. Why do you suppose that is? Indeed, it would not be so that we can ignore it or twist it to fit into the tiny boxes of our theological opinions. We should let God's Word say what it says, accept it and not try to change it to fit into the box of our personal or denominational dogma.

And then let's not forget that several portions of the book of Proverbs are identified as instructions from the author's mother, particularly the final chapter. Additionally, Miriam, Moses' sister, wrote and sang a song to praise God for His deliverance, which enlightens and instructs us all—or are men supposed to skip over those verses? While these women may not have always been standing before men when they taught, their teachings have nonetheless been read by teachers and pastors worldwide for thousands of years.

I think that, to a great extent, the involvement of women in "ministry" (not pastoring or deacons) depends on culture. Suppose a culture, being only infused and not yet saturated with the gospel, does not permit or strongly encourage women in leadership or public service (Islam, Hinduism, Buddhism, etc.). In that case, it is perhaps best that women do not take public leadership positions. For me, I don't care if a woman *preaches* (and by that, I mean "exhorting" or "encouraging"); remember, the specific issue in Scripture is not *preaching* but *pastoring* or being a *deacon*. Still, they certainly evangelized and taught men like Apollos and other women as well. Doing so was expedient and served as an example for younger women. After all, what can a man possibly have to teach a woman? (Any husband can answer that, and the answer is a resounding "Nothing!")

There may be just the slightest possibility that we have allowed our culture to define our doctrine. Let me give you an example. In the same passage we use to insist that women cannot preach; it also says that they are not even allowed to speak. For some reason, we insist on one and ignore the other. Women speak in church; they sing, and they teach. Even in our most strict church fellowships (or camps as they are often called), women still serve as teachers in Bible colleges, Sunday schools, etc. They may encourage the congregation before singing. They may even participate in discipling new converts. To me, stifling the wisdom of godly women from being shared is not wise. Pastors and missionaries rely significantly on the wisdom of their wives. If we believe God's Word, then we must not change definitions.

Excluding women was restricted only to the offices of a pastor and deacon. Some argue that it was an implied restriction to the Corinthian church. To them, I respond (not argue) that none of Paul's epistles were written to a woman leading a church, only to men. Paul saluted them and honored them, but he never addressed them as the pastor or leader, even though the church may well have been meeting in the house of a woman, like Lydia in Philippi.

I cannot rewrite Scripture, but I would rather listen to an insightful woman than an ignorant man. If I may use an analogy, I don't care who cooked the food; all I care about is how it tastes, and is it nourishing.

Maybe I'm wrong. Hang with me because we may be able to agree on a solution.

I think it would be difficult for a woman to simultaneously be in a position of spiritual leadership publicly and still demonstrate an attitude of submissiveness, but that is probably more due to my Baptist upbringing than to specific Scripture. Again, I am distinguishing between proclaiming God's Word as a *witness* and shepherding a flock of believers as a *pastor*. Though pastors in our culture are often called preachers, they are two distinct callings. Pastors do preach, but preachers do not necessarily pastor.

Again, we cannot ignore the Bible when it referred to Philip's daughters as being evangelists. We can say the term only means a soul winner, but God uses the term to define one of the gifts HE gave to enrich the body in Ephesians 4. It takes the participation of all these gifts to bring the believer and thus the congregation to spiritual maturity. In our culture, the idea of a woman's being an *evangelist* is also rejected because we think an evangelist is a man, typically a retired pastor, who goes around preaching in churches. That's a cultural definition that is far from being biblically accurate. Our misunderstanding of what an evangelist is biblically causes us to restrict women from being what God permitted them to be, just as our misunderstanding of what a missionary is limits the number of biblical missionaries who are serving. President Obama said, "Elections have consequences." So, does redefining biblical definitions—more on that in a moment.

I think it helps to look not at what the missionary is (man or woman) but at what they do biblically, and then determine which gender is naturally best suited for that calling. In the New Testament, there are three primary stages in developing a church (congregation): inception, maturity, and reproduction. To accomplish those three stages, God gave the new church four gifts to enable this process that are listed in Ephesians chapter 4.

1) Apostles, from which the word *missionary* is derived, meaning "a special messenger with a special message." The apostle was the groundbreaker. They did not go, as a habit, to preach where people knew of Christ, except to visit; instead, they went where Christ was unknown and unnamed. That is why Paul said he did not build upon any other man's foundation. Others (those who followed) would build on the foundation he and other missionaries had laid. The one who lays the foundation is the missionary. He boldly goes where no man has gone before (Final Frontiers missions' statement).

Being an apostle had nothing to do with authoring Scripture. That is a misconception easily proven; Barnabas is called an apostle, but he didn't write any of the New Testament. On the other hand, Luke wrote two books (Luke and Acts), but he is *not* called an apostle.

Peter was the one who established the criteria and qualifications of being an apostle. But some apostles, such as Barnabas (as far as we know), never knew Jesus (as far as the biblical record goes). Some men knew Him, traveled with Him and witnessed His post-resurrection ministry who were not called apostles. This would include most of the 120 witnesses whom Christ discipled and others like Lazarus, those on the road to Emmaus, Nicodemus, Joseph of Arimathea, and the thousands that saw the post-resurrection Christ.

God seemingly dismissed Peter's requirements by establishing Paul as an apostle. Like all the supposed Peters (popes) who followed him, Peter did not necessarily speak for God.

Some of the apostles mentioned in the Bible beginning with Jesus Himself in Hebrews chapter 3 include the Jewish men, Paul, Barnabas, and James, the brother of Jesus. There were also Gentile apostles, including Apollos, Epaphroditus, Andronicus, Junias (whom some believe to be a woman but cannot ascertain for sure), Silas, Timothy, Silvanus, and two unnamed apostles.

We know of these because the majority of them are Gentile converts referenced by Paul. But was Paul the only apostle to produce other missionaries (messengers/apostles)? I think not, since the command given by Christ was not only to go but to produce more messengers who would do likewise.

Let's remember that the definition of the word *apostle* is "messenger." There is no doubt that Christ's chosen and trained disciples were superior to any of us. Still, we are nonetheless messengers called of God to deliver the same message they delivered. To put it simply, every president is not George Washington, but every president is still a president.

For some reason, at some time in my lifetime, the definition of *apostle* changed for Baptists, and we no longer use the title. We run from it and reject it. However, giving only a minimal amount of effort to research, will reveal that until the mid-twentieth century, the first missionaries to a specific region were called "the apostle to...." That's how we referred to Hudson Taylor, David Livingstone, David Brainerd, Adoniram Judson, and others.

The Scriptures are complete, but our Great Commission has yet to be completed by any generation since Christ gave it. If we would only use the pattern of global evangelism given to us of each of us doing our part, we could finally honor Him by fulfilling His command.

2) Prophets were traveling preachers. The third epistle of John refers to them (what we today call national preachers) and commanded the church to support them on their way. John even threatened to discipline the self-righteous pastor who refused to do so and was evicting members out of the church who refused his command, helping them anyway. The unjust pastor wanted all the sheep's wool (financial giving) for himself. These prophets followed the apostles chronologically and taught more Scripture to the new converts, grounding them in truth.

Remember, the apostle's purpose was to break ground so others could reap the harvest. Paul even said some plant, some water, and some reap, but God gives the harvest. The prophet was not there to *foretell* the future, though some like Agabus did, but rather to *forth tell* the truths of God's Word. According to their ministries, most ministers today that we call *evangelists* are actually, and more accurately, "prophets." Let me explain.

3) Biblically, *evangelists* were not retired pastors going from church to church holding revivals; they were men and women who evangelized and were exceptionally gifted in doing so.

During my first exposure to New Testament missions, some national preachers in Asia asked me, "In your country (America), why would an evangelist preach in a church, since the people there are already saved?" Good question. Truthfully, it is just another example of where we have altered a word's definition (just as we have with the term *missionary*). Having changed the entire meaning and thus the specific training and preparation needed has thereby diminished the results.

The evangelist was a specially gifted preacher/proclaimer/soul winner who would enter a field that the apostle had already plowed, and the prophet had already watered (water of the Word). He has come to reap the harvest. The evangelist is the harvester who reaps where others planted. This is not to say that the apostle and prophet never won souls; this is only a generalized example. Some people in the hamlet, town, or region were already saved, but most had only heard a little or had only begun to hear and consider the gospel. They still had questions that needed answers, doctrinal concerns, and fears of conversion. God gifted the evangelist to answer those questions and concerns and reap a harvest as He gave the increase.

4) Pastors naturally followed. Why? It is natural that once the scattered sheep and lambs are together, the flock increases. If a shepherd does not come along, the wolves certainly will. His job then was to *complete* ("perfect" in the KJV) the work that had been begun by the *apostle* ("missionary"), the *prophet* ("traveling preacher, exhorter"), and *evangelist* ("real-life, aggressively convincing soul winner"). The pastor's function was to mature the sheep by keeping them grazing in green pastures and refreshed by the still waters. He was to mature them to produce as much wool as they could—not for their benefit nor

his sustenance, but for the kingdom's sake, and to duplicate themselves by birthing more sheep and creating more flocks. His tender example before them, his familiarity with them, and his care and instruction for them would produce more missionaries, prophets, evangelists, and pastors in perpetuity. That's why our churches exist today. Think of it, just as we all came from Adam and then Noah, so every congregation that has ever or will ever exist comes from the same first churches in Jerusalem and Antioch. They faithfully produced *missionaries* ("apostles"), prophets, evangelists, and pastors who are teachers of the Word. The dominoes will never stop falling.

Now having set the stage by defining and elaborating on the biblical definitions, let's get back to the conundrum at hand.

I feel there were particular circumstances that Paul referred to in Corinth where he so strongly admonished women to keep silent in the assembly. I believe that in Corinth, there were obvious cultural reasons, and to be sure, the church there had a multitude of sins and difficulties to overcome. There is a reason that Paul stayed in Corinth longer than in any other place.

Nonetheless, it is significant to note that we never see Paul writing to a female pastor or apostle, or preacher. We know for sure biblically that females were evangelists and teachers—even teachers of men and preachers. Isn't it interesting that those who preach loudest against women preaching or teaching men sit under female teachers in Bible colleges? I don't think we will ever have a complete and acceptable answer to this conundrum until we mature enough to be more concerned to know the truth than to fit what we consider the truth into our cultural boxes. Those who reach that point before others will be labeled as liberal heretics for many generations to follow.

Today, the title *missionary* has lost its biblical meaning and is used by any person doing ministry who wants to receive support. Many churches support missionaries to the prisons, the military (only to the *American* military for some reason), the county fairs, truckers at truck stops, the hospitals, abortion clinics, and even missionaries to the garment industry on Manhattan. There are also *missionaries* in the legal arena, construction, airplane pilots, mechanics, orphanage workers, and Christian schoolteachers. The list could go on and on. I would say that most of these ministries are needed and worthy of support, but they aren't missionaries unless they are involved in planting churches. Remember, Luke helped Paul for years, but he was never called an apostle. The surgical nurse most certainly helps the surgeon; he/she hands him the instruments he needs but does not perform the surgery. *Helping* and *being helped* are not the same.

Years ago, missionaries saw the validity of using the influence and energy of women to advance the gospel in new lands, just as Paul did in the first century. However, they knew that the term *missionary* could not be applied to them, though they helped perform that function simply because of the common understating of the sending churches regarding women in ministry and because they were helping in the process—not performing it. This in itself was a conundrum. The women were helping and the missionaries needed their help, but they also needed to fund them and knew they could not use the term *missionary.* What did they do?

China Inland Mission, now known as the Overseas Missionary Fellowship International (OMF), and others considered this concern over women in ministry. They adapted a non-threatening term to describe them so that it could be possible to appoint them as teachers and evangelists and to raise support for them without creating a controversy. They wisely did so, not by arguing the point or the need but simply by creating a new title that no one had ever used. They called them "Bible women." They didn't pastor churches, but they preached (evangelized and taught) in homes and villages, in a subordinate role under the pastor and church leaders. They did ministry as *Bible women*, which was, in essence (without the title), a female assistant pastor, an assistant missionary, an assistant preacher, an assistant evangelist, or an assistant anything you needed. They were able to pull this off without alienating the sensitivities of the churches back home. As a result, even today, the strictest churches then and now that would never allow a woman to preach, teach or even pray in a church service, will willingly support a woman as a missionary, who will be doing all that and more elsewhere. And by the way, a hundred years after Hudson Taylor invented the term; it is still used today by women doing ministry all over the world. The term only began to fall out of use with the Pentecostal movement's rise, which encourages women to be pastors.

Today, most American women who wish to serve use the term *missionary*, which has become widely accepted. However, in reality, their service description more closely fits that of a Bible woman since they are neither planting churches nor pastoring. I know that some of you will say, "But, Jon, that is not biblical; there is no calling in the Bible for a *Bible woman.*"

I appreciate your point and praise your devotion to the written Word, for, without that, we shall most assuredly go astray. But let me remind you of something, as gently as I can—many functions and positions in churches today are not mentioned in the Bible, yet we assign them a title, a job description, and even a salary. Think about these titles and descriptions as examples: senior pastor, executive pastor, assistant pastor, associate pastor, youth pastor, children's pastor, and senior's pastor.

I hear you saying, "Yes, but they all have the word *pastor* in them."

True, but what about these: minister of music or worship leader, secretary, bus director? All of these titles are commonly used in our churches. Then there are other ministry functions in Christendom outside of the church, including Christian school principal, teacher, coach, professor, camp director, house parents, and administrator, to name only a few. Why then would the title *Bible woman* be unacceptable and all the others okay?

May I summarize it this way? There is a big difference between being unbiblical (going against what the Scripture teaches) and non-biblical (issues that are not referenced in Scripture). We know from our understanding of Scripture that it is unbiblical for a woman to be a pastor. Still, the Bible tells us they can serve in ministry and gives examples of their serving as evangelists and teachers—even teachers of men.

Without a doubt, Lydia, the first European convert, helped Paul organize the church in Philippi. It is assumed that she used her house as a meeting place and possibly helped finance Paul's work there. For all we know, she was host to the apostles, giving them a place to live. The Scripture neither confirms nor denies these suppositions, but it is a logical assumption based on others' examples in Scripture. One thing for sure and without exception is that all of Paul's churches were house churches. Like everyone, Lydia had or lived in a house, and she was the first convert and a convert with means.

ELIMINATING THE CONUNDRUM

Suggestions for Missionaries:

- When presenting your work and in your letters, be specific about your activity. Explain what it will and does include, at which church you will be or are serving, and who the pastor is that you will be or are assisting. An occasional note from him explaining your service and its profitability to him and the congregation would be an excellent boost for your ministry.

- Consider your opportunities. Is presenting the gospel to a man allowed? Well, of course, it is. The Scripture commands it. What about two men at a time? Three? What about a group of men sitting around a table or working in the street? How many men are too many for you to evangelize at one time? Hopefully, you don't have such a number in mind. Remember, the Bible tells us that Philip the evangelist had two daughters, and it says that they were evangelists too. Whether man or woman, you don't have to be a pastor to serve God effectively.

- For some reason in our culture, preaching implies a congregation in a church setting with an elevated platform and pulpit. Don't let Western culture handicap your serving in other lands, particularly if they are not Western countries. Despite the influence of our culture, preaching is simply declaring God's truths—nothing more, nothing less, nothing else. Be sensitive to the culture you are in and use every opportunity given you to be a witness. In India, for a man to speak to a married woman is inappropriate; thus, the pastors always take their wives with them when witnessing. They will speak with their wives beside them, making it culturally acceptable, or have their wives speak to the ladies.

- Men, make use of the tools God has given you. Women can be an incredible help with advice and instruction, not to mention their organizational skills, willingness, and desire to serve the Lord.

Suggestions for Churches:

- If this is a problem for your church, and you know of ladies you would like to help but cannot because of tradition or understanding, try explaining and using the term *Bible woman* and see if it would be acceptable.

- Remember, for ladies to be evangelists is biblical, so don't hinder them from doing what God made them both to do and to be.

- We are involved in spiritual warfare, yet we deny active-duty service to over half of our soldiers, based only on gender. Is that what God intended? Can we not allow women to serve Him without having the position and title of pastor? They have unlimited energy, wisdom, and desire; they have a strong motivation for souls with compassion known by few men. Let them serve. There is more to ministry than just pastoring and preaching.

- Encourage your ladies and girls to be involved in the activity and service of the church. Scripture overflows with examples of women possessing courage and wisdom. They both led the Jewish people (Deborah) and saved the Jewish people (Esther), not to mention the many references of them caring to the needs of Jesus himself and his disciples.

- God put it in the hearts of women to be sympathetic and benevolent servants (not slaves). As girls, they served their parents and siblings. As young ladies, they served their hardheaded husband and unruly children. As elderly, they serve the body of Christ, as Anna served at the Temple in Jerusalem. God put a heart of devoted service in women, whether as a mother, a doctor, a teacher, or a leader. If we forbid them to serve God, then they will find someone or something else to serve. Don't take away the tools that God has put in His toolbox. Put more into it.

A Final Word

Having said all I have said, let me conclude with this brave summation: As for the conundrum, *"Can a woman be a missionary?"* I will defer to the teachings of your shepherd. My job as a missionary is to clear the ground for grazing and birth the sheep; it is the pastor's job to feed them. My purpose is not to convince you but to make you think. The Holy Spirit is the One who guides us into all truth. (This is a convenient cop-out on my part, to be sure!)

#9
Should a Missionary Be Sent by a Mission Board or by a Local Church?

Explaining the Conundrum

Once again, I'm going to get myself in trouble no matter how I respond to this conundrum. Thus, I will try to do so entirely from a biblical perspective using observation and analysis and not my personal interpretation and opinion. As I begin, I can almost see the opposing armies of varying opinions gathering in front of me on the battlefield of my mind, anxious for the trumpets to blow and the battle to begin. And to be honest, as I studied this question, my own opinions were shaped and shifted by what I discovered.

Among Baptists in recent years, this issue has shifted from one of option or opinion to conviction. It is one of those few things that guarantee the missionary either the loss of support or the loss of opportunity to get support, depending on which side he stands. The issue of who "sends" has now, for some, evolved into a doctrine. For that reason, for some it has become sacred ground that dare not be invaded. But since I was asked, let me share my thoughts, which I am confident many of you will feel are wrong. To you, I would ask prayer for my ignorance. And if you are one of my supporting churches and have strong feelings on this matter, I beg you to skip this discussion altogether—(so I don't lose your support).

Please take a moment to reread the conundrum carefully.

Did you? Good, now here is my honest answer. No—or better yet—neither.

Before you start boiling the oil and plucking the feathers, give me a few moments to explain my point from Scripture. Remember, I have also made shifts in my thinking on this subject based on verses that I had never carefully studied.

Examining the Conundrum

What does the term "sending church" mean? Truthfully, I can only guess since technically, it does not appear in Scripture. I know some will disagree since the church sent out Paul, but that verse refers to the verb *(to send)* rather than to an adjective of a *(sending)* church. Before those veins on your neck pop, let me explain, and you'll find that I am not a heretic after all.

In decades past, a missionary's home church was logically his sending church. The two terms of "home" and "sending" were synonymous. At that time, *sending* meant that the local body was giving their endorsement to the man and his calling. As a body, they were willingly sending him out, away from them, to do the work of a missionary.

Over time, and in my observation, with the rise of church-based Bible colleges, young men (like me five decades ago) left their home churches to be trained at schools based out of other local churches. During their four years of study, that church became their "home" church. By the time they prepared for deputation, they had virtually lost all contact with their previous home church, visiting only once or twice a year during holidays. In many cases, as in mine, the church had a new pastor that I had never met. Missionary candidates, not wanting to abandon their allegiance to home, family, and friends, would list them as their *home church*, then list their college-based church as the *sending church*.

The ability to quickly raise support is dependent on the missionary's personal contacts, thus, the need to associate with the college-based church and its network of pastoral alumni, supporting churches, and friends. The idea behind this was that the original home church could provide some support, and the pastor could also encourage his pastor friends to support this young missionary his church had produced. On the other hand, the college-based sending church can expose the missionary to an endless supply of pastors to contact, along with a weighty letter of recommendation from the college church's home pastor, the head of the missions' department, and the president of the college. These references then doubled or greater his supporting raising contacts. Frankly, it is a great arrangement that has proven to be an effective, support-raising strategy.

On the other hand, mission boards sometimes consider themselves to be the *sender*, though they do not like to use that term. The terms of *home church* and *sending church* have thus become *ipso facto*, the domain of churches.

It is only logical to ask, *"How is the sending church distinguished from other supporting churches?"*

This conundrum presents a good question since almost without exception, neither the church nor the board sends the missionary on his way; they only help to do so because technically, doing so would mean they are footing the bill and providing for all of the missionary's needs. The home church merely endorses him and his intention to go but seldom fully supports him. In fact, their support is likely at a level less than some of his other supporting churches. The board never gives financial support—only credibility and endorsement. So why the confusion? After all, Paul emphatically stated that he was *"sent not by man but by God"* (Galatians 1:1).

Logically one would think that if a church were the sending church, that would mean they are literally sending him—spiritually, physically, and financially. However, the term has morphed to mean that they stand behind his decision and calling and choose to acknowledge it publicly. Sadly and unfortunately, rarely does the home or sending church give any more to "their own missionary" than they do to the strangers they support in other lands. In reality, every church that supports the missionary is technically making the same claim by their actions; thus, they are all *sending churches*.

Exposing the Conundrum

To do this, we first have to ask, *Is this a doctrinal issue, or has it only masqueraded as one?*

According to Galatians 1:1 and Acts 13:2, Paul was not sent by a church or by *his* home church; instead, according to Scripture, he was *set apart* or "set free" by them. In other words, an examination of the verb in this passage shows by its very definition that they freed Paul and Barnabas to do what the Holy Spirit had collectively informed the five of them (not the church as a whole) that He wanted Paul and Barnabas to do.

The act of setting them apart was not philosophical, as it is today, nor was it one of an ongoing association with that church. Rather, it was an agreement, endorsed and informed by the Holy Spirit, to free or release them from their assigned duties in that congregation. The Bible defines those pastoral duties as preaching, teaching, prayer, and the congregation's oversight.

Of significance to note is the "church" did not set them apart; according to Acts 13:1, it was the "prophets and teachers" who apparently jointly shepherded (pastored) the church. If not, then the church pastor was not present during this event and had no voice in the decision. These two prophets and teachers' offices refer to two of God's five gifts to the churches for their inception: maturity and reproduction. (See conundrum #8 for more detail.) Pastors and teachers were the final gifts God gave to the churches, and most would agree that the teacher is not separate from the pastor. The office is often debated today as pastor-teacher (position and job description) rather than as pastor *and* teacher.

At the time, the churches had what some call a "plurality of elders." Acts 13:1 lists the five Antioch elders as follows:

1) Barnabas
2) Simeon, also called Niger, who some speculate came from Nigeria
3) Lucius of Cyrene (modern Libya)
4) Manaen, who was raised with Herod Antipas (Antipas, also called the Tetrarch, was raised in Rome and was a friend of Drusus, the son of Tiberius)
5) Saul, now known as Paul.

This decision came not in a church service or a business meeting but instead when these five men (and no others that we know of) were deep in a time of prayer and fasting. Then the Holy Spirit revealed His will to them—not to the congregation. We can speculate that they later informed the congregation of their submission to the Spirit's guidance without asking their approval or consent.

Let me put it this way: Paul and Barnabas were part of a five-man pastoral team leading the church. While seeking God's will, the Holy Spirit impressed all five of them to release Paul and Barnabas from their local duties so that they could go abroad to spread the gospel to the Jews and Gentiles alike (read the context in chapter 12). They obediently separated (dismissed) them having no recorded consultation with or permission from the congregation. (Absent a discussion and vote of the congregation, one might jokingly suggest here that it was not a Baptist church.)

Here Are Some Facts to Ponder:

- The church leaders in Antioch, Syria (now southern Turkey near the Syrian border) were from Cyprus (Barnabas), Libya (Lucius),

Nigeria (Simeon), Jerusalem/Rome (Manaen), and Tarsus (Paul). None were from Antioch, which at that time was a major cosmopolitan city on a trade route from northern Persia (Phrygia) to Rome. The church at Antioch was primarily evangelizing the Jewish population. All of these men were Jews. Interestingly, being from Tarsus, Paul was raised geographically and culturally closer to Antioch than the others.

- Even though four of the five men on the pastoral staff were from other countries, none of them were classified as *apostles* ("missionaries"). They were classified as prophets and teachers.

- By this commission from the Holy Spirit in Antioch, we see that the Great Commission given by Jesus was not only for His disciples based in Judaea (as some teach) but for *all* of His disciples based everywhere.

- Both Paul and Barnabas had already traveled to Jerusalem, a city in a different region and territory than Antioch's. Still, at that time, they had not yet become apostles. That did not occur until they were set apart and ventured out. It was not a title they received because they felt a calling; it was a position they earned by fulfilling the call. In other words, they did not tell the people what they were planning to do once they raised their support; they just went out and did it.

The word *separate* in verse 2 means "to set apart." In context, it meant to set Barnabas and Paul apart from their local fellowship and their obligated services at and for the church in Antioch, allowing them to follow the Spirit's leading into unevangelized areas. At this time, Paul and Barnabas had been in Antioch for a year, serving the church, having returned from an eventful trip to Jerusalem. Let me explain.

James's death and Peter's arrest occurred shortly before Herod Agrippa had left for Caesarea, where he would perish. And since it was the Passover season, Barnabas and Paul were probably in Jerusalem when James was martyred, and Peter was imprisoned. Thus, it is possible, if not likely, they were a part of the prayer meeting in John

Mark's home, beseeching God for Peter's release. If they were not in Jerusalem during these events, they arrived shortly after that. Paul and Barnabas were undoubtedly in Jerusalem when Herod Agrippa (nephew and brother-in-law of Herod Antipas, and childhood companion of Manaen) was struck down by God in Caesarea and died. They left from there with John Mark, the young cousin of Barnabas, and moved to Antioch, where this story takes place.

Did you get all that? If so, here is another puzzle at the least and a seeming contradiction at the most. Verse 3 says the church leaders "sent them away" (this is from where we get the idea of a *sending church*), but verse 4 clearly says they were "sent forth by the Holy Spirit." Since God's Word never contradicts itself, we need to do some research to understand what is being said; otherwise in our innocence and ignorance, we may end up creating a doctrine that God did not intend or inspire.

The verb *sent* in verse 3 is the Greek word *apelusan*, which means "to freely and fully release or dismiss," as in being released or dismissed from an obligation, a contract or a relationship. In short, the leaders of the Antioch church *released* and *dismissed* Paul and Barnabas from their current ministerial obligations, so they could follow the leading of God's Spirit, which was "sending them forth or sending them out" *(ekpemphthentes)* to Cyprus and beyond, to "preach the Word of God." Though in English the same word *sent* is used in both verses, in the Greek text, two distinct meanings were given by using two separate verbs, one to *release* and the other to *send forth*.

Note that the Holy Spirit sent spiritually mature, ministerially experienced men, who took with them a young novice, unable at the time to endure the hardships of missionary work. John Mark was not "sent" by the Holy Spirit; he was recruited as a helper by Barnabas and Paul.

Technically, the act of a church's *sending* a missionary is the church's acknowledging and submitting to God's desire to physically (for a time at least) separate the man from that particular location to serve Him elsewhere. They then officially release him from his local ministry obligations to do so.

Without realizing it, this is precisely what happened to me when, as a pastor, I informed my congregation that I felt God had revealed His will to me as a missionary. They knew that was my calling and that I was temporarily serving them as their pastor while I waited on the leading of the Holy Spirit. That leading became evident to our church leaders at the same time that it was impressed on me. As a result, not wanting to lose their pastor, the church asked me to remain as their pastor, with the liberty to be gone up to nine months of the year doing missionary work. But realizing that God does not partially call, He fully calls; they submitted their will to Him then *dismissed* and *released* me with tears. When they did so, under the leading of the remaining pastors, this small church emptied their building fund account to support my family for three years. (I accepted the funds at a discounted amount but never used a dime for my family. It all went into the ministry. Like Paul, I never went on deputation but spent my full time in His service.)

In regard to being called and being sent, it should also be noted that Paul emphasized in Galatians that he was an apostle (from whence we get the word *missionary*), not *of men*, neither *by men*, but by Jesus Christ and God the Father. In Romans, I Corinthians, II Corinthians, Ephesians, Philippians, and Colossians, he emphasizes that his calling, sending, and service were not from man but *for* and *from* God. So, in essence, biblically, the church *dismisses* the servant from his local and obligated ministry so that He can be *sent* forth by the Holy Spirit to follow His Wind, wherever it blows.

So, whether you are the home church, the sending church, or the home and sending church, be careful not to spend so much time at the "home plate" of terminology that you fail to set your missionary free to knock a grand slam for the Lord's team.

ELIMINATING THE CONUNDRUM

***Suggestions for Missionaries*:**

- Know whom you are sent out by and then be released to do what God has called you to do and go where He leads you. Financing should never be a barrier to His sending.

- If you don't have valid ministry obligations for the church to *release* you from, consider it more biblically appropriate for you to go as a recruit while you strive to become a missionary. There is no shame in that.

- Keep in mind that between his journeys, Paul spent a great deal of time back in his home church, serving. You don't have to be on the field nonstop.

- Consider that we don't have a single example in Scripture of God's calling a missionary to one single place and leaving him there. Your calling is to "go" and go and go, leaving behind you the converts you have won and discipled and the congregations you have planted and trained to continue the same pattern of multiplication. Stay in one place is not wrong, but it is not a requirement.

- Impress deeply into your consciousness that if you are sent to be a missionary, you are sent to be a church planter and discipler. This was what both Paul and Barnabas did together and after their separation. The other three men in the Antioch leadership were foreigners to Antioch but were not church planters. As far as we know, they stayed in their positions in a foreign city (Antioch) because that is the nature of pastors. They shepherd the sheep, and you cannot do so distant from the flock. Their example proves that you can legitimately be a foreign pastor without being a missionary. A missionary is not affected by his location; he is affected by his job description—a transitory, church-planting pastor and discipler.

Suggestions for Churches:

- There is no sin in saying you are a missionary's sending church. You may not find the term in a biblical example, but it is certainly not anti or un-biblical. It is semantics that, to most, don't matter; however, to those like me, who like to do research, seek answers, and commonly ask "why," it is both interesting and significant that in Scripture, there is a difference to be made between *a sending church* and *a sending Spirit of God*. It is advisable to understand the scriptural principle behind the "sending" as *dismissing* and *releasing* instead of sending as the approving and calling authority.

- When you release a missionary, you release your authority over him. Some would say that is not true. I say prove me wrong with Scripture in black and white—not by opinions, "principles," or so-and-so says. If his spiritual maturity is such that he still needs to get his orders from his pastoral staff back home, then he is far too immature to be a missionary. I have sometimes seen pastors in America who try to control and influence the work of the missionary. If you do that, then you are stepping on the feet of the Holy Spirit. Your job is to release him from local obligations in your church, to pray for him, and if you wish, to support him in his endeavors for Christ, but you are not to attempt to control him, refrain him, or to be his master.

We should keep in mind the difference between *counsel* and *control*. I have counseled missionaries who have to consult with their sending pastor to change the hours of their services, allow me to visit them, or start a new ministry in their church like a bus ministry. How could a pastor living a thousand miles away in a different culture, who has never left his own land, have any legitimate discretion to tell you what to do in your ministry, with your people, in their land and culture? It is absurd and prideful. Wisdom for counsel is one thing; domination for control is another.

- We need to understand and teach that missionaries are not

subordinate to pastors. They are a distinct calling and a distinct gift from God to the church; in fact, they are His primary gift. Without the missionary, there is no church and no need for a pastor. The home church pastor will not call the missionary for permission to lead his church, so the missionary should have no obligation to seek his former home pastor's approval.

As I said at the beginning, if you still disagree with me after reading this, then I will gladly (for the sake of your support) disavow all I have written until you change your opinion. Then I will return to my heretical ways. (Just kidding.) Seriously though, I would hope that no church would threaten the support of a missionary because he disagrees with them on non-essential teachings or issues. You will never find a man who agrees with you 100 percent. And if you do, check with him next week to see if he or you have not shifted slightly.

When I transitioned from simply reading to contextually studying the Bible in-depth and meditating on it, I found that many of my long-standing opinions changed. In contrast, others became more cemented in my heart and mind. This conundrum of debate over being sent by a church or a board serves as an example.

#10 At What Age Should You Drop the Support of a Missionary? At What Age Should You Begin Supporting a Missionary? Should You Support a Single Missionary?

Explaining the Conundrum

This puzzle is an issue of support regarding age and marital status. Most people do not consider these factors when offering support to a missionary—those who do generally decide from personal opinion rather than a scriptural foundation.

If a person is mentally or physically disabled so that they can no longer function as a missionary, perhaps that should be considered, but to disqualify a man because he is too old, too young or single is an unwise decision. Former President Donald Trump clearly illustrated that age has nothing to do with energy. He seemed to function in his mid-70s better than I did in my mid-30s. If age is to be a factor in your decision, it should be applied individually rather than across the board.

I will say this. Those who support me personally are getting "more bang for their buck" now than they did thirty years ago. My level of accomplishment and sphere of influence has dramatically increased due to my longevity. Most of us slow down when we get old because our culture has conditioned us to do so. Others do so because of affliction. But some of us have the attitude that was well put by Pastor Jack Hyles, who was known for saying, "I would rather burn out than to rust out."

Age drives the car down the highway of time, and, due to mechanical problems or running out of gas, some of us are forced to pull over sooner than others. But as age drives, experience and wisdom ride along on the back seat, warning of potholes and upcoming detours. Never discard a missionary because he is too old, too young, or single if he is still accomplishing what he was sent to do.

Examining the Conundrum

Some Relevant Background:

I officially began my life in missions at the age of thirty. I never did deputation and often turned down support offered me, asking the church to give it to one of our national church planters instead. My decision doesn't make me righteous; in fact, it only revealed that I was ignorant.

In time I realized two things that now seem as constant as gravity. First, the more churches give "to me," the more funds I had to do the ministry's work. Second, whenever I turned down the support offered, the church would seldom give it to one of our men as per my request. The result was that my family unnecessarily suffered for many years. After all, since most missionaries fund their ministries from their "personal" support, I could have done the same. While I still do not actively seek personal support, I also no longer turn it down when offered (hint, hint).

Since 1992, I have acquired ministry support from roughly 98 percent of all the churches I have spoken at (from the church or a family in the church), while my "personal support" is barely equal to that of a novice missionary in his second year of deputation. But don't be alarmed, like Paul, I have learned how both to "abound and to abase." I have no unfunded needs allowing any new support designated for me to go 100 percent to the ministry. By God's grace, Nolin and I live with a perpetual abundance (for now).

When I became a missionary at age thirty, many churches felt I was "too young" to support. At that time, over half the missionaries were in their fifties and expected to retire within a decade. The typical "face" of a missionary was about the age of 45 to 50. I was a baby-faced young man touting an unproven (and supposedly new) concept of missions. (I also had a beard, and in the mid-1980s to 1990s, many still considered that to be a sin.)

Any missionary will tell you how difficult it is to go to a church as a stranger and gain their support. Usually, if they do give support, it is for one of several reasons:

- The pastor knows your pastor.
- The pastor has been encouraged by a pastor-friend in a quid-pro-quo arrangement.
- The pastor likes your mission board.
- The church has funds available, and you gave an excellent presentation and have a lovely family.

On the other hand, being green and ignorant, I went to churches as a stranger, with no referral (except a letter from Curtis Hutson). I asked them not to support me but a stranger in another land whom they will never meet. My business plan was ludicrous. If I had thought about it, I would never have started Final Frontiers. But God used my ignorance for His purposes. Today, many new missionary candidates are in their mid-twenties; thus, the "face" of the "typical" missionary is now much younger than it used to be. It is easier for young men today because some churches prefer youth and zeal over experience and accomplishment.

At that time, I also began to see many missionaries in their sixties who were retiring and coming home. As a pastor, I often wondered why these missionaries would walk away from a lifetime ministry, so I began investigating the phenomenon. I learned that missionaries retired, for the most part, not because they wanted to but because their mission board required it. For example, as late as the 1990s, many mission boards had a mandatory policy requiring retirement at age sixty-five. When the missionary reached that age, expecting him to be obedient to their retirement policy, the board would send notices to his supporting churches telling them that "Missionary Smith" was no longer a part of their ministry. The board would offer no explanation or encouragement to continue his support, only their announcement of their abandonment of affiliation with him. Of course, this would cast a negative shadow on the missionary in the minds of his supporting churches, wondering why a board would break fellowship with a missionary. And I can tell you from painful experience when bad news is circulating; few pastors call to ask why or what, they assume "where there's smoke, there's fire."

As a pastor, that policy seemed ungrateful, considering all the missionary had accomplished, spiteful because he would not submit to their calling him home (when God called him there), and evil, that they would intentionally handicap a servant and a work of God. Missionary Smith hadn't done anything wrong. He could now speak the language better than he ever has, he knows the people and culture better, has more contacts, he may be training more preachers or starting a new work, his house is mortgage-free and his life, for the past thirty to forty years, has been there—not in the USA. In fact, in his mind, he is an American by birth but a part of that country's people by choice. There is no logical reason for him to quit; to the contrary, his ministry is more vital now than ever. The only thing he did wrong was living to be sixty-five. That last candle on his birthday cake sent him home. And what if he should decide to stay on and continue where God put him?

No problem, except that the letter his board sent out will typically result in his losing between 30 and 50 percent of his support—overnight. Happy Birthday!

The good news is that most boards have acknowledged we now live longer. As mandatory retirement was changed from 65 to 70 in much of the business world, mission boards also made the change. Why follow God when you can follow man?

To be honest, if the missionary foresaw the inevitable and contacted all his supporting churches in advance, he would likely save his support. Still, for those churches who dropped him though learning he plans to remain, the likelihood of regaining their support is extremely slim because the funds have already been assigned to another missionary—or the building fund.

Exposing the Conundrum

When Is Young Too Young?

I don't think youth should be a factor. If you agree that a missionary is not an American pastoring in another country, but a church planter who starts new churches, trains men to pastor them, then moves on to start another—support should have nothing to do with his age and everything to do with his *activity.*

For the sake of argument, I am responding to the conundrum by assuming that we are referring to a biblical missionary (a continuous church planter) and not a "traditional" missionary (pastoring in a foreign country).

We all agree that Timothy was a young man, as was John Mark, yet Paul was eager to have both of them on his team. Sure, John Mark was sent away for a time, but you find him later serving alongside Paul's comrades in the epistles, and Paul referred to him as a "partner" in ministry. Perhaps as a youth, he could not handle the cultural challenges or Paul's leadership style, but that would not necessarily be due to age. I have seen many men in their early twenties who proved their calling by successfully planting churches. At the same time, I have also seen teenage boys who were vital on a church-planting team. Fifteen-year-old Franklin Rivera, the son of a Honduran church planter, is such a young man.

When I was fifteen years old, I attended the Forest Hills Baptist Church in Decatur, Georgia. Curtis Hutson was the pastor, and at that time, he was still "Pastor" and not yet "Dr." Hutson. I was impressed by God's hand on him, and by my exciting recommendation, the following Sunday, my family attended. The following Thursday, Pastor Hutson visited us in our home, and that Sunday, we joined the church.

Immediately after the service, the bus pastor, Johnny Stancil approached me and asked if I wanted to work in the bus ministry. My immediate reply was "yes," though he had to tell me what that was since I had never heard of it. Because I lived near a particular bus captain and would need a lift to visit each week, he assigned me to work on a brand-new bus route that covered the areas of Grant Park and Cabbagetown in downtown Atlanta.

The bus captain of route #5 was a short, grinning, balding man named Tommy Tillman. God would use him to change my life. He taught me bus ministry and street preaching. Brother Tommy taught me to visit all day and even into the night. We would even knock on doors at midnight, waking up people to invite them to ride our bus—eight hours later. During the summer months, he would pick me up on his way to work, and I would spend the day visiting and soul winning on our bus route. After work, he would find me and take me home. On the days that he could not, my brother Ben would take his place. I would visit the area every day, all day, often with Ben by my side. It was my ministry, my service for my Lord, and it had become his as well.

If you know Johnny Stancil, ask him what my nickname was in the mill-community of Atlanta, and he will tell you it was "Cabbagetown King." Some even wrote it on the walls as graffiti. He still calls me that today—over fifty years later. (The route was so successful I was told that in a few years, it multiplied into fifteen routes.)

One summer day, Tommy told me that he had heard of villages of people in Mexico that were part of the old Aztec nation. He wanted to move there to reach them and asked if I wanted to go with him as his "Timothy."

My immediate reply was, "Absolutely."

We made plans to discuss it with my parents later that evening. (It was, I think, 1971, and I was 15 years old and between the tenth and eleventh grades at the time.) When he got to my house, he went in to talk with my mom and dad. They both knew that my calling was missions, and they were accustomed to my friends and me coming home at 2:00 a.m. from soul winning in downtown Atlanta among the alcoholics, prostitutes, and hippies. On Sundays, our family dinner was always around 3:00 because my dad would not let the family eat until I got home from the bus route.

After hearing Tommy's plan without any hesitation, my dad said, "Yes, Jonny can go."

I spoke up and asked, "What about school?" to which my parents said, "You can go to school in Mexico." From that moment on, I was on my way to Mexico, but for whatever reason, Tommy's plans changed, and he did not leave for another few years. At first, he moved to Leeds, Alabama, and started a new church while I was in college. Then he again targeted those same Indians living in Belize. From there, he evangelized on the ships in the New Orleans harbor. While doing that, some men serving on a ship told him about lepers in South Korea, so he left to evangelize them. While there, he learned about the lepers in Thailand and moved there—which is when I met up with him again in 1986. Since that time, he has continued working and expanding the gospel into Mongolia, helping his son Mitch, a missionary. (Mitch and his sister Paula went to high school with me, but in different grades.)

Are you bored yet? My point is, you are never too young to *learn* missions by *helping* a real-live missionary. It is logical, though, at such a young age, that like the Mormons, the family should support their young son on the mission field—just as they would if he were still at home. While there, he can still do schoolwork and even get a college degree online. Then, if he needs support, he can begin deputation—not as an inexperienced novice but as a young, veteran missionary with years of experience and significant accomplishments to verify his value and worth of support.

During all this time, the young apprentice had already learned the language, customs, and culture and had by necessity worked with a team, if only one other man, and had not floundered by being alone.

Again, *traditional missionaries*, if only by example, are taught to fellowship with others but work alone. After all, you don't want someone else telling you what to do. *Biblical missionaries* always work in teams. Simply follow the life and pattern of Paul, and that principle will be evident.

My feeling is that if a man is going to serve as a traditional missionary, meaning a pastor on foreign soil, then he needs first to have some years of pastoral experience under his belt in his own culture. He should be competent to teach and counsel from Scripture on subjects, such as raising children, teenage dilemmas, husband/wife relationships, finances, etc., that require experience and maturity that he has not yet gained. If he has not yet done it in his own country, culture, and language, why do we expect him to succeed in another? If, however, he is going as a biblical missionary, he needs only to perform the abilities God has given him in conjunction with the others' abilities and experiences on the team. He is a church planter, not a pastor; thus, age becomes irrelevant.

When Is Old Too Old?

As long as a man feels called and can perform the task's requirements, he is not too old. I am 65 years of age. I cannot do today what

I did at the age of 35. I cannot hike up mountains; diabetes will not let me go days without food, arthritis screams at me if I have to spend a night on a hard floor or sit too long in a car. My hearing is failing, and my memory has become unmemorable. Am I too old to be a church planter (missionary)? Not by a long shot!

During my 2018 summer trip to Honduras, I helped start a new church with no intention of doing so. I stopped along a dirt road that had a dozen or so houses that I could see and began talking to a few people. Unaccustomed to that, they came out to see who I was and what I wanted. I didn't "preach" to them; I merely conversed with them—like Paul did in his initial contacts, always coming back to the message of the cross. That day I lead several of them to Christ, so I offered to return and teach them and asked where we could do so out of the blazing heat of the sun.

Five families offered their home for our meetings. When I returned, I brought several Honduran pastors with me, and eventually, one of them decided to conduct regular services for the growing congregation. Within two years, that church had started another church in a nearby village and was evangelizing another community for a third church. Could I have done it without help? Absolutely, if I lived there and had the time, but the task of a missionary is always training, always motivating, always moving on, and always encouraging others by his example, and by stepping back to let them do what he has been doing for decades.

When Paul entered a town, it was not to get *the* job done; it was to get *his* job done, plant a church, appoint a pastor, and then move on to the next town. But what about the new converts? Don't they need to be discipled and grounded? They do and feeding the sheep while the missionary moves on to produce new sheep is what the pastor is for. It's a team effort that works well and, when done correctly, will turn the world upside down.

We often teach that the missionary's job is to replace himself. That is true, but the motivation is not for retirement but multiplication, accomplishment, and the Great Commission's fulfillment.

One of my friends was Randall Stirewalt, who passed away in 2019. We have worked with this missionary in Kenya for decades. In their May 2018 monthly letter, Randall and his wife Phyllis mentioned that they were now nearly 70 years old. He also wrote that in May they had started two new churches. Randy could do this because he understood church planting is a team effort; it's more like volleyball than tennis. He trains the young men for the ministry, then sets them up to spike the ball by targeting a village, taking them with him to evangelize it, herding in the new sheep, and appointing a shepherd from among his Timothies. Then he moves on to repeat the process with the rest of his trained men and any new Timothies he has attracted.

You cannot do what Randy was doing if you are not actively and consistently training men, targeting villages, evangelizing, and…moving on. That is actual missionary work. Sure, you may also pastor a church for a time, but you're not a missionary if that's *all* that you're doing; you're only a pastor on a foreign field. Having a sending church does not make you a missionary. A board's approval does not make you a missionary, having $7,000 a month support does not make you a missionary, and having a prayer card and a foreign address does not make you a missionary. So then, what does? Your actions are what make you a missionary. If your ministry is confined to one church or a dozen churches so that you are no longer doing the work of church planting and discipleship, then you are not a missionary, regardless of youth or age. If you look like a duck, waddle like a duck, and quack like a duck—you're not a missionary.

Moses was not a missionary though God sent him to go to a people to bring them to Him. He was already 80 years old when God called him. For that alone, he would never be accepted by a mission board today. But it was the elderly Moses who knew the God who could part the seas, drop manna from the skies, flow water from the rock, and talk with a man at Sinai. Sure, younger Joshua took over eventually, but he was at least 60 years old himself when that occurred and possibly closer to 70.

Truthfully, the advantage of youth is youth itself—the energy, zeal, and determination. But that same youth is also the detriment—a lack of experience, responsibilities at home, temptations, pride, eagerness to achieve no matter the cost, and the willingness to cut corners. In Scripture, these youthful attributes are why you always see the young man, despite his ability, being in submission to the leadership of the older, experienced, successful man. Often young men are unwilling to do that because they don't know such a man personally, or they are captive to their ego and desire for fame. And we all know what comes after pride.

Our continuing and widespread problem, the misunderstanding of what biblical missions are, has led us to many problems. Pastors much teach this biblical pattern, and Bible colleges emphasize what a missionary should be and do. Until they do, we will continue to send out well-meaning but unqualified men who are satisfied with shepherding existing flocks rather than starting new flocks and training new shepherds.

What About Supporting Single Missionaries?

Some insist that Paul was never married. Others say that Paul had been married because it was a prerequisite that only married men could be part of the Sanhedrin. If so, then what happened? Did she die? Did she leave him because of his new faith? Did he abandon her to do ministry?

We don't have the answers to those questions, so we logically surmise that he was either never married or that his wife was no longer a part of his life due to death or her desertion after his conversion. Frankly, I feel that we should simply assume that his wife had passed away, having no evidence to the contrary. There is just no logical, historical, traditional, or cultural reason to suspect that he had never married. It defies logic.

The requirement for supporting a missionary should not be age, health, funding, or a pleasing presentation. The requirement should be a calling verified by experience. And if you are planning to support the man, do so until he stops doing what you are supporting him to do. Hopefully, that will be his entire life.

Off the top of my head, which has become barren over past decades, I cannot think of a single apostle or a fellow-minister of Paul whose wife was referenced, other than Aquila's wife, Priscilla. Yes, Peter must have had a wife since he had a mother-in-law, but what was her name?

This observation does not discredit women or lower the status of their place in ministry. Scripture is full of the names of women who accomplished great things for God; it's just that the Bible does not mention these men's wives. Why not? Possibly because doing so was not relevant to what was being taught. In our day, it is culturally typical and expected for a preacher to refer to his wife. But that was not the culture of the day. If you examine Roman culture at that time, you will learn that save for a few exceptions, women were relegated to a lower status. In many places, they were not even allowed to leave home alone without being considered immoral. In my case, I enjoy having my wife with me while I travel to other lands. I love seeing the expression on her face as she encounters new foods, dress, and cultures. However, because of the danger, I don't take her to some countries.

I concur that a single man will have to endure temptations that a married man can withstand, but that is not to automatically assume failure because of marital status. He can endure temptations, loneliness, etc., because he has the zeal to work longer and harder. Besides, there is the fact that unlike us today, missionaries did not work alone; they worked in groups or teams of men and even ladies. Read in Paul's letters how he salutes the ladies who helped him, worked with him, and now assist in those local house churches. The Bible contains multiple examples. The single missionary had no lack of companionship, and he had little opportunity for the interference of temptation, Demas being the exception.

Besides this, in I Corinthians 7:7, in context, Paul encouraged men to remain single so that they could give more time to the ministry's work, rather than having to share time with family. Some say that we should not support a single missionary; Paul said that he wished all missionaries were single. So then, since God did not command either way, whose opinion should we value most—yours or Paul's?

Since I am driving this wagon, I am entitled to give yet another opinion based on my decades of observation. I have known many single men who served God with great zeal and great effectiveness. I consider a handful of men—both married and single—in our generation to be all-stars of missions. However, to me, one man stands above all others. I am so proud of him and, at the same time, so jealous of all he has accomplished. When we stand before our Lord, I hope to receive a few crowns to lay at his feet, maybe even a small basketful. However, in the celebration, I expect a delay as the angels unload truckloads of crowns for this man's honor. It is a good thing that we will return our crowns to our Lord after receiving them; otherwise, this man's mansion will fill with his from floor to ceiling.

I would love to take the time to tell you why I feel this way and to introduce you to him, but his work is so secretive that exposing it would harm it and him. I know that some of you have already concluded of whom I speak. If you have not, contact me personally, and I will share both his ministry and his name with you. And then, unless you are certifiably crazy, you will want to support him as well.

Indeed, if there has ever been another Paul, he is it. We are honored to serve this single missionary (by choice) as he serves our Lord.

ELIMINATING THE CONUNDRUM

***Suggestions for Missionaries*:**

- You got support by convincing the churches of your calling. Now keep it by showing them that you deserve it. Churches often have to drop the support of some of their missionaries. When this occurs, they look for reasons to drop you and not to drop you. Final Frontiers will often maintain support when a church has dropped most or all of the others they supported. Why? Because they believe in what we are doing and because we demonstrate that we are continuing to do it. We have sometimes gone from being one of the ministries a church supports to being the only one. As their members fell away, they had no choice but to drop one missionary after another, but because of what we do, how we do it, and the fact that we don't hide it under a bushel, they determined to keep us supported while dropping all of the others. In several cases, when their church disbanded or they sold their property, they gave the proceeds to our ministry, knowing what we would accomplish with it. Make a reputation for yourself that attracts churches to want to support you and keep supporting you.

- How do you create that trust? Do not barrage your supporting churches with daily Facebook postings of your family on vacation or pictures of the plate of food you had that day. Also, do not indulge in online political debates. Avoid judgments like posts saying, "if you love Jesus, you'll forward this message to ten other people." Give regular postings or emails with substance that accompanies a photograph or a video (a short video, well done and filmed without palsy and fish-tailing). We usually do this once a week. Try to make the substance readable in a two- to three-minute sitting and make sure the photos are clear and interesting.

- Remember, your supporters need to be *reminded* of what you have done, see what you are doing, and *hear* what you plan to do. Missionaries often make the mistake of talking too much about their plans and too little about their actions and accomplishments. Don't give a sermon outline or a video of you preaching for an hour. Simply mention where you went, what you did, what the results were, how you intend to follow-up, and what, if anything, your supporters can do to help you.

- Attract and encourage young men and teenagers to come work with you during the summer to get experience and learn what missionary life is all about.

Suggestions for Churches:

- I would highly recommend that all churches disregard age and marital status as a disqualifying factor. Look instead for *evidence* of the calling, experience, and accomplishments. To do otherwise is to take a chance. The wise man never bets on a three-legged horse.

- In each case, ask yourself, *why did we choose to support this missionary?* If you see or feel he is slipping from that expectation that prompted his support, then share your concerns with him. Be quick to improve your relationship and understanding of his work rather than being quick to drop his support. At the same time, be a good steward and do what is right. No missionary "deserves" support; it is your gift to him. You gave it for a reason with an expectation. If he is not fulfilling the expectation, then you are released from your obligation.

- Make sure each missionary knows what you expect from them in accomplishments and in reporting. Do not be lenient with this expectation. Make it a contract between your church and the missionary. Have them sign it and receive a copy. If they break the contract, further payment is suspended until improvement or dropped due to breach of contract. Wake up, churches! This is our Father's business! Operate it as a spiritual business. If you consider this to be too harsh or too much work, you need to restudy the meaning and purpose of stewardship. Remember, Paul dropped a missionary—John Mark. Later in life, when Barnabas had further trained him (and no doubt Peter also), and John Mark had matured and improved, Paul invited him back as a team member, saying that he had become "profitable" for Paul's ministry (II Timothy 4:11).

- When considering initiating support, enquire:
  1) Has the candidate ever been involved in starting a church in his own culture? If he has not or cannot do so among his people and culture, what makes you think he can do it in another?
  2) Can the candidate introduce you to another man whom he has won to Christ, mentored, and who is now successfully serving in the ministry or as a layman? If he cannot, why would you support him to do something overseas that he has never done at home?

- When considering continuing your support, ask the same two questions. Is the missionary fulfilling the purpose and calling of a missionary? If he is, then help him; if he is not, give him a probation time to improve and demand improvement or the loss of his support.

- If you are supporting men, women, or organizations from your mission account that do not and likely never would meet the core requirements of a missionary, then consider forming a separate Ministry Account and support them as ministers of the gospel, not as missionaries.

- Consider sending your young men to work an entire summer with a successful missionary. Doing this will help young men solidify their calling or realize what they felt was a burden—not a calling.

SECTION THREE

Great Commission Conundrums Regarding ACCOUNTABILITY

A leper, India

#11
How Can a Church Feel Confident the Missionaries They Support Will Not Fail, and What Should Be Done If They Do Fail?

Explaining the Conundrum

It is necessary for a church to feel confident that they have made a correct decision after electing to give a missionary monthly financial support and continued prayer support. Such confidence excites the church as to their influence abroad and encourages them to give and do even more. But what if there is a case of a missionary failure? Do you 1) confront and correct it, or do you 2) deny and cover it up? Frankly, I think the first choice is the only answer, but the second is usually preferred unless the failure has to do with doctrine or morals. So, how then do we handle this dilemma?

Examining the Conundrum

To begin with, we have to define the term *fail*. Usually, it is applied to a missionary's having to quit the ministry due to immorality. Some would say it also applies if the wife has sinned. However, a man who returns home permanently because of illness is not a failure. Still, I would wonder if doctors could not have treated the illness in that land so the family could remain there serving and training. I would not automatically call a man who voluntarily quits because of age a failure, but I would certainly wonder why. I have met so many couples who "used to be missionaries," but no longer are, and I cannot imagine what could have pulled them away from the land they claimed God called them to, sent them to, and which became their home for decades. Yet, how blessed we are to hear of missionaries' wives, who after their husbands perished or were martyred, returned to the same people in the same land to continue reaching them for Christ. I am not judging anyone, so please don't judge me; I am merely asking questions that in my mind need answering. Perhaps if everyone's case is different, then everyone's call can also be different.

By the way, I am not a judge or jury; I am a curious missionary looking to increase our forces with qualified candidates, not dilute them with missionary wannabes or shrink it with the loss of those still capable of serving. No one must answer to me, except me.

God called Paul to both the Jews and the Gentiles. That included everyone on the earth. But we typically feel called to reach a smaller and specific *ethnos* or people group for Christ. Some stay with these large groups and evangelize throughout their lands, while others move on to another *ethnos* living elsewhere. Both are biblical and legitimate.

So, I submit, since every missionary's case is different, who then gets to define the term *failure?*

Every missionary and pastor probably can and certainly should be able to answer that question based on their understanding and experience. But since I am the only one sitting here at the keyboard, let me give it a shot.

I would suggest that failure can be, and in the vast majority of cases, is much more than a doctrinal change or an immoral act. In reference to failing as a missionary, here's my definition: *failure* is "a continuous pattern of not performing the duties expected of his service due to ignorance, inability, laziness, misconduct, or abandonment."

A weak character could cause these conditions, as a family problem, a lustful or envious heart, depression, an inability to adapt to the culture (this is the number-one cause given), too much self-reliance and not enough on the Holy Spirit, or any other number of things.

Exposing the Conundrum

From the Missionary's Standpoint:

Before a church determines that a missionary they support is failing, he should first be made aware of their purpose in supporting him. He may be failing in discipling men for ministry but have enormous crowds when he preaches on the street or has a vast bus ministry in his church. What you call failure, he may not.

As missionaries, we know our supporters expect us to "go" but other than a quarterly letter—not what they expect once we arrive. Most church members have no idea why they are supporting a particular missionary; they just are. Maybe it's because their church wasn't yet supporting anyone in that country, maybe it's because of the Bible college he graduated from, maybe he was referred by a trusted friend, or he is the nephew of a faithful (big giver) church member no one wants to offend.

There could still be other reasons. Perhaps the missionary had a pretty wife with a bubbling personality that the elderly in the church fell in love with. Maybe they have a disabled child, and the church felt sorry for them (as they should), but they forgot that sympathy might demand an offering but does not necessitate support. After all, a hospital is nearby with unfortunate cases to whom they give no attention. Maybe the missionary has been on deputation for five years and has only gained support from a few churches and was discouraged; they felt sorry for him, so they took him on for support. I have seen these given as reasons to support a missionary.

At a minimum, the church should expect specific results, a quarterly update, or even an annual Skype call to the congregation. If he is willing to jump through their hoops and later fails to do so, he is in breach of contract. At that point, the church should contact him with a gentle reminder, offer a second chance, then see if he improves. If not, drop his support altogether. I would suggest churches put all their expectations in writing and have it signed by the pastor and each missionary they support. In this way, while going from church to church, he doesn't forget who expects what and ends up accidentally losing support.

From the Church's Standpoint:

I would also suggest to churches that you do not get too specific while listing your expectations. Most missionaries will have from 50 to 150 supporting churches. If only half require specific "expectations" that are not of common concern to the other supporting churches, the missionary becomes handicapped by the contractual agreements and unable to fulfill the purpose for which he is there. He will have to spend a great deal of his time writing 150 different specific reports every quarter.

Keep in mind that it is not a sin to drop support. But on the other hand, dropping support should not be done lightly. Churches often drop the support of their missionaries because they acquired a new pastor, and he has "favorites" from his past church that he wants to help. He justifies this decision by declaring that since he does not know the missionaries the church has committed to, then how can he support them. It is as if he alone has the spiritual discernment to know whom to support—not the pastor who started the church nor the pastors who preceded him, nor his deacons, nor his trustees, nor the members—only he has that knowledge and right. But at the same time, he will not consider dropping the mortgage payment or any other commitment the church made before he arrived.

The church's commitment to supporting should be as binding as their commitment to pay the utility bills and the mortgage. The church voluntarily committed themselves to a life-time obligation of his family's support unless the missionary breached the requirements for such. But if the church gave no requirements or expectations, how can he breach them? You don't stop paying the light bill because there was not enough money; you find the money. No one put a gun to your head to get you to pledge support (well, there was that one time when…), so fulfill your vow before the Lord.

Missionaries are not chess pawns to be moved around and discarded as we play at world evangelism. They are (or should be) highly trained, experienced, gifted servants of God; after all, if the Lord must equip a man to serve Him in his own culture, how much more if he is serving God in a strange and distant land.

On the other hand, a missionary who is not "missionary-ing" and fails at his calling has no right to expect a lifelong welfare check from 150 churches looking for results. They don't support you so you can live in a country you love; eat exotic foods; enjoy the climate, culture, and history; and revel in unscheduled vacations. When John Mark failed, Paul sent him home, where he received more training and became "profitable" for the ministry. Today, we would feel sorry for him, saying he meant well and continue his support. If our supporting churches would do as Paul did, it might eventually make great missionaries out of some of us too. But it would certainly free up wasted missionary support—millions of dollars annually—that could be given to men who both need it and deserve it.

But I have strayed from the point. Let me return to the issue of failing as a missionary. I must understand and acknowledge that before I can begin to fail a supporting church back home, I must have already failed my Lord. The first step is to repent, then to do the works of repentance. Do your job. Do what you said God called you to do or go home.

If churches supported missionaries to evangelize, plant churches, disciple converts, and produce more preachers, a simple, two-page report form (such as we use for our national preachers) would do the trick. It would display to the supporting churches whether or not the missionary was a success or a failure.

Since I mentioned it, you might be curious about what our quarterly, two-page "National Missionary's Report Form" encompasses. Before they reply to specific questions about their family, ministry, health, plans, etc., they answer the following four, simple, one-word-answer questions:

In the last quarter:

1. *How many souls have you won to Christ?*
2. *How many have you baptized?*
3. *How many new villages (areas, barrios, etc.) have you evangelized?*
4. *How many new churches have you started?*

Now here is the best part: the next sentence says: *If the answer to any of the above questions is "zero," explain why*. It's not that we expect a preacher to start a new church every three months; most could never do that. But it's our way of reminding them each quarter that we expect them to be working—not sitting in their home or office writing Sunday school lessons. (You can find thousands of those on the Internet, free of charge.)

Now, I know what some of you are thinking; *"What if writing Sunday school lessons is his ministry?"* Easy question, easy answer. If that is his primary ministry, then he isn't getting support from us. We only support men who are "actively and consistently involved in church planting and discipleship." Anything else is permissible but is considered an extra, a need for ministry, not the purpose of ministry. If the tail begins to wag the dog, then Spot will have to look elsewhere for supper.

By now, you know I believe that biblically, missions is church planting and discipleship. Still, most churches continue to consider other endeavors as "missions" rather than "ministry." I think a church could do both, funding each from separate accounts, one for missions and one for ministry. The church can decide if they want their giving to be a 50/50 split or a 90/10 split. By doing this, they will never "accidentally" forget to fund one or the other or get too out of balance. The tail will never wag the dog.

Many churches support more mission headquarters, children's homes, Bible colleges, defense funds, rescue centers, etc., in the USA than missionaries overseas. Yet all that support comes from their "missions" budget. Don't you see that by changing the definition of "missions" and "missionary," we have destroyed the Great Commission's global outreach in exchange for funding local, needy and worthy ministry causes? Does this funding please God?

Considering failing in missions, maybe it's not so much the missionary who has failed but some of his supporting churches.

For the sake of this conundrum, let's just assume I'm speaking to a typical American church that believes missions is anything and everything done off-site…

- A youth trip to New York City to pass out tracts while visiting the Empire State Building and the Statue of Liberty
- The downtown rescue mission
- Restocking a food pantry
- Supporting American preachers who incorrectly call themselves "missionaries" and do nothing more than pastor a foreign church that they did not even start
- Supporting orphanage workers, legal staff and attorneys, schoolteachers, airplane pilots and mechanics, camp directors, groundskeepers, foreign office staff, retirement homes, children's homes, etc.

If you believe as I do, you agree we should support all these entities, but they are *ministries* and not missions since biblically, a missionary is a church planter like Paul—not a pastor like James. That being the case, a simple "report form" like the one I have already detailed should be enough to see if each missionary is succeeding or failing.

However, if I cannot convince you and you feel that anything and everything outside your church property is missions, then you will need to find another way to determine whether or not your missionary is failing.

I submit that with all your supported missionaries, consider that our *progress* is typically more critical than our *process*. Let me explain. Perhaps you support a missionary in Brazil. The process by which she got your support is that she is a teacher at an orphanage. You love children, so that need sparked your interest. How then do you develop criteria by which you determine if she is a success (worthy of continued support) or a failure (deserving to be dropped)? I call this determination the *progress*.

Typically, the answer is that as long as she sends quarterly letters, it is enough. But what was your purpose for supporting her? Was it to receive quarterly letters or for her service? A typical response may well be, "She works at an orphanage; isn't that enough?" Great, so does the cook, the janitor, and the administrator, but you don't support them. So, get more specific. How many children is she caring for? What is she teaching them? What impact is she having on their lives? How is she helping the local church? Has/is she training a student-teacher (and if not, why not)? How many student-teachers has/is she training? These concerns are more important than which curriculum she uses, does she like her roommate, or has she met a young man yet? These issues reveal her ministry progress, allowing you to feel better about supporting her and maybe helping with a project or taking a team to visit the field where she labors.

Historical Note: *Many early British missionaries to Africa were single and had no intention of ever going home, and since they had given their lives to reach that tribe, they married local girls.*

Here is another example of *the process*: perhaps you are funding a small Bible institute in Uganda that is training pastors and church planters. What is the progress by which you determine continued support or cessation of support? What is important to you: how many students they have, what courses they offer, their holiday schedule, whether it is a two-, three-, or four-year course, if the buildings are made of bamboo or concrete block, or do they have a scholarship program? Or is your *ministry progress* concerns better to address? What is their doctrine, how many churches have their graduates started, and what is the attrition rate of the "preachers" they graduate? (What percentage of their graduates remain in ministry compared to those who get a diploma and then go into the secular world?) Can they help other pastors and missionaries in outlying regions of their land by opening satellite campuses?

So, in Conclusion:

To answer the conundrum, you as a church or family have to decide two issues first:

1) Why are you supporting missions in general?

2) Why are you supporting each missionary in particular?

If your concept of missions echoes mine, that task is easy. Is the missionary/national preacher winning souls, baptizing converts, planting new churches, and training men as pastors to lead those churches? Is he sending you regular reports (you define *regular*, but quarterly should be acceptable)? If he is accomplishing this criteria, he is a resounding success—no matter what else he is doing. And if he is not, he is a failure who should receive a loving warning, some spiritual encouragement, and a second chance to be conformed to the standard he claims God called him to—a missionary. He may benefit from a visit from another missionary who can help him understand his purpose and function and help him find ways to overcome whatever is hindering him. A pastor may do this as well, but it would mean more coming from a fellow missionary. (And I offer myself to that end.)

You can determine if a missionary is succeeding or failing by merely defining the purpose of his support and having him held accountable to you with regular reports. Logic and fairness dictate that if the missionary is doing what you are supporting him to do, you should continue his support. If he is not doing what you are supporting him to do, he should be first encouraged and then motivated, and if you are still not satisfied with his performance, he should be dropped.

In that event, I would recommend you be lenient with him, remembering he is out of the country and has little means to replace your support. You may want to give him a year, so he can contact other churches to take his place or even wait until he returns home on furlough. It's your call but remember the Golden Rule because you will most certainly reap what you sow.

The following is yet another logical question: what about men who don't produce because they are in countries where it is harder to be productive? We already established that everyone's case is different. In some countries, evangelism is like giving milk to a baby, get it close enough, and the infant will find the bottle and go to sucking. In others, it's like trying to feed a toddler who doesn't want to eat. Some of it may go in his mouth under protest, but most of it will be on his shirt, the floor, and you.

I acknowledge that every field is different. However, I do wonder at times about men who have no fruit at all after many years. God put us in the vineyard to produce fruit. If a missionary has no fruit, he probably has not been trained well. Even in a Hindu, Muslim, or Buddhist land, you can win souls. The method may be different—no tract, no going door-to-door, etc., yet the message is the same. In the hardest of lands, you should first develop a friendship, and that accomplished, most will be willing or eager to hear your witness. Since God's Word does not return void (without results), if you have no results, you are likely either not planting seed or not giving them water and fertilizer. Build relationships with your neighbors, employees, and contacts like your barber, the mailman, the milkman, your kid's teachers, the parents of their friends, the gas station attendant, the butcher, baker, and the electric meter reader, etc. I guarantee you that people want to know you, but in most cases, they are too shy to make the first move. You make it, then reap the rewards.

Even the missionary's children play a part in the ministry. Some missionaries insist on having homeschool, but why? It's not wrong, but here's a thought to consider. If you put your kids in the neighborhood school or even in a private school, they will make friends and have ministry opportunities. If not, they will become those weird kids on the block who look different, talk different, dress differently, and have no idea what is going on around them. The others won't even want to play with them. Where is the witness in that? They need not only to learn the language but also the culture. If you feel your children are too spiritually weak to resist exposure to the unsaved children, then come home, lock them in a bubble until they are grown, then go back to the mission field. Let this sink deep into your DNA. You cannot win the nationals or be accepted by the nationals if you do not become one of them. Or at least that's what Paul said.

People like to cite the fact that Adoniram Judson was in Burma for six years before he had his first convert. That was his fault, and he later acknowledged it. However, in the following six years, he had a multitude of converts. It took him time to learn, accept and adopt the Burmese culture, and only in doing so was he able to learn how to communicate effectively and culturally. Once he learned, he was off and running, not only producing converts but teaching them how to do the same. During his first six years, the message was not the barrier to success; it was his method. Let me explain further.

Recall that daily, dressed in his eighteenth-century American attire, Judson sat on his porch, preaching in Burmese to those who would gather to hear him and reject his message. What happened? One day his only convert told him that the people standing around were not Burmese; they were from the Karen tribe (pronounced *ka-rin*) and could not understand what he was preaching. They barely spoke the Burmese language.

When the convert, knowing their language, translated for them, they asked Judson to go with them to their villages, and he refused. Still, his helper went for a weekend trip that lasted several months, going from village to village, winning thousands, and planting churches. By the time Judson died, he had dedicated his life to the Burmese people, translated the entire Bible in their language, and developed the Burmese Primer that 250 years later is still used in their elementary schools. After his death, while preparing his biography, I believe the church attendance records revealed over 90 percent of the converts in Burma were not Burmese; they were Karen. Still today in Burma, they are known as the "Baptist tribe" and have won many other tribes to Christ, particularly the Chin and Kachin. After the Vietnam War, tens of thousands of Karen living in Vietnam and Laos migrated to our West coast and established Karen churches there as well.

One of the most fruitful areas of conversions in the world is Andhra Pradesh, India. In the 1990s, the State was considered the fastest-growing region of Christianity in the world. But 150 years ago, when missionaries first started going there, well, it was a great place to go if you wanted to get sick, discouraged, tortured, and killed. My point is that somebody has to break ground with the gospel, plow the soil of men's hearts, and plant the seeds for a later harvest.

The church always referred to such men as "the apostle to the ____." Keep in mind the Greek word *apostle* is from where we get the English word "missionary." Missionaries should always seek out those who have never heard the gospel because no one has yet gone to tell them. The evangelists, preachers, pastors, and teachers follow behind them (Ephesians 4), building on the foundation for which they died.

Latin America is another classic example. South America is a relatively difficult region to evangelize, steeped in Roman Catholicism, animism, and ancient witchcraft. Central America has somewhat the same language, food, culture, customs, and people, but evangelism there is like picking ripe fruit from a tree. The difference is that the Central American Mission (started by C. I. Scofield) specifically and aggressively targeted Central America. Their missionaries were soul-winning church planters who were often beaten and killed. Even 40 years ago, Baptist and evangelical pastors were still being imprisoned in Honduras, and 20 years ago, Mayan preachers in Guatemala were still being stoned. (All of this happened at the instigation of local Catholic priests.)

Nonetheless, today, the gospel covers Central America, not as a thin cotton sheet but as a heavy woolen blanket. South America did not get the same attention (process—sending missionaries) and has not produced the same result (progress). So, whereas today Central America is now mostly evangelical by choice and conversion (even if they are Catholic by birth), most of South America remains highly Roman Catholic.

Missionary, the point is, while you may feel that you are not yet reaping a successful-looking harvest, are you at least preparing the field and sowing the seed for the harvester who will come after you? There is no failure in that. You cannot reap a harvest from a field that is not plowed and sown, and to do that, someone must first "break up the fallow ground." You may not see the harvest here, but you will see it there—*"Well done, thou good and faithful servant...."*

Eliminating the Conundrum

Suggestions for Missionaries:

- Remember that part of our ministry is to help the local churches that are funding and feeding us. Whatever you can do to help the pastor boost the mission's awareness, involvement, and missionary funding should be prioritized. The following are a few examples:

- Make sure you send quarterly reports, if not more often. I produce a 24-page quarterly magazine for our entire ministry, write one or more weekly news alerts for the Internet, and send out a quarterly letter to my supporting churches and friends. On top of that, I edit letters from our foreign workers so their sponsors can understand them in English. I write books of my own; edit others' books; and develop and approve curriculum, podcast materials, and video teaching scripts. I also spend about three to five months a year out of the country and multiple weekends (and weeks) speaking at churches and conferences. I also teach as an adjunct missions' professor in various colleges and institutes worldwide, yet I will typically plant one or more churches a year. I am a little bit busy, and truthfully, I do a lot of this in the early morning hours when I can't sleep or can't sleep any longer. I'm getting old and getting tired, but if I can find time to do all this, you can write a one-page letter every three months. If not, you reveal that your sponsors are not your priority; only their money is.

- With the advent of smartphones, you have no excuse not to make short, unscripted videos and send them to your mailing list. If there is a flood, send a clip and tell how you are using the calamity to help others and spread the gospel. If you visit a school, send a clip. If you visit an orphanage, talk about the kids and that ministry and what you would like to do to help them.

In 2019 while my wife and I were in India, we visited a leper colony and were burdened (not called) to start a feeding center for their children. I calculated that I needed $1050 a month ($12,600 for the first year). I didn't have a sufficient surplus, so Nolin showed me how to post pictures on Facebook, shared what we would like to do and asked for help. Within 48 hours, three people had committed the funds. In mid-2020, I found we needed to provide food and water across the Islamic Middle East and North Africa for 325 families whose husbands were martyred for preaching or smuggling Bibles. That's well over 1,300 people in need. They are our people, so I prepared a short, unscripted video and mentioned that we needed a bit over $15,000 a month for the next four months at least ($62,000). Within two weeks, we had it all and more. I am not a master fundraiser; I wish I were. Frankly, I'm a beginner compared to others. But I have learned a few lessons over the years that may help you:

1) Be as brief as possible with requests (that is difficult for me) and as infrequent as possible. I get calls from around the world almost every day, but I never answer some of them—those who only call to say, "give me," and with whom I have to struggle to get a follow-up picture or report.

2) Be honest in explaining the problem, the project, the need, the solution, and the steps to the solution (The same process I am using in addressing each conundrum).

3) Speak or write from your heart. We are missionaries; we are not politicians or used car salesmen (no offense intended).

4) Please don't overdo it with constant requests, or they will stop opening the letters you send. I'm sure I send too many, but after over 35 years of building a network, we have found that everyone has something they are interested in helping with, while no one wants to help with everything. It may be kids and not preachers; it may be Bibles but not bicycles; it may be film evangelism but not tract distributions. Someone is always interested in something and looking for an opportunity to help. This is true whether you are talking about families who donate or supporting churches. If you follow those steps and build a long-standing relationship of trust and confidence with them, they will rush to help you with your projects.

- If you feel you are failing or beginning to fail, seek help—especially from someone who does not stand to benefit from your failure (like a fellow servant who wants to "inherit" your facilities if you give up and go home). I have traveled to many counties only to help a struggling missionary. I don't have all the answers, but I can fake them. (Just kidding.) However, after all these decades, I have many answers and even some proven ways to implement the solutions. And if I don't by now, I never will. (If it's true that you learn from your mistakes, I'm a genius.) I am happy to serve God's servants. That is my secondary calling, my first being church planting. I can come to your field, or you can come on one of mine.

- Finally, recognize that all who go are not called; many felt a burden and mistook it for a call. If that is you, own up to it. You are not a failure, you did something others were afraid to do, and you did it because of your love for the Lord and souls. Okay, you got there and figured out this is not God's will after all; then find out what His will is and do it. It may yet be in that land, and if not, go home with your head held up high and serve God there. You have learned an important lesson that you can share with others. Or, stay there, get a job and be an exemplary layman to the churches in your adopted country. The truth is you may be more of a blessing as an employed or self-employed layman than you ever would have been as a foreign pastor or a missionary. Sometimes while watching a football game, the announcer will talk about a quarterback initially drafted for another position. His successes and failures while trying revealed his greatest potential. (Get my point?) Find out what God made you for and do it. Anything else is simply a waste of the dirt He used to make you.

Suggestions for Churches:

- Be fair. While you're "determining" the missionary's validity, keep in mind that every field is different. In some, you may struggle a year to win a convert, while in others, they line up on the street outside your house, waiting to be evangelized.
- Find a way to discover what your missionaries are doing and

producing. As I discussed in an earlier conundrum, you may want to set up a spreadsheet, making it easy to observe at a glance. If you have a missions' director or secretary, let them do the work; after all, that's why they get paid the big bucks, right?

- Don't burden the "producers" with long, frequent, and detailed reports and questionnaires. Accept their quarterly letters unless an issue arises and stick to the issues that concern you regarding ministry activity.

- Don't frequently ask them for additional information and videos so that you can share it with your church when they never see any benefit from taking the time and expense to do it. I have one supporting church that does this to me frequently, yet despite my dozen requests over the years to drop by and give an in-person report, they never invite me. Obviously, they are not trying to help me build my work; they are trying to get me to help build theirs. (And that's fine too; we're all in this together.)

- Develop whatever level of accountability necessary to make your people feel confident in missions, missionaries, and your church's missions' program. One of my upcoming books will exclusively address this subject, Lord willing.

- Whenever a missionary comes to your church, if you desire stewardship that produces accountability and trust, it is imperative that the pastor or someone sits down with each selected missionary and clearly explains to them the following four essentials:

  1) How much your church will give him and how often, i.e., monthly, quarterly, etc.

  2) When the support will begin, i.e., the month and year and when he can expect to receive his first support check.

  3) Why the church wants to support him, i.e., give him a reason, not just "because." (Was it his ministry presenta-

tion, his character, his experience, his board, the country where he plans to go, etc.? Let him know so he can use that knowledge to improve his ministry presentation at future churches.)

4) What your church expects of him in return for support, i.e., length of time to his departure, the minimal activities you expect him to do—church planting, soul winning, etc., how often you expect a report, who to send it to, and so forth.

#12
How Do We Really Know What the Missionaries We Support Are Doing? Can Accountability Really Exist When Supporting Someone in Another Country?

Explaining the Conundrum

Being curious about the life and ministry of those you support is natural. Unfortunately, reports sent to supporters often lack substance. They seem more like a page from a diary than a report on production, performance, or even activity.

While admittedly, most church members are not interested in missions, a few live for it. When writing the pastor, keep him and those missions-minded people in the forefront of your thoughts. They will read what you write and pray for you, and when there is a need, they will lobby the church on your behalf. Hold yourself accountable to the churches generally but hold yourself accountable specifically and purposefully to the pastors and those who eat, sleep and drink missions.

In this two-part conundrum, the two are so aligned that I felt the need to treat them as two parts of one issue, which is probably the most crucial issue regarding both the giving and receiving support—and that issue is accountability.

EXAMINING THE CONUNDRUM

Webster defines *accountability* as "the quality or state of being accountable; an obligation or willingness to accept responsibility or to account for one's actions."

There are two sides to this coin of missionary accountability. Some assume missionaries are energetic, self-sacrificing, workaholics, and I have met many like that. In contrast, others contend that missionaries, excuse me, *moochonaries* (as we are sometimes called), are lazy, indifferent, overpaid, whining failures living in mansions with servants. Unfortunately, I have met a few of those too, but neither of these two assumptions describes the typical missionary's life and activity.

The truth is that most missionaries are like many aspiring entrepreneurs. They are hardworking individuals with grand visions of success rarely accomplished because they either dreamed too big or didn't take the steps necessary to reach their goals. They have not yet learned you don't build a house all at once; you build it one brick at a time and refuse to accept the adage, "you have to crawl before you walk."

Remember President Clinton's famous line while under his impeachment trial? "That all depends on what your definition of the word 'is' is." *Working hard,* I have learned, is another term open to an individual's personal definition. A missionary may feel he is working hard because he preaches three times a week and prepares each sermon with lengthy Bible study. While across the country in a different town, another missionary preaches the same number of times and has a Bible institute with classes five nights a week and an orphanage with thirty children to teach, feed and raise. He, too, feels he is working hard. The reality is, if the missionary does not tell you what he is doing, you have no way of knowing. And even if he does, you don't know if he is being sincere or is, as we say, just *speaking evangelistically* (which is a religious idiom for the word "exaggeration").

In other words, just because a man claims to be working hard doesn't mean he is. It could mean that what he calls "working hard" is different from how others define it. The only way you could know would be for each missionary to give you a short but detailed report on what he is doing. Then you can decide if he is working hard or hardly working.

Such accountability is not so difficult with church staff. You see what time they start and finish their work, how well they do it and how profitable it is to the church. But for a missionary, you receive a quarterly letter that often gives no mention of ministry accomplishments but includes intricate details of family news. That should not be considered accountability by anyone's definition.

Over the decades, I have heard some people say missionaries are incapable of service; they are nothing more than men who could not make it in America as a pastor, so they went abroad to be a missionary. I admit among the thousands of missionaries I have met, I have met a few men who qualify that condemnation. I agree too that it is a possibility but not a probability and seldom a reality. I must also say to the supporting churches, "Shame on you if you send your 'undesirables' to other lands rather than keeping them at home and helping them overcome their inabilities. Are you trying to diminish the cause of Christ?" This scenario usually occurs when a man is so boring in his preaching that you cannot bear listening to him longer; thus, he is not "apt to teach," so you send him overseas. How wrong!

Now, let's start with the second question in our conundrum. "Does accountability *really exist* when you are supporting someone in another country?" For me, the most crucial concern in this question is not the noun *accountability*, but the adverb *really*.

Depending on what you as a missionary can do (and report) and what you as a supporter expect to receive, there are different levels of accountability. For example, our director in the Middle East cannot always write letters "on time." He may be in any number of countries, traveling under different names with different papers, having to depend on landlines that are usually tapped, and being followed and/or hunted by the secret police and/or various militias. At those times, which can last for weeks, putting anything in writing or on the Internet is difficult and dangerous. He has a daily or weekly scheduled time to communicate with me via burner phones, but depending on his report, I sometimes cannot safely relay the news to his supporters. For that reason, he occasionally loses the support of churches that expect a bi-monthly or quarterly letter, regardless of his life-threatening circumstances. They either cannot or will not accept his inability to report "on time." Policies on reporting, it seems, are not flexible. In this case, he realizes that he is obligated to report, and he certainly has a willingness to do so; the problem is that his circumstances sometimes forbid him from doing so.

Other missionaries I have spoken with do not see the report process as an obligation. Instead, they see it as an infringement on their time, incorrectly thinking that if God led the church to support him, then they should do so—no questions asked, no report expected. He seems to think they should be thankful for whatever information he gives them whenever he gets around to giving it. Most missionaries, thankfully, have much more intelligence than that.

Years ago, we began supporting some preachers in Azerbaijan. These guys were titans as national missionaries, and I truly felt it an honor to be a small part of their ministry. However, it was not long before we realized they were not reporting. I called their leader and spoke to him about it. He abruptly and quite rudely told me that they don't work for man; they work for God. He added that they would not be held accountable to man, and if I didn't like that, I could drop their support. I did, but not because I wanted to, not because they didn't deserve it, not because they didn't need it, and not because they failed to understand the importance of reporting for accountability's sake. I dropped them because, without reports, there is no accountability. We have a policy in our ministry forged on hundreds of disappointments over decades that policy is "no report, no support." When faced with a time limit that determines if they will ever get another support check, it is incredible how men will find time to write a report. It's virtually miraculous.

Some missionaries acknowledge their obligation to report but are unwilling to take the time to do so, putting it off to do other things. Usually, these are good men who feel they don't have a "gift" of writing, so they put it off as long as they can or ask their wife to write it for them. Often, their unwillingness to prioritize the reporting process leads to extended periods with no accountability at all, especially if the wife also doesn't have a "gift" for writing.

Still, others have nothing to write about from a ministry standpoint, and it shows in the content (or lack thereof) of the letters they do write. If you are accomplishing something, then you have something to write about. And if you are not, then you don't. Again, the contents of the letters reveal the relevance of the labor or lack thereof.

Exposing the Conundrum

I have heard many churches complain that they don't know what a particular missionary is doing because the letters are infrequent, and the information is vague. They naturally doubt that he is doing anything worthy of their support, but they continue to support him without seeking to decipher or correct the problem. This is poor stewardship of their mission's funding.

On the other hand, every church has a different idea of what they think the missionary should be doing. He cannot possibly please all the churches all the time, and he is a miracle worker if he can genuinely please most of the churches, any of the time.

The missionary is living in a strange land with a strange language and, worse, a strange culture. It takes time in other lands just learning to live. When living in Honduras, I can recall that I had to allow at least up to two hours to make a deposit or withdrawal at the bank. As Americans, we know what we want, and we want it now. It takes an entire personality makeover to realize that the rest of the world does not function that way, and they are not concerned with accommodating our whims. And the more you act like their lack of action bothers you, the slower they get. The same is true with the postal service, any dealings with government officials, and virtually any time you need help from an employee at a store. Missionaries know all about these cultural obstacles; supporting churches don't.

In Augusta, Georgia, our annual power loss lasts about two seconds. In developing nations, they may last two months. If the missionary is dependent on the Internet for accountability, both he and his supporters are out of luck.

What about mailing the reports? First of all, that would cost a fortune. Second, you would probably never get them. In the five years I lived in Honduras; I received delivery of only two letters—and both of them were from Cuba. I had to go downtown to the (only) post office in the capital to mail a letter. Though it was only about five miles away, such a trip would take half a day between travel time and standing in line to mail it. (Think about your typical DMV wait time and multiply it by ten).

My attempt with these explanations is not to justify the missionary who is not reporting, but rather to help those who receive your mail daily by walking from your front door to the curb to understand that what we take for granted is different overseas.

Admittedly communication is more manageable now as many countries have Internet connections that are as fast or faster than we have in America. Unfortunately, some missionaries think they satisfy the need to justify continued support by their daily Facebook posts of family activities and their Instagram photos of the cafe latte they are about to consume. In particular, young missionaries tend to think that frequent Facebook posts are in and of themselves "accountability," which is an incorrect assumption. Sponsoring churches want to know what you are doing to further the cause. Regularly reporting that information, taking responsibility for what you do or don't do, is proper accountability. If you are providing it, this type of accountability should lead to continued and increased support, and if not, to discounted and discontinued support. (That is if churches are doing their job as stewards of their missions giving.)

Truthfully, for the missionary who wants to provide accountability and the church that desires to have it, the main hindrance is the lack of communication between them. By that, I mean each needs to know what the other expects.

This communication can get complicated. Consider that if a typical church gives $100 support per month (many give $25 or $50) and a typical missionary receives $5,000 in monthly support (a low amount for the average missionary), he has 50 supporting churches. Suppose he has to customize separate reports for all 50 churches, fulfilling their particular "need" for specific information, and it takes just 30 minutes for each custom report to be processed. In that case, he will spend 25 hours writing reports. That's half a workweek. That's not accountability; it's bureaucracy!

In our ministry, we developed a reporting procedure for overseeing thousands of quarterly reports for decades that still functions well today and frankly has been copied by many other ministries. (You can read about it in detail in conundrum #11.) If churches adopted ours or a similar plan, the missionary could fill out one form online in less than ten minutes and send it to all his supporters with the click of a mouse with photos and/or video clips attached. And since the form is online, it needs only to be filled out once. Our computer program then sends it to all the relevant donors. (We do this using a program my son-in-law, Michael Horne, wrote.)

Our quarterly report starts by simply asking these questions—in the last quarter:

1. *How many people have you led to Christ?*
2. *How many did you baptize?*

3. *How many villages did you evangelize?*
4. *How many new churches were started?*
5. *If the answer to any of these was zero, EXPLAIN WHY.*

We are supporting them for ministry results—not for the thrill of living overseas. (And yes, some of us do consider it a thrill—not a punishment.)

It then asks for them to write a short, personal greeting of appreciation for the support, a list of prayer requests or particular needs, and news of any plans or special efforts they are about to enact. We designed the report for accountability, so the donors will know they are getting what they are paying for while not taking a lot of the missionary's time.

Our Quarterly Report Form is not an epistle; it's a two-page report. In our case, we support the national missionaries for a cause, which is to be a witness, a discipler, and a church planter. We don't care about their garden, their kids' grades in school, their difficulty learning a new language, or how much gasoline costs. We don't care if the kids have new friends, the wife found a new piano student, or that they don't have an AC in their home office. And may I suggest that if those are the sort of things a supporting church is looking for, you need to reexamine your purpose in giving missionary support. And if a missionary thinks that is what his supporters want and need to know, he has missed the entire point of why God called him to be a missionary.

For relatives who may want that type of information or maybe even a home church, Facebook posts are great. But if churches in America are looking for cute stories and comfortable missionaries, then we have disgraced our Lord's commission and deflated the purpose of missions to the point that we no longer even vaguely resemble what God meant and made us to be.

When our military located Osama Bin Laden, they sent in the Navy SEALs. Their commanders and national leaders monitored the event listening for every word, every update, and every action. You know what they saw and heard, but what if the SEAL team members had taken the time to Instagram a picture of the compound, or how scary it was to enter the house. What if they stopped to take a selfie beside each victim or sipping a bit of Pakistani coffee with Osama's cup? Their friends back home may have gotten a kick out of it, but the reprimands from their commander would not have been worth it. We didn't care if they were comfortable, well-fed, enjoyed the flight, or if the weapon was too heavy. And neither did they. They were eager, well-trained, and hand-selected men sent on a mission with a specific purpose. That is precisely what a missionary should be and should be doing.

Okay, the second part of the conundrum has been put to rest. Now, to the first, "How do we *really* know what the missionary is doing?" (There's that adverb "really" again. I stress that in both questions because anyone can tell you what they are doing, but that doesn't *really* mean they are doing it—even if they have photos.)

I once knew a man who was a missionary beginning deputation to a country in South America. He was a friend I had known since Bible college. He had gone there to scout out the land for several months and had come back home to raise support. In doing so, he showed pictures of church services with himself standing behind the pulpit preaching, and other pictures of people getting saved. In still others, he had his arm around male converts who were now serving God. He made constant referrals during the slideshow that these were churches he had started or helped to start and men he had won to Christ. The implication was, "I am doing such a good job that your church should support me."

Listening to his presentation, I was stunned. As I said, this man was my friend, and I knew that he had only gone to that country for a several-week survey trip. I also personally knew the hosting national pastor that he had gone to visit. That faithful South American brother had spent more than a decade starting and building that ministry. He had started the churches shown in the photos long before the missionary had even graduated from Bible college. This national pastor had sent the same photos to me more than three years earlier, telling me the location, naming the converts, how they were doing, etc. They were part of his application for support portfolio. Incredibly, the very man that the missionary on deputation had supposedly led to Christ was already a deacon in the church. I had an old photo of him being baptized many years earlier before this missionary candidate had ever been called to mission's work.

The presentation was all lies, yet, this man raised his support, moved his family there, and returned home to pastor in less than three years, abandoning his missionary calling because of the fear of civil unrest ravaging the country. Why was he able to do this? Because as a rule, churches accept the word of a missionary, and if he has a photo or a video to back it up, they receive his words without question. (This is why I never travel alone, why I let people travel with me, why I help them with their trips without me, and produce so many articles and reports that can be verified.) We don't even use photographs that are not ours without acknowledging the source.

You may wonder where his board was when all of this deception was taking place? You are not alone. A mistaken assumption prevails that a mission board's purpose is to verify their missionaries' reports are authentic and accurate and ensure they are worthy of support (this is administration and accountability). Wrong. I don't know of any that do that. Responding to a concern or an inquiry, they may investigate the occasional missionary, but not as a general practice. They know nothing more about the missionary than what he has written in his letters, and that only if they are receiving and reading the letters. In our case, we have staff who read every report every quarter, and if something looks strange or questionable, we find the answer before sending it to the sponsor. (We like to know the answer before you even know there is a question.) If we can do that with a staff of two, couldn't a large mission board do so as well?

I once visited with a missionary in the Ivory Coast affiliated with one of the largest independent Baptist mission boards in existence. In his 23 years of service in the Ivory Coast, he told me that his board's West Africa Director had never visited him. I'm sure the churches who supported that "West Africa Director" as a "missionary" responsible for the oversight of the missionaries in West Africa had no idea that he wasn't doing his job. And if the president of the mission board didn't know what his appointed director was or was not doing, how in the world could he possibly know what the individual missionaries were or were not doing?

I revealed that lack of accountability to illustrate that, in my opinion, the only way to really know what any missionary is doing is to follow these suggestions:

- Ask questions.
- Verify the answers as best you can.
- You or a small delegation from your church go and visit him.

I feel it is risky for a church to support more missionaries than the staff or a capable church leader can visit at least every three to four years. The pastor or church representative needs to see it with his own eyes, take his own pictures, and personally meet the converts. If you have concerns, hire a bilingual speaker to accompany you. During the week, you or the missionary can possibly lead them to Christ. (You can find them online, at universities, or language schools.)

If you make one widget a day, you can oversee the quality. If you make a hundred, you may be able to, but at some point, you need quality control and an employee who oversees it. The same is true with a church's missions program. If you support too many to adequately oversee the quality of the workers you support, delegate regions or countries to staff or a trusted member. It's all about accountability.

By the standard method of accountability, churches get a quarterly form letter that virtually none of their members will see or read. As a result, there is virtually no ministry information or positive missionary exposure to the church body. By our method, the church would get a firsthand, exciting and sincere report from a fellow member who visited the missionary. Imagine how their experience will ignite fervor for missions in your members. And you can do the missionary a great favor by giving him a video copy of your member's report to the church that he can send to all his other supporting churches.

Improving accountability will accomplish two things. First, it will enhance the missionary's work by holding his feet to the fire, both in performance and reporting, and second, it will increase your church's zeal by giving them a reason to be excited and get more involved.

ELIMINATING THE CONUNDRUM

***Suggestions for Missionaries*:**

- Be open and honest with your reports. Do not be shy about mentioning problems and even setbacks, especially if you can show what you learned from them.
- Reports are not your enemy. They are the mightiest tool you have to promote and fund your ministry.
- Remember that you are supported for a purpose. Demonstrating that you are fulfilling that purpose is not conceit. (David never played down killing Goliath, and he didn't only talk about it either. He had many successes and many failures. He mentioned both, and we love him because of it.) If no one is there to tell the story for you, then you must tell it as humbly and honestly as you can. Don't let history be lost by your not recording it.
- Though I don't recommend you do this, I write a 24-page, quarterly magazine that goes to everyone on our mailing list, showing them precisely what we have done, what it accomplished, and what we plan to do next. I used to do it monthly, but in my old age, I've gotten

lazy. I started doing this in 1986 when "cut and paste" literally meant "cut and paste." Now it's an easy process. I also do a quarterly personal letter for those who support my wife and me. I also do at least one email project a week that is from two to four pages long. All of these have either photos or a video link. The point is, if I can do this, then you can write a compelling one-page letter every three months.

Suggestions for Churches:

- Ask questions. If what you are receiving in reports does not meet your expectation, be fair and let the missionary know. He could probably benefit from your suggestions.

- Someone with a curious nature should read every report you receive. Look for patterns, questionable facts, and inaccuracies. You may need to choose different people for different regions. While it should not be your intention to pick at everything reported, you should at least be conscious of spotting apparent, questionable data. For example, if a missionary says he is leading ten people to Christ every week, but the church is not growing in attendance after several months, something is wrong. Perhaps he was trained as an evangelist and did not attempt to baptize and disciple the new converts. Help him overcome this deficiency.

Years ago, we received a report from a supported preacher in Africa who typically led about twenty people to Christ each quarter. His report stated that he had won over 800 souls that quarter. I immediately emailed the director for that group and asked him to verify the number, thinking perhaps he meant 8 or 80. I assumed it was a mistake and needed clarification to edit his report before sending it to the sponsors. The director told me that they had a month-long street preaching campaign in their city, explaining the large number. My job was to question the report. After receiving the explanation, I wrote a note on the report to the sponsors explaining why the number was both large and abnormal. Not only did they appreciate my note, but also that they didn't have to contact me to get the answer. I had rightly assumed if it caught my eye and that I needed an explanation, it would also catch there's. And it did.

- Inform each missionary if their reports are or are not of the caliber you expect. Give suggestions; just don't go overboard. Everybody has an opinion of what others should be doing, but you, as a pastor, know what your people need to hear.

#13
What Do Churches/Church Members Think Missionaries Do and What Do They Really Do?

Explaining the Conundrum

Everyone has his own idea of what heaven is like—and we are all wrong. After all, according to the Bible, man cannot even imagine what God has prepared for us. Likewise, everyone has his own idea of what a pastor's daily life and routine is like, and they are probably all wrong as well. Most people think pastors only work on Sundays and Wednesday nights. They have no concept of what his position requires and the hours spent weekly in study, counseling, visitation, and witnessing, not to mention carefully overseeing a legal corporation, a body of needy believers, a staff, and the properties they jointly own.

Even so, most people have absolutely no idea of what a missionary does. Stop a moment, close your eyes, empty your mind—no, not that empty—and imagine "a missionary." What do you see? What does he look like? What is he wearing? What are his tools? What did he just finish doing, and what is he about to do? Now, strut around the room, crowing like a rooster, and when I snap my fingers, wake up!

I told you most people have no idea what a missionary does.

Examining the Conundrum

But everyone has his idea of what the life and daily routine of a missionary should be. It depends on how long they have been in church, the various missionaries they have met, and the books they have read. After thirty-five years as a missionary (and over ten before that as a pastor), I have learned the following generalizations: pastors do far more actual "work" than their members imagine; missionaries do far less "work" than their supporters suspect.

Now before you tar and feather me, give me a moment to explain. Please remember—I AM A MISSIONARY—so I know a little about the subject and have the authority to speak specifically as a participant, not generally as an observer.

Pause for a moment again, close your eyes and go back to that image you have of what you think missionaries look like and do.

- Is he an average-looking guy or some ministry superhero?
- Is he dressed in a suit and tie or wearing khakis and a sports shirt?
- What's on his head—a baseball cap or a mosquito-netted, pith helmet?
- What's in his hand—a smartphone or a machete?
- Where does he sleep—on a bed or a mat?
- How does he travel—in an SUV or on foot?
- Is he preaching all day, every day, or only on Sunday and Wednesday?
- Is he starting new churches/congregations or just pastoring an established church with the same congregation, year after year?
- Are his evenings spent in Bible study and discipleship or on Netflix and relaxation?

- Does he eat hamburgers and pizza or monkey brains and a roasted dog?
- Has he witnessed to every family on his street, or does he not even know their names?

Whoa, big boy, before you go on the offensive, let me state that I am not judging anyone, so if I may quote perhaps the most outstanding pastor and orator of the twentieth century, Dr. R. G. Lee, "Don't get mad, I'm just asking."

If you're like many Christians who grew up in the church, based on your experiences attending mission conferences and your pastor's sermons, a missionary is likely either to fit into the image of one extreme or the other. And if you are one of the few who have spent time on a short-term missions trip and you still have the lesser of the two visions, then we as missionaries are really in trouble. After all, if churches support us to "go into all the world," and we don't even go into our own neighborhoods, what impetus remains for churches to continue our support? The quick answer is "none."

Exposing the Conundrum

The truth is no one can study all day, preach every evening, pray all night and last for more than a week. It reminds me of the man who preached, "Let's stand shoulder to shoulder, back-to-back, look each other square in the eyes and march forward for the Lord." The concept sounds great, but it's impossible to do. Missionaries are people too and have all the limitations any other human has. Yet, we are called on and expected to accomplish more each day than others dream of accomplishing in a lifetime—simply because we are missionaries.

So, what do you think missionaries do? Again, that depends on the individual missionary. In my book, *The Great Omission*, I tell this story:

In 1992 I spoke at a church mission conference in Londonderry,

New Hampshire. I was the keynote speaker for the week, which was becoming more common as our ministry was getting exposure. Each evening, while I tried to motivate the members to support missions, various other missionaries were downstairs teaching the children about missions and their personal ministries. During the conference's closing service, the pastor called all the boys and girls to the platform to tell what they had learned about missionaries that week and show the drawings they made to illustrate what the missionaries told them. When the question was asked, "What do missionaries do?" I pulled out my pen to take notes, thinking it would make an excellent subject for a future book. I still have these notes to this day. The response from the children was threefold. "Missionaries," they said, and I quote word for word…

1) "Kill snakes."
2) "Work in the garden."
3) "Don't get enough people to come to church."

The understanding was wrong, although beautifully illustrated with crayons. But what was even more wrong and devastating to the cause of Christ and missions, is that the missionaries they had listened to every night from Sunday through Friday had given them that impression. Keep in mind that incident happened in 1992. Those "kids" are now thirty-five to forty years old with kids of their own. I wonder if that has been their lifelong impression of what a missionary is and does? Is that what they have now taught their children about missions?

We sometimes kill snakes; we do work in the garden, weather permitting, and often we don't get enough people to come to church. But is that the sum total of who we are?

Some missionaries work tirelessly planting numerous churches, training scores of young men to be preachers, and pastor several churches simultaneously. They attempt much and accomplish much. Others "study" all day in their home office and pastor a little church of twenty people started by someone else when the missionary himself was still a toddler. They attempt little and accomplish even less.

I encourage all churches to establish a committee of missions-minded, intelligent people and ask them to develop a mission policy for your church. This policy, approved by the pastor and both understood and accepted by the members, will guide you in what type of ministry you support, what type of missionary you support and how you hold them accountable. (I am currently writing a manual for churches on how to do exactly that.)

So, how do you get started on such a project? Go to the members of your church and ask them the same question I asked: "What do you think missionaries do?" or better still, "What do you think a missionary should be doing, and why you think that?" (Have them read my book, *The Great Omission*, as a starting place.) None of us can live up to every person's expectation in every church, but the Bible reveals some practical things that a missionary should be involved with, if not every day, at least routinely. If a missionary is fulfilling those functions and the work is not growing, find out why. If, for example, a missionary says he goes soul winning every week for five hours but rarely has anyone converted, ask why? Here are some possible reasons:

- Perhaps his area is challenging, such as France or England, where there are so many atheists. (See if you can help him find some useful tracts, booklets, or videos. Inquire of more successful missionaries and pastors in the same region and ask them why they are successful. Ask them to teach the missionary, offering to pay their travel costs and expenses, of course.) At Final Frontiers, we do this regularly, so, for example, a group that is deficient in one area (like baptisms) can receive tutoring from the leader of a group with more success.)

- Perhaps he is using culturally unacceptable methods such as knocking on doors. In some cultures, it isn't polite to do that. In others, the wife will never open the door if her husband is not home, as doing so would spoil her reputation. (Suggest he speak to the national pastors and ask them how they do it.)

- Perhaps, because of how he dressed, he is perceived as a Mormon, and the people prefer to avoid them. If you look closely, we Baptists look just like Mormons with one exception; we have the same pants, shirt, tie, and the same haircut. We wear black and white and dress better than the ones we are trying to reach. We even carry the same KJV Bible. We don't have a name tag, but this is a slight difference for most to notice, so they confuse us as Mormons. (Suggest that he dress more casually as the locals do; thus, his appearance is neither threatening nor opulent. Remember, Jesus didn't wear a tie; you don't have to wear one either.)

- Perhaps he is dressing too nice. He appears to be a wealthy man canvassing in a low-income area. The people feel they cannot relate to him or they are unworthy to speak to him. They may feel that he is flaunting his wealth. (Encourage him to become all things to all men and copy the styles of those he is trying to reach, i.e., don't wear a kilt in Kenya and don't wear one in Scotland on a windy day.)

Though it sounds silly, the solution to non-productivity could be as simple as taking a bath, using deodorant, spraying on some cologne, and sucking on a breath mint. Just because you like to go *au natural* does not mean those around you like it.

It is not an issue of the missionary's being a failure. Instead, it is an issue of your determining what you expect from the missionaries you support and following up to see if they are meeting your expectations.

As you adapt this policy, future missionaries will know what you expect and have the opportunity to reject your support if they feel they cannot comply. Current missionaries should, of course, be allowed an appropriate amount of time to adjust their schedule and activity (or lack thereof) to meet your newly pronounced and possibly inexperienced expectations. Remember, he is on the field partly because of the verbal contract you made to support him. If you are changing your support requirements, then ethically, you should fulfill your committed term of support before punishing him for non-compliance. Again though, be practical and be willing to listen and learn from what he tells you. Ask the Holy Spirit to guide you in determining if his responses are questions or misunderstandings and if his explanations are reasons or excuses. Your expectations should be his acknowledgment of a job well done by biblical standards, not an opportunity for you to increase his workload by compiling detailed data.

Remember, you cannot expect a man to go soul winning 24 hours a day. Even the Lord took time off to go fishing, go to parties, fellowship with friends, read, and rest.

The truth is, if we want to educate our members and our children about the work of missionaries, then we need to know what they actually do—not what we imagine they do.

What Does the Bible Teach a Missionary Should Do?

If you read the Scriptures concerning Paul's ministry, you will have the most concise illustration given. In short:

1) He worked with a team that included his perceived superiors or equals (Barnabas and Silas). He did not lord his position over anyone in an attitude of superiority.

2) He worked with his disciples—always learning and always emulating what they learned from him in word and deed. He instructed them in Philippians 4:9, *Those things, which ye have both* ***learned****, and* ***received****, and* ***heard****, and* ***seen*** *in me, do: and the God of peace shall be with you.*

3) He planted many churches but may have never pastored one for a lengthy period, with the most obvious exception being Ephesus and Corinth, which had two churches, Corinth Upper (I Corinthians) and Corinth Lower (II Corinthians). He revealed to us the four gifts

of the church in Ephesians 4, but he never once referred to himself as being the gift of a pastor, only of an apostle, which is the Greek word from which we get the English word, "missionary."

4) He turned newly established churches over to his disciples and the churches' trained men (the elders), then moved on to start more churches.

5) He taught not only doctrine but also day-to-day practical ministry.

6) He did not rely on support (but accepted it). He went where and when he felt led to go. If support was lacking, he went anyway, working with his hands to provide for both himself and his team.

7) He listened and consented to the advice of others, even those with less experience than he.

8) He reported his activity to his friends, supporters, disciples, and the churches he started, with astounding detail.

What Do We Expect a Missionary to Be?

I am listing here several basic qualifications.

- *He should have **experience**.* Scripture commands us not to lift a novice. Make sure the missionary has some experience in ministry already. If he has never started a church in his own land, why do you think he can start one in another land with a different language and different culture?

- *He should be **qualified**.* Does he meet the biblical requirements for a preacher? In the past, missionaries were considered inept preachers; that is to say, they were going overseas to preach because no church at home would tolerate their inabilities. Missionaries should be our best—not our worse. They are being sent to war (spiritually) and should be trained and proven.

- *He should be **self-sufficient**.* Does he have skills to fall back on when necessary? If not, he will quit. Paul was able to literally "set up shop" wherever he went and had daily, all-day access to customers and shop owners to whom he could witness and where others could find him if they had questions. His self-sufficiency allowed him to meet and disciple Aquila and Priscilla, who later did likewise with Apollos. Though a missionary may have full support, it may be lacking or cut off. What will he do then: stay where God called him or go home?

A missionary's primary function is to win souls, disciple converts, plant churches, and train others to take over. Then he is to move on and repeat that process, taking some with him and sending out others with their own teams. Anything else (even social ministries) should be for either personal fulfillment, financial survival, or to benefit the missionary's primary function. This concept of what a missionary is and does, although biblical, is so far removed from our missionary culture in the United States that to teach it, as I continuously do, brands you as either a heretic or someone who hates missionaries. So then, what do church members, and sadly, most pastors, think a missionary does?

Misconceptions About What Missionaries Don't Do:

- Most pastors and church members do not know that statistically, most missionaries will never start a new church in their entire career.

- They don't realize that most missionaries are only pastoring a church in a foreign country. It usually is not a church they started but one started by a national or another missionary many years earlier. They are not planting new churches; they are pastoring existing churches.

- Most of those supported as missionaries are not even preachers, much less church planters. They are doctors, nurses, children's home workers, pilots, airplane mechanics, schoolteachers, bookstore operators, college teachers, etc. For example, the Southern Baptist Convention has long been the largest denominational missionary force globally. Several years ago, a friend told me that though they don't know us, they coincidently adopted our view of what a missionary is supposed to be (a church plater). After making that determination, they called home all their "missionaries" who were not church planters. That cut their missionary force by some 45 percent. They now use their designated missionary funds to support missionaries (dedicated church planters), not support staff, which are needed and worthy of support, but not from missionary funding. Just as you don't use your tithe for other purposes, like your kid's college fund, your utility bill, etc., no matter how worthy, we should not use funds designated for missions for any other purpose than actual missions.

As for what missionaries really do, you have to take it on an individual basis. In our ministry, we have general requirements that if a man does not meet, he is not or is no longer supported.

1) He must be doctrinally sound. (I like to say jokingly that means he is wrong about the same things we are wrong about.)

2) He must be morally pure.

3) He must have a verifiable track record in planting churches and training men for the ministry. (To qualify as a Final Frontiers missionary, he must have already, without support, started at least two churches and have at least one man serving in ministry whom he won to Christ, discipled and trained, which confirms he is not a novice.)

4) He must be a part of a local accountability group of preachers. (We don't support lone rangers as there is no accountability.)

5) He must agree to filling out and returning our quarterly report forms. (Failing to fulfill this requirement is automatic grounds for us to drop his support.)

And after we have determined a man is qualified, he is told that his continued support is dependent on his meeting continued requirements. What are those requirements?

1) He has to remain actively and consistently involved in church planting and discipleship of others.
2) He has to fill out and return their quarterly Missionary Report Forms.

To determine this, we use the Missionary Report Forms that have already been discussed. The data is entered into our program on each preacher, giving us a "lifetime" analysis based on his quarterly reports of what he has done and is doing. We keep a digital copy of every report and photo he sends us. If needed, we can compare his activity to the other preachers in his accountability group and compare one group to another. We do this to target trends or weaknesses, so we can send an "expert" from one region to help out with a group in another region, as earlier discussed. Sending a local to help them is better received and more cost effective than sending a foreigner. There can be justifiable resentment when a man from another country, culture, and language asserts mastery over another culture. An invitation to fix a problem is different from an inexperienced and unknown foreigner's insinuation that he can fix it.

This data accumulation since day one is how we can report the astounding numbers that we have. Keep in mind that all those we support are church-planting missionaries, so we would expect them to do exactly that. And when you consider our network of national church planters has grown from 6 in 1986 to over 28,000 in 2020; then you can understand why we have the results we have.

How Should You Expect a Missionary to Be Accountable?

We are speaking here of him reporting to his supporters. When doing that, he should be like:

- A *politician*, always ready to talk about what he is doing

- A *pastor*, realizing the truth will always be revealed
- A *publisher*, refusing credit for what others have done and not claiming their accomplishments as his own
- A *prisoner*, grateful to those who provide for him and always bound up in the service to which Christ commissioned him.

ELIMINATING THE CONUNDRUM

Suggestions for Missionaries:

- Give reasons for what you report if they are needed. I failed to heed my own advice, and my failure hurt our ministry. Late in 2019, I temporarily suspended one of our nine feeding centers in Honduras that was requiring us to give food bags to those children rather than feeding them at our tables. Several detailed, legal reasons for doing this allowed us to protect that particular location from lawsuits and our property's potential loss, saving us a fortune. However, due to legal issues, the expected three-month diversion lasted six months before we were able to return to normal. (Then Covid-19 hit.) However, I did not inform the sponsors of this temporary change as I felt they were more concerned that we fed the kids than where we fed them.

A disgruntled former affiliate informed a few sponsors that I had "closed" the feeding center and implied I was trying to hide it. They wrongly assumed it was a permanent closure and that I was absconding with their donations. As a result, we lost several sponsors, even after they learned the truth. That man had maliciously spread gossip. He was trying to start a feeding program and was attempting to redirect their support to his. A few sponsors believed him and further spread his untruths without ever contacting me as the Scripture requires.

In truth, I sparked the whole ordeal by not being upfront with what we were doing and why we were doing it. My intention was not to conceal the situation, just the reality that I cannot disclose the purpose and reason behind every decision I make. The volume of our work is too large and in too many countries. I have to make daily and even hourly decisions that sometimes have lives in the balance. My mistake was thinking our ministry and I were highly trusted by this sponsor, having supported us for years and visiting our feeding centers at least five different summers. I was wrong. As the time stretched out, I should have sent a note informing the supporters of what we were changing, why we were changing it, and when things would go back to normal.

- Sharing precious family moments may be of interest to some of your supporters, but not to all. Be sure to put some meat on the bones of your letters.

- Understand why you are being supported and try to adapt your letters to address those points.

- Realize that pastors back home need encouragement too. They have to endure people wondering why the church is spending so on missions when they have their own needs. Give them something they can use to justify their vision for missionary support.

- Demonstrate in all of your letters precisely what you are doing, how well it is progressing, and what could help you do more. If you have to kill a snake, then, by all means, kill it (and take some good pictures too). If you are growing a garden, tell them how you gave away produce to a hungry family and how that brought them to Christ.

- Remember that God may use your letters to influence a young child who will someday turn the world upside down. Don't let your letters be a bore; let them be an extension of your ministry. They are your legacy in print.

Suggestions for Churches:

- Analyzing your supported missionaries' productivity and methods is not an issue of your telling the missionary there what to do and how to do it. Don't present yourself as his master, possessing a superior knowledge of his situation which you cannot possibly have, but rather as a partner sharing concern and offering possible solutions.

- Please don't be shy to ask questions when you have them. People like to talk about their ministry, and missionaries are no exception. Ask their opinions, ask about their observations, ask why this, why that, etc.

- If a missionary fails to communicate his work with your people regularly, kindly point it out to him. Frankly, if you feel that way, other pastors probably do too. You are doing him a favor by telling him what is lacking in his letters and making a few suggestions. Hopefully, he will see it as a helpful critique and not as hurtful criticism.

- When taking on a missionary for support, be sure to tell him what you expect in regard to his labor and reporting. Don't hold him to a standard that he is ignorant of.

#14
If the Missionary's Letters Are Meant to Provide Accountability, Why Do So Few Write Good Letters, and Why Do Pastors/Churches Seemingly Not Care?

Explaining the Conundrum

I continuously hear remarks from pastors about the lack of substance in many of the letters they receive. Some missionaries, however, excel at writing good reports. Over the past decade or so, missionaries serving with FBMI (Fundamental Baptist Missions International), for example, have become excellent writers. I don't know how this happened, and though I hope I had some small influence with the ones I have counseled, I suspect the board's leadership (Darrell Moore previously and Mark Bosje currently) realized there was a problem and promptly fixed it.

I have been blessed reading many of their letters that seem always to follow a specific pattern. First, they give a brief greeting from their family and perhaps mention a blessing or problem, then they move on to talk about a new work in which they are involved and give the testimony of one of their converts; finally, they close with a ministry need for which they humbly seek help. But they don't just tell what the need is; they tell why it is a need and how to resolve it. To me, this is incredible, astounding, and an example for all missionaries to follow, and admittedly, many already do.

This writing method excellently highlights a vital principle—if you don't realize there is a problem or choose to ignore or excuse it, you will never repair it. On the contrary, if you recognize the problem and fix the problem, you will enjoy the benefits.

EXAMINING THE CONUNDRUM

I see three basic answers to this conundrum—the long, the short, and the simple. The long answer is: pastors, why do you have three congregational songs, two specials, and an offering before you preach? (Oops, we're supposed to be talking about missionaries, and I forgot you're not supposed to answer a question with another question.) Let me try that again. The short answer to both is **tradition**.

That's the long and the short of it. The simple answer is that missionaries usually are not taught to write informative and motivating letters, and churches do not expect them to. Now that we have defined the problem (inadequate letters) and the cause (lack of instruction and expectation), let's look a little deeper.

Writing letters and reports are all about accountability. So far, our journey for accountability has taken us only one step and already we have to pause, wondering where to go from here. We need to dig deeper to find the root causes of our problem; only then can we seek the best solutions and decide how to resolve them. So, let's look at the conundrum again. "If the missionary's letters are meant to provide accountability, why do so few write good letters, and why do pastors/churches seemingly not care?"

In my thirty-five years as a missionary, the reasons I have encountered for this conundrum are legion, but they typically fall within several common categories.

Category One: *Inadequate Training*

How many times have you heard this answer? "That's not the way we have always done it."

1) Missionaries learn from missionaries, who learned from other missionaries, etc. We do reproduce after our own kind. The missionaries I have influenced (and likewise, mission boards) highlight their ministry results over their personal or family trivia. That is because I emphasize that churches are supporting the missionary for ministry results and not for an ongoing family blog. Therefore, they need to know if they are getting what they are paying for. If you take time to visit Facebook pages, websites or read the "prayer letters" they send to the churches, you will find that as much as 90 percent of the missionaries you support have not yet learned this simple fact. Their letters seem more like pages from a diary than progress reports.

2) Missionaries also learn from mission board leaders who may have never served as a missionary. They are usually well-meaning pastors and can only see missions from their point of view. Missionaries like myself, who have experience as an assistant pastor, a pastor, and a missionary, see our responsibility and training needs from multiple viewpoints. What about those who lack experience? My question is, why would you expect a man who has never pastored, worked for a pastor, started a church, or trained a man for ministry in his own country, culture, and language, be able to do so in another?

3) Then some missionaries have only *studied* missions in college. Their only experience is a two-week "survey trip"; thus, they must rely entirely on the stories they can remember their instructor telling them and the books they have read.

The solution is to send and support men with successful ministry experience in their own culture and adequate time serving as an intern on the mission field. The missionary-in-training can accomplish this standard by spending the summers of his college years with missionaries or by interning after college for a year or two. Another idea is that students majoring in missions spend at least one semester of their four years getting practical training from a missionary in the country they intend to make their home. As I have already mentioned, consider that of all the missionaries who make it through deputation, survive their first four years on the field, then come home for furlough, 55 percent quit and never go back to the field where supposedly God called them. Knowing this, you will begin to understand why I put such importance on training and experience. Simply put, let's let our missionaries learn to crawl and walk before we expect them to run a marathon.

CATEGORY TWO: *An Abundance of Ignorance*

There is a misunderstanding of what churches want to hear from the missionary. Some pastors want their missionary letters to be a family letter that gives family details. This is usually when the pastor personally knows the missionary because he is a family member or a friend, a former church member, or an old college roommate. The pastor knows the wife and kids and has a special interest in them personally, apart from ministry. Though this happens frequently, it is far from typical. Unfortunately, this familiar style of missionary letter has for some reason become the rule, rather than the exception.

And let me rush to say that I am not discouraging the use of personal information. That can be a blessing to the people who read it. What I am speaking of is the ordinary reality of when that is all the letter contains. If reading missionary letters is any indication of what the missionary thinks the church wants to know about him and his ministry, then we can summarize the church is interested primarily in:

- The missionary children's birthday parties
- The weather
- The difficulty in learning the language
- The death of the family pet

- Assorted Facebook posts with photos of what they have been eating, a recent potluck dinner with strange recipes
- The ever-present need for a new SUV or four new tires

The other side of the coin is that what the missionary typically *does not mention* is what he must think the supporting churches *are not interested* in hearing, including the following:

- The number of new converts
- Testimonies of recent converts
- Men in training for ministry
- How they used your support to help others
- New churches or works being started, etc.
- The four new tires needed by a poor preacher who works with him

Though we cannot know anyone's heart and should therefore avoid all efforts of judging motives, we can logically assume at least two possibilities for the cause of the problem:

1) What the missionary writes about is what he thinks the church wants to hear about
2) The missionary is oblivious to what his supporters want to know and only writes about what is important to him. If that is the case, then he has a problem.

Let's look at this conundrum logically for a moment. We rate a baseball player by his batting average. We rate a quarterback by his total yards passing and running. We rate a talk-show radio host by the number of his listeners. We rate an author by the number of best-selling books he has written (I obviously have a very low rating). We rate a singer by the number of top ten hits they have acquired and a military sniper by the number of his kills.

A car salesman validates his worth by the number of cars he has sold, an insurance salesperson by the number of policies he has in force, a truck driver by the number of miles he has driven, and a McDonald's by how many hamburgers they have sold. (I remember when they advertised "over one million sold," and now they probably sell that many worldwide every day).

So, I ask you, by what measure should we validate a missionary's worth or accomplishments?

CATEGORY THREE: *The Belief that Pastors Are Satisfied with Their Letters*

Let's be honest, pastors, if you don't tell the missionary that his letters need improvement, more detail, or a moving reflection of his ministry, then who will?

As a missionary, he may be a mature believer in Christ, but that does not mean he is an expert on everything he does. You are his brother, perhaps his elder brother. Do him the favor of schooling him to produce a more enlightening, entertaining, and informative letter. This will not only bless him and you, but it will also bless the other churches that get his carbon-copy quarterly report.

I frequently receive letters from people who like my writing, yet many also include a "but...." They encourage me to correct my spelling, my grammar, and sometimes, even my position. These generally come from lifelong friends, new readers, and most often from English teachers. I'm never offended, though sometimes I am embarrassed. (I now use Grammarly, though I realize a computer program cannot think.)

Years ago, we could not print clear photographs in our *Progress Report* (our free, quarterly magazine now available in print or online). They were so awful that I had to explain what was in the picture. One day I received a letter from an old friend who asked me if I was doing it that way on purpose so people would feel sorry for us and donate more money. (If so, my tactic wasn't working.) The sad truth was, I was doing the best I could, and my best was not nearly good enough. However, her gentle prod led me to find better software eventually and even a professional printer who could do our entire run-in full color for only $50 more than I had been paying for two colors. Later, when a few others mocked our layout and graphics quality, I began (and still do) to study other magazines to see what they do concerning page layout, etc.

I spend many hours every quarter writing, doing layout, choosing pictures, etc., then I send it off for proofreading and additional editing. (We sometimes still find errors after it's too late.) After all that work and all those hours, I want to make sure that you have a product that you can enjoy and understand that will motivate you. Otherwise, I'm wasting my time. Missionaries, you should feel the same about your quarterly letter—even if it's only one page.

The list of reasons why missionaries sometimes don't write good letters could go on and on, but I think I have made my point. My question then to the missionary, to the pastor, and to the church members who fund the missionary's budget is this: in your opinion, what accomplishments would validate the worth of the missionary getting your support? Figure that out, and you'll know what the missionary should be writing about; and if he is not, then why not? And while you're at it, why not suggest it?

EXPOSING THE CONUNDRUM

Now let's look at a few possible reasons why the missionary does not write compelling letters to his supporters.

Reason #1—There is a misunderstanding for some missionaries as to why they receive support. Thus, there is no motivation to write compelling letters.

After talking with hundreds of missionaries, I have concluded that many of us (missionaries) have misunderstood why churches choose to support us. We think it is because they love us (or maybe our cute kids), or that we are so exceptional, and they can see that in us (that applies primarily to me—my mother always said I was special), or we are from the right board or school, or we worked with a famous pastor. The truth is, those are components of the reasons for supporting us—but only components. They are not the full picture.

Here are a few more parts of the puzzle you may have overlooked as to why you get supported:

- Missionaries taken on for support at a mission's conference are usually supported simply because the church had enough funds to take on "x" more missionaries. Those who were able to show up for the conference automatically got support; those who didn't show up didn't get supported. It's a right-time-right-place thing. Their quality or qualifications are seldom considered; they were merely available to attend the conference. Pastors often advertise this fact to potential missionary attendees, and thus they show up not caring whether or not they speak—and rightfully so.

Several years ago, I met a missionary who confessed that he ONLY goes to church if it is having a mission conference. His logic was, why waste time driving around America speaking for five to thirty minutes at services, hoping you get support when you can stay home and attend conferences and be virtually guaranteed support? If nothing else, he was a smart cookie.

- The church wants to support a missionary in a particular field. Because you happen to be going there, you get their support. For example, if a church supports ten missionaries already and eight of them are in Mexico, you would probably have a better chance of getting support if you were going to Kenya or any place other than Mexico. If not, do some research, congratulate them on their burden for Mexico being equal to yours, and encourage them to support you because you are going to a different area of Mexico than the others they already support.

- Sometimes the church happens to have extra money they want to give to missions. So, they need missionaries to give it to. About thirty years ago, I knew of a church in the Midwest that came into a significant sum of money for missions—so much so that at the rate of monthly support they gave (which at that time, I think, was $50 per month per missionary), they had funds available to take on the support of 64 more missioners. To make what in their mind was the wisest decision as to whom to give that support to, the pastor called the president of a large mission board, who promptly pledged to send him the names and prayer cards of (guess who) 64 missionaries from his board. This pastor knew me intimately but, for whatever reason, did not consider supporting me nor any of our men because, at that time, he was not certain nationals could be trusted. They later supported me temporarily when my father confronted this young pastor whom he knew well and rebuked him for supporting strangers over someone he had known for years—me.

My point is that there can be many reasons why you get support. In my case, I am so old (but still functioning like Moses and Caleb), I have been doing this for so long, and I have had so many pastors join me on missions' trips that, based on our ministry reputation, we often get new supporting churches by word of mouth. And if you last long enough, that will happen to you too. Work hard and be patient.

But we missionaries can also lose support much easier than we got it. I know one missionary who recently lost a great deal of support because of two primary reasons. First, he left the field that the church was interested in reaching, and second, because he left the format of ministry his supporting churches were interested in supporting. He shifted from being a church planter to doing another type of ministry. We, as missionaries, often think that churches support us because of us. That isn't always true. They support us because we are doing what they want to see done. Stop doing what they are paying you to do and where they are paying you to do it, and they will almost always discontinue your support.

Generally, a missionary eventually gets support from a church after giving his presentation for one of three reasons:

- One, he has a unique ministry, e.g., he works with lepers.
- Two, he has a unique location, e.g., he serves in a remote jungle filled with headhunters.
- Three, he has a unique presentation, e.g., a professionally designed, interestingly scripted, and emotional as well as logical display. This used to easily be accomplished by using video, but now everyone has a video presentation. I have found most of them are incredibly dull, uninformative, and cookie-cutter.

"Churches-will-never-support-plain-Jane" missionaries with a "vanilla presentation" and not-so-cute kids like they will the young, thin, salesman-type missionary with a darling wife and precious children. But be warned; there will always be another "younger you" who has cuter kids, a thinner wife, and a flashier presentation. To get support and keep support, you have to show your value as a missionary and validate your worthiness to remain on your supporting churches' support list.

Reason #2—There is a misunderstanding about the purpose of their letter writing. It is not just to fulfill an obligation but to be the pastor's partner in motivating and producing future missionaries.

There is another overlooked point to make about letter writing.

We, as missionaries, should be busy reproducing ourselves. We know that applies to our work on the field, but we forget that it also applies to our influence at home in our supporting churches. Our presentations, Skype interviews, and most certainly our reports, weekly, monthly, or quarterly, should always be designed to encourage, interest, and involve the readers in missionary work and support. The letters should make them eager to offer themselves and their children full-time, part-time, or as summer interns in missions.

We, at Final Frontiers, annually host what we call *Visionary Trips* to many lands because we want pastors and church members to travel with us, see what we do, how we do it, where and why we do it—what I call the "Adverbs of Missions." We want them to understand our work and become interested in and burdened for missions as a result, so they will go home and infect their fellow church members with the missionary virus. When this happens, our ministry benefits, to be sure, but the real benefit goes to the supporting churches. The pastor no longer needs to beg for missionary funds; he merely needs to lay the need on the table and watch as members rush to meet the need. I have never had a pastor tell me that his church's missions giving went down after we presented our ministry, or they visited us on a Visionary Trip. Pastor Anthony Lamb in San Antonio, Texas, told me years ago that their missions giving shot up 400 percent after I had a conference at his church. And this did not include the support given to Final Frontiers and Touch A Life (two of our primary ministries), which was an additional nearly $700 a month.

Why is that? It is because we know what pastors and members want. They want results. They want to know that what they give is bringing souls to Christ, not just taking the missionary's kids to McDonald's.

Then there is yet another, all too common reason that missionaries fail to write good letters:

Reason #3 – They are sometimes or at times overcome by an occurring obstacle—procrastination. Several things can cause this:

- *They haven't or feel they haven't done anything worthy of mentioning.*

The bottom line is simply this: if the missionary is doing something worth talking about, he'll talk about it. If he isn't talking, he probably isn't doing.

- *They are too lazy to take the time to report.*

If the missionary is accomplishing great things for God, but he cannot take the time to be accountable to his donors and let them know that their funds are producing fruit, then, in that case, he has no reason to expect those donors to have the time to send him any more support.

- *They feel they lack the ability to write a good letter.*

The old excuse of "I'm not good at writing" pops up over and over until the wife comes to the rescue. Don't get me wrong, I love to hear a word from the wife and get her perspective and wish more missionaries' wives would do that, myself included. Still, when I get letters the missionary himself had no part in writing, it makes me wonder why he had nothing to say to me for the past three months. And missionaries, keep this in mind: if you write quarterly letters and your wife has to do it for you one quarter, that means your supporters do not hear from you *personally* for SIX MONTHS. Don't be surprised when your support is diminished.

When I was first getting started as a missionary, I consumed as many missionary biographies as possible. Because of that, certain features or aspects of various missionaries from bygone ages greatly impacted what would become practice and policy—not just for me personally but also for Final Frontiers. It also shaped what would become our quarterly report form.

We all have heard of Hudson Taylor, who started the China Inland Mission. Few know of a young, British missionary named James Fraser who joined the team long after the mission was started in the early twentieth century. He was born in 1886, precisely one hundred years before the founding of Final Frontiers.

He gave up all to follow his calling.

In 1906 he attended Imperial College in London to study both music and engineering. Still, after being infected with an acute case of foreign missions, he left in 1908 to join the China Inland Mission and was stationed in Yunnan, a southern province of China along the border of Burma and began to work with the locals in that mountainous region.

As Paul realized by his Macedonian vision, James understood he was not so much called to a place as to a people.

After arriving there, he noticed men and women dressed differently from the Chinese, who also spoke a different language. He set out to learn it and spent the next thirty years with this tribe called the Lisu. (A Lisu missionary was among the first six men Final Frontiers supported in 1986, and we still support him today; and though he is very old, he is still very effective. His name is Boonroat Premsanjaint. He calls himself Luke Bee, which I believe you will agree is much easier to say. His children also serve in ministry. James arrived in China in 1910, and the Chinese Revolution started the following year. For safety, he moved across the border into Burma.

He used every means possible—the unconventional as well as the unheard of—to reach them.

Realizing that the Lisu had no written language; and transferring their knowledge of nature, religion, culture, and history by song, he began to teach them the Bible by making choruses of the passages. Simultaneously, he developed an alphabet for them, the principles of which many other missionaries still copy called the Fraser Script. In effect, he used English letters and assigned them to various sounds in the Lisu language. When our 26 letters were not enough, he would turn an "A" sideways using it for another sound or lay a "B" on its back for yet another. Eventually, he translated the New Testament for them. I have personally seen his songbooks and New Testaments used in mountaintop Lisu villages in Thailand. When we helped facilitate the Akha Bible translation, an oral language with no alphabet, the national scholars used the Fraser Script, based on Akha sounds, to develop a written language for their tribe.

Fraser was so successful that by 1918 his success had lit a fire in his converts' hearts to evangelize their tribe resulting in the baptism of over 600 people. He expertly organized the converts into local house churches, which became a pattern that all the other tribes in the region emulated, including the Akha, who taught me that pattern as a young missionary. His work was so successful that in the 1990s, the Chinese government acknowledged that the Lisu Tribe (in China) was over 90 percent Christian. By 1955, ten years after his death, the total conversion number among the Lisu was over 100,000.

Unfortunately, he did not believe in helping the converts build buildings or support them as missionaries or pastors. Since the Bible condemns neither, especially the last (it encourages doing so in III John), I do not know his motivation. After all, if we can give them ourselves, give them the Bible and give them discipleship, why can't we give them our pocket change to support them as missionaries, especially when we are supported as one? What James accomplished in China was magnificent, and I must remind you that at that time, missionaries themselves had precious little to live on. Unfortunately, his evangelistic impact did not motivate fully evangelizing the Lisu of Thailand and Laos. Perhaps if some Lisu men and women had been "sent" as missionaries as Paul charged us, that story would have been even more marvelous.

He produced many detailed letters and drawings.

I learned many things from James Fraser, but one of the most significant was his emphasis on writing to his supporters back in England. Sending only one letter to the chairman of his supporters and having no means to duplicate them, they would gather regularly to read together what he had written.

James would write lengthy, detailed letters explaining the crops they grew, how they built their houses, and how they wove their clothes and fashioned their shoes. He would describe the dresses of the women and the toys the children played with. As somewhat of an artist, he would do his best to illustrate these things in his letters, even using paints to imitate the colors and designs of Lisu fabrics. As a result, his sponsors became enamored with the Lisu people. Their interest went far beyond James and his future wife and family to concerns for the people whose testimonies he shared and the well-being of their tribe.

Learning this taught me as a young missionary to insist that my letters contain a little about my family and me and a lot about the people we were trying to help, support, feed, and evangelize. To this day, my letters and stories are long and involved because when I write or speak, I want the reader to feel like I have transported them to that place and that time. Knowing I needed to do that, I prayed that God would enable, equip and gift me with that ability. That is why we have always used photos and videos. I have often told my kids I hope someday, like sounds and images with video, we will have the technology to reproduce the smells of the mission field, so when you see us on video walking through a slum, you can smell the garbage and the black-waters too. Imagine as our national minister in a village; you can catch a sniff of the pigpen and the sweet smells of a leechee orchard, a wild orchid, or the diesel fumes of the old clunker that passes by.

The more I can help you know them, see them, smell them, feel them, understand them, the more you will pray and give to help us reach them.

James Fraser died in 1938 at the age of only 52 of cerebral malaria and was buried where he had served. What I have shared are only some of the things I learned from James Fraser that have shaped my life. I hope that I can have an equal effect on young missionaries just getting started or yet to be born.

His most remarkable works involved the conversion of the Lisu people, the translation of Scripture, the writing of songs, and the transformation of oral languages into written languages, discipleship, organizational skills, and the young men he trained for ministry. But we would never have known about any of these accomplishments were it not for his missionary prayer letters to his supporters.

(His primary biographer was the daughter-in-law of Hudson Taylor, who used his letters and diaries to tell his story in her 1944 biography, *Behind the Ranges*. Later, his daughter Eileen Crossman wrote *Mountain Rain* in 1982, using much of Mrs. Taylor's research.)

ELIMINATING THE CONUNDRUM

***Suggestions for Missionaries*:**

- Look in the Bible. What kind of letters do you read? Paul wrote doctrinal letters, but Luke wrote letters of activity in the books of Luke and Acts. The epistles do not typically motivate us for missions; they instruct us how to plant and grow the national churches and address their doctrinal and cultural problems. Consider then that the motivation to be a missionary and to support a missionary comes almost exclusively from the book of Acts. Write accordingly.

- Remember, it never hurts to throw a few personal messages in your letters. Some churches want to know a little about you, your family, your trials, and your health. Satisfy their concerns too. And by the way, write them at least every quarter unless you have a church that requires more frequent reporting; anything less is insulting.

- Don't expect your supporters to have to hunt you down on Facebook to see what or how you're doing. Send them an email directly and tell them. They'll appreciate it and so will your bank account.

- Any good letter should try to include emotional aspects. Help your readers to laugh and cry if you can. Don't be shy about admitting your failures, blunders, and mishaps, but show what you learned from them and how the Lord used them for His glory. On the other hand, don't be shy to talk about your successes. It's not prideful if you're not telling it pridefully. Every great character of the Bible admitted his failures and boasted in Christ for his successes.

- Always remember, the quarterly letter is not about you; it's about what you are accomplishing because of *their* support.
- Remember also that your letter's purpose is not to give the churches something to read but to give them something to respond to.

***Suggestions for Churches*:**

- Let your missionaries know how often you expect to hear from them. Make sure you encourage them to comply. You may even consider having a simple contract with them, stating you will support their family at "x" amount of funding for "x" number of years *if* they stay in contact with you every "x" months. If they fail to do so, withhold their support until you hear from them. If this becomes a pattern, then a character issue needs to be addressed. At that time, you may need to help them acknowledge their weakness and overcome it or drop their support altogether.
- Do not create additional forms for your missionary to fill out. They should not have the time to do the paperwork. And if they do somehow have the time, they may not be doing the work they are paid to do. On the other hand, if it has a vital function, other than data harvesting, ask away, but try to keep it as short and straightforward as you can. Please don't give missionaries homework assignments that require hours of research and writing. Suppose a missionary is busy planting churches and training men. In that case, he does not have time to write doctrinal or topical dissertations, simply because you want to impress him with your knowledge on various subjects or shame him on his lack of knowledge. Are you supporting him to be a Greek and Hebrew professor, an authority on eschatology, angelology, and apologetics, or to be a church planter?
- If a missionary fails to mention matters vital to you, drop him a note via email to explain why it is important and ask specifically for that information. Request that he include it in future letters/reports if it is not convenient to give a direct reply at the moment.

SECTION FOUR

Great Commission Conundrums Regarding PHILOSOPHY

A woman devotee worshipping her gods, India

#15
Since Missions Is Defined Biblically as "Church Planting," Why Do So Few Missionaries Plant Churches?

Explaining the Conundrum

We have already discussed that statistically most missionaries will never start a church in their lifetime. They have a title that implies productivity that they will never achieve, yet we continue to call them by that title and support them as if they are fulfilling its demands. The issue at hand is, why don't they?

These men are not swindlers or con men. They are ignorantly doing or not doing what they are supposed to be doing. We support them generously because we swim in the same pool of ignorance. Some of us in the deep end and some in the shallow. Would we support a missionary doctor who never treats a patient? Would we support a missionary teacher who has never had a student? Would we support a missionary pilot who has never flown an airplane? Then why do we support missionaries who have never started a church or produced a Timothy?

You say it is because they pastor churches. News flash! Pastors pastor churches; missionaries start churches for pastors to pastor.

But before I get off the subject and talk too much about support, let's return to the issue at hand, why don't missionaries start churches?

EXAMINING THE CONUNDRUM

First, let's establish that we have misunderstood the Great Commission. We have heard, taught, and believed that it is a command to go soul winning. As a result, we "win souls" by the tens of thousands but never see them get involved in a local church. We leave the new converts as sheep without a shepherd, as students without a teacher, as babes without a parent. Then we wonder why our churches don't grow.

I was trained as a boy to win souls, and from the age of 12 to 17, when I left for Bible college, I had records (a soul-winning diary) of having won several thousand to Christ. By the time I had graduated from college four years later, I had accumulated a list of slightly over 25,000 conversions. I was a fanatic.

I would go soul winning frequently. One Sunday afternoon, at age 16, while coming home from church, I remember stopping to witness to some teenage boys playing on the street. They all prayed with me. (I drove past their homes every time I went to church, and it never occurred to me to invite them along. Soul winning was the only important thing to me.)

I would often get in the car and ask the Lord to lead me to someone He had prepared to hear His gospel. Within a few minutes, I would see a man taking a walk, or boys playing basketball in a schoolyard, or just felt led to approach a house and witness to the entire family. After each event, I would record the day and number of how many "got saved." In the beginning, I would write details about the people, but as time went on, I begin to record only the basics of date and the number of converts.

The problem was that except for those who would ride my bus to church, I rarely ever met one of my converts after winning them to Christ. I often wondered about their well-being but felt that was between them and Christ. I had done my job.

On one occasion, I felt the need to evangelize in a particularly hazardous area of Atlanta. I was sixteen and had just started driving.

Racial tensions were high, but it was my pattern to go into the African-American neighborhoods because I felt they were more prone to accept my message and because I didn't know of anyone else targeting them. It has always been in my heart to go to those who others overlook or ignore. Perhaps it was because I felt the call of God to be a missionary at the age of eleven—to take the gospel to those who had not heard it. During church visitation programs, we were always targeting the white neighborhoods and avoiding the black. I wrongly concluded that African Americans had no exposure to the gospel, so I went to evangelize them.

I know that in this era, some will accuse this as being an example of racism. Keep in mind it wasn't this era; it was fifty years ago. I submit that a white person who does not care enough about a black man to witness to him is a racist. Furthermore, any person who thinks evangelism of a people is racist does not understand the basic definition of missions. Does a missionary go to Nigeria to evangelize all the Chinese living there? Does a missionary go to Albania because he has a burden for Brazilians? No, he goes to reach those who he feels have not had proper exposure to the gospel.

That day was the first time in my life I truly felt fear. As I entered the apartment complex, I prayed for safety. I got out of my car, and for the first and only time in my life, I felt my knees knocking together. Frankly, I was scared to death. However, using what little faith I had (and God used episodes like this in my life to build my faith), I began going door to door witnessing. In the next few hours, I had several converts, among them a teenage girl, slightly older than me.

About eighteen months later, I was on a date with my girlfriend, Donna Hutson (now Donna Janney), the daughter of my pastor, Curtis Hutson. We were going to the memorial park in Kennesaw, Georgia. That was the last stand for the Confederate forces before General Sherman annihilated Atlanta. Being a history buff and enjoying time with Donna, I decided to visit the park. On the way there, we stopped at a

McDonald's to eat. While in line, we both noticed a young black lady about four people ahead of us, who kept turning around and staring at me. Finally, she spoke to me, asking, "Is your name Jonny?" I answered affirmatively and she continued, "You don't remember me, do you?" I had to apologize to her because I had no idea who she was. Then she said something like this: "I used to live in the ____ apartments in east Atlanta. [Though she named them, I no longer remember.] About two years ago, you came to my house and led me to Christ. I started going to church and have become a faithful Christian. I never thought I would see you again. I just want to say thank you."

After eating, I again walked over and said goodbye to her, and that was the last time I ever saw her. However, that day I was impressed with the reality that some who pray continue in their faith. I wondered how many others were part of a church and how many I had left for the wolves to devour. I comforted myself again with the reminder that my part is to witness, and God's part is to mature them. I lived the next ten years with that misunderstanding of the Great Commission.

In my mind, the missionary's value was determined by how many people he persuaded to say a prayer. It was not until 1986, when national and tribal preachers tutored me in Thailand, that I realized the Great Commission has several components that, if performed, will bring the world to the feet of the Savior.

Preaching or witnessing is not the end; it is the beginning. After that, we are to baptize the new converts and teach them (discipleship) to do likewise with their converts. This is best done by gathering these new converts into an assembly, in a home, or under a tree where you regularly instruct them. That is what the Bible calls a "church." Being successful in the first step is terrific, but you need the help of others to accomplish the other steps. That is the imperative of working with a team as Paul did. If you are alone, then you must be willing to slow down and do it all yourself.

I believe this is an example of the gifts God gave to the church in

Ephesians chapter four. I was, by all means, an evangelist. I was zealous bringing men, women, and children to Christ—but I was an absolute failure at discipling anyone. If I had done my part, not alone but in tandem with others who could preach and teach and pastor these converts, then the body of Christ would be blessed and multiplied as my converts were brought to maturity by those who were gifted to perform those tasks: the pastors and teachers.

God devised a marvelous plan for fulfilling His will, but I didn't see it, so I continued using my plan for the next decade. I realized that while I was faithfully adding converts to my roster, I could have multiplied them. This is why we emphasize supporting church planters and not just evangelists, preachers, or pastors. They are winning souls, assembling them for baptism and teaching, then training them as disciples (followers) to go and do likewise. They don't need a corporate document or a building with a steeple and pews. They win souls, return to their homes to disciple them, and in doing so, win the family, the extended family, and the neighbors to Christ. In turn, they produce more "leads" than the church planter can handle on his own. So, he trains his converts by doctrine and by example to do likewise. That is why our network of preachers average a new church planted every five minutes.

The Great Commission instructs us to preach to the unreached, understanding that we are only the messenger—not the Savior. Our attempts to notch our spiritual guns with large numbers of "pray-ers" do not impress God. It is nothing more than zeal without knowledge. What could be more shameful for us than while we energetically fulfill only one-third of His commission, we ignore the rest and pretend we have fulfilled it all?

Our first charge is to preach so that the Holy Spirit, through the spoken Word of God and the "foolishness" of our preaching, may stir the hearts of mankind to repent and turn to Christ. But that is the beginning and not the ending. From there, we are to baptize them, obviously with a thorough understanding on their part as to why we are performing this ordinance, and then we are to teach them—not just soul-winning but "all things that I have commanded you." One commission—three commands.

If we understand His Great Commission, we must realize that one man cannot fulfill it all. As a missionary, I cannot go into all the world if I must stay in one spot for years to teach all He commanded us. God knew this, so He established a process of growth for His church's perpetual existence and reproduction by giving gifts to the body of Christ that would help them fulfill His commission. A pastor is not a missionary, and a missionary is not a pastor.

Exposing the Conundrum

My purpose is not to cast blame but to open eyes. In Western Christianity, three primary issues reveal why missionaries do not plant churches—why we don't do what we say God called us to do.

1) We are not taught to by our churches or colleges.
2) We are not expected to by our boards.
3) We are not required to by our supporters.

We no longer understand or teach how the Bible defines a missionary and his purpose as separate from the other "gifts." If you don't understand what you are supposed to be, how can you know what you are supposed to do?

We have lost the understanding of what missions is. Most church members, and even pastors, think that a missionary is simply someone who goes somewhere else to preach. Somewhere other than home. He, in effect, is nothing more than a pastor in a foreign land. But the New Testament tells us that missionaries were not the only "travelers"; they were followed by teaching prophets as well as evangelists. Pastors were also appointed, bringing solidity, leadership, and loving care to the church. As a result, regions formerly a mission field had become a "home base," sending out missionaries, preachers, and evangelists to reach and develop other, unreached regions. This method produced results that excited the believers to do more. Like knocking over the first domino and eagerly watching the others fall one by one, they "turned the world upside down" using God's method.

Assuming that we know better than God how to do His work on His planet, we have redefined and thus diminished the very meaning of being a "missionary" to that of being a foreign pastor in a host country. What have we done? We have moved a domino out of its position, handicapping God's method. If they fall now, it is a miracle indeed. And that is why most missionaries, in their entire career, will not plant a single new church. They will be satisfied to pastor an existing church someone else started, believing they have fulfilled their calling.

I know this teaching angers some, and you ask, "What's wrong with pastoring in another country?" I would answer you by saying nothing at all is wrong with it. Pastoring is honorable; it is righteous, it is even necessary—it is just not missions.

Honestly, do you think a foreigner (American) can pastor a flock better than a national? I'm not talking about having more education or more money; I'm talking about shepherding the flock. How can the foreigner fully relate to his congregation? They work for a living; he receives his income from America. They struggle to buy food and clothes for their children while he has an abundance. They never get a day off, much less vacation, but he can take off all the time he wants. They are answerable to a boss or a pastor, but he is answerable to no one. And after working for four years as their pastor, he has to leave them (furlough) and gets an entire year off with pay. When he returns, if he returns (55 percent don't), the man who toiled in his place as the pastor is once again pushed aside.

I'm not saying that any of this is wrong; I'm simply pointing out how difficult it is for a foreigner to pastor a congregation with nothing in common with him other than two eyes, two ears, a nose, a mouth, and faith in Christ. Still, some do accomplish it.

If serving as a missionary and not a pastor, these personal differences do not matter. He is there as a messenger from God to perform a singular, temporary task—to plant a church, begin the discipleship, train the converts to do likewise, appoint a pastor, and then move on. Since he is always on the move, he has no home church to support him, and thus receiving support from abroad is neither illogical nor offensive. On the other hand, pastors should be supported by their congregation. This was Paul's method. Why do we oppose it?

I grew up believing that a missionary looked like me and went to preach to people who did not look like me. I was so wrong. Paul did not look remarkably different from any group of people he preached to. They ate the same foods, wore the same clothes, and though they were multilingual, they all spoke Greek. Their only difference was they had an incorrect knowledge of the true God and His Son. So, he went to turn them from idols to the living God, from performing sacrifices to accepting the sacrifice of Christ, from darkness to light.

Missions and missionaries have been shaped and led by reason, not biblical examples. Logic says that some soldiers battle and others peel potatoes, but they are both soldiers. Some team members hit home runs while others sit on the bench, but they are on the same team. Some astronauts fly spaceships while others do science experiments, but they both work for NASA. This logic explains the various "types" of missionaries—the teachers, children's workers, mechanics, doctors, and preachers.

It is logical, but I argue against the logic (man's reasoning) with the logos (God's thoughts put to words).

Timothy, Titus, Luke, and others traveled with Paul. They worked side by side with him, sharing in ministry, but were not called *apostles* (missionaries). They were the missionary's *ministers* (helpers). Paul told Timothy to pastor; he also sent Titus to his home country of Crete to pastor and establish churches in every town. Luke was known to all as a doctor who traveled with a missionary but never claimed to be one. Aquila and Priscilla moved with Paul and set up a shop to support themselves while strengthening the local church by discipling converts and training preachers like Apollos. Mark ministered to Paul's physical needs while in prison. Others carried messages from Paul to the various churches. So, we see that children's workers, teachers, builders, pilots, and doctors may *minister* their gifts and callings alongside a missionary (church planter). Still, they have their individual profession and unique ministry, which they perform for the team's benefit and the body of Christ. Their task may assist the missionary; it may comfort the missionary, bind his wounds, transport his equipment, and repair his car. But it is not missions.

Consider this: when these same dedicated people return home from the field and begin to minister in their local churches, do we then stop calling them missionaries and call them pastors? Why not? First, there is more to pastoring than simply helping out in the church. Second, they are neither trained nor experienced as a pastor. Third, they would never presume to call themselves a pastor; fourth, the pastor would never allow it. He would say it is wrong and has no basis in Scripture, and he would be correct.

Besides these four reasons, it is primarily because we understand the biblical calling and purpose of a pastor. Still, unfortunately, we no longer remember the biblical calling and purpose of a missionary. That understanding has been lost for many decades. So while we elevate one title (pastor) and would not presume ourselves worthy to accept it, we denigrate the other title (missionary) as if anyone can do it and that it is not a unique gift that requires God's calling.

The Result:

Because of this misunderstanding, for several decades, we have sent out men whose ministry more resembles pastoring than church planting. The tragedy is they won't even know that they were supposed to plant churches. They don't know what a biblical missionary is commissioned to do. No teacher ever took the time to instruct them, probably because most teachers don't know themselves.

We have been taught that being a missionary is, at most, pastoring or serving in another country while getting paid by the churches back home. No wonder the national churches often don't understand the purpose of tithing; they have never had to pay a salary for their pastor; his supporting churches in America took care of that. Now that he is gone, they don't know what to do. They have never had to pay a pastor, a light bill or a water bill, repair damages, purchase chairs, upgrade the PA system, etc. The missionary gladly did all that because he was able to. He had raised not own his personal support but also his ministry support as well. Missionaries unintentionally raise the national churches and their members under a ministry plan that cannot reproduce itself. When the missionary leaves, the church often dies. I have been told this worldwide by missionaries and national pastors and have seen enough empty buildings to believe it.

Fortunately, this is not an absolute fact, but it is common enough that it has become an expectation. We blame the national Christians, but where is the blame for the missionary who preached to them for three decades? Upon retiring, he had to request his mission board to send a replacement because he had never developed a single Timothy of his own.

If he only received an average of $5000 a month and was there for thirty years, then what in the world was he doing all those decades that justified the $1,800,000 he received in support? Some of you wrongly think that I am suggesting that we stop supporting missionaries. On the contrary, I suggest you stop supporting men who aren't, men who are not doing what they are supposed to be doing and what you are paying them to do. Give those funds to men who are and do and will—no matter their skin color or nationality. American and otherwise, red, yellow, black, or white.

How This Happened, Both Historically and Today:

(The following is a quote from one of our podcast episodes.)

In the 1700s, missionaries were defined as being church planters in other cultures. These other cultures were generally in foreign lands with foreign customs, foods, lifestyles, and languages. Sometimes, like in the Americas, the cultures were different but not so far away. They were often less than a day's walk into the forest. Such missionary endeavors to the American Indians were carried out in the Northeast by missionaries like David Brainerd and in the Southeast by missionaries like John Wesley.

As they ventured farther into the forests, they left behind small tribal churches, sometimes led by tribal preachers and sometimes by other foreigners. Usually, their efforts produced congregations that developed needed ministries like schools and orphanages. Such worthwhile ministries were first staffed by ministers (laymen), not missionaries. In time, the staff of specialized workers such as doctors and teachers would outnumber the church-planting missionaries. Because of this and the need for these workers to be supported, it did not take long before the term *missionary* had morphed from being *church planters* to becoming merely *church workers*. From there, the term *missionary* took another hit to its original definition, in that missionaries almost ceased to be church planters and became virtually, without exception, church pastors and workers.

Today, statistically, most missionaries will never plant a church. They will serve only as a helper or an assistant pastor until the senior missionary retires or moves on, then they will take his place. For this reason, most people today who claim to be and are supported as missionaries are only pastors or workers.

Two missionary misconceptions are prevalent today:

1. All missionaries are church planters; this is *factually* incorrect.
2. All missionaries don't have to be planters; this is *biblically* incorrect.

This does not mean he may not work an outside job as Paul did, teach at an institute, or even serve temporarily as a pastor while the congregation finds one. A missionary may temporarily wear many hats, but his primary function and driving motivation is starting new house churches and seeing them mature into effectiveness, producing more men just like him.

The end of all I have tried to say is this—to fulfill the Great Commission, pastors need to educate their congregations that a *missionary* is not a *church worker*; he is not a *church pastor*; he is a *church planter*. For the most part, missionaries do not plant churches because they were never taught it is their primary purpose, and no one ever showed them how. And seemingly, the churches who support them don't seem to understand this either.

ELIMINATING THE CONUNDRUM

Suggestions for Missionaries:

- As you read my comments, did you feel anger or a spark of excitement? If anger, I apologize; I must not have expressed my feelings adequately. First, please do two things: pardon me and then ask yourself if and where I have misinterpreted Scripture or history? If you don't acknowledge a misunderstanding, how will you correct it? I once received a phone call from a missionary who read my book, *The Great Omission*. He started by saying he had thought himself to be a missionary but, after reading, determined that he was not and asked what advice I could give him. Our conversation went like this:

1) I asked, "Do you agree that a missionary must be primarily, among other things as necessary, a church planter?" He answered, "Yes."

2) I then asked, "Do you believe God you called to be a missionary?" Again, he answered, "Yes."

3) I responded, "Then start planting churches." And he did.

Okay, so you weren't taught in your college what a missionary is supposed to be. So then, are you a missionary or a pastor? If you want to pastor, that is fantastic, even if you want to do so in a foreign land. I have two ethical suggestions:

1) Do the best you can but be honest with your people, so they don't think by your example that a missionary is a pastor. Help them understand the biblical difference.

2) Be honest with your supporters so they can decide if they want to support you as a pastor or allow your local church to support you. Just be honest. God never blesses dishonesty, and He uncovers everything we try to cover.

If you're sure of your calling, then be sure of this as well: you will never stop learning and never stop discovering truths in God's Word until you begin to ignore and excuse those truths. I hope you become a successful missionary, an example for your people to follow, and for those here who know you to emulate. If God called you, He created you for the excellent work and honor of being on His global church planting team. It is your "high calling in Christ Jesus." Don't despise, belittle, abandon, or reinvent your calling, and don't let anyone else do it either.

Suggestions for Churches:

The solution to this conundrum is quite simple: return to the biblical pattern God gave and Paul exemplified for successful missionary ministry.

- Teach the biblical difference between being an overseas pastor and a church-planting missionary. A shepherd is a shepherd and may never plant a church. If that's what you want to support as a missionary, go ahead, but remember, we cannot deviate from God's plan, purpose, or pattern and expect His blessing. He may wink at our ignorance, but He never excuses our disobedience.

- Instruct the non-productive missionaries you support and

encourage them to discover or re-discover their calling and purpose. Then hold them accountable as you would a paid staff member at your church. Remember that you should be supporting them to do what God wants them to do (church planting and discipleship), not what our tradition has taught them to do.

- Reorganize your missions' program. As I have already encouraged, just as your church has a mission fund or budget, you may want to develop a ministry budget as well. Support your missionary church planters from the missions fund and support other worthy ministry personnel from your ministry fund. You don't expect a young lady serving in an orphanage in Africa to be planting churches. Support her for what God called her to do. Are you supporting a missionary to pastor a single church of thirty people (or 3,000 people) year after year? Examine the missionary letters, and you may be surprised to learn that you have been doing exactly that. Support and expect your missionaries to be starting new works and training new pastors. If he is not doing that, then why are you supporting him?

- Keep in mind that missionaries are people. They do what they were taught, whether in a classroom or by those who went before them. Don't rush to drop their support but do inform your supported men what you expect. A sincere, Christ-like challenge could be all that is needed to spark a flame that will burn for as long as they live. And remember, give them time. It took you this long to learn the difference; it will take them some time as well. They have probably never heard this "new" (as old as the book of Acts) concept of missions.

Pastors, Let Me Help You…

I am in the process of writing a manual for churches on how to establish and maintain a biblical missions program. If you are a subscriber to our free, quarterly *Progress Report*, you will be advised when it is ready. You can register at our website: www. FinalFrontiers.world.

#16
Is It Always More Effective or Better Stewardship to Support a National Instead of a Foreign Missionary? If so, Is There Any Legitimate Purpose Left for the Traditional Missionary?

Explaining the Conundrum

In the past forty years, the biblical and philosophical movement of supporting national preachers has not only gained traction but has also overcome all the previous obstacles and prejudices that first opposed it. Whereas in 1986 you could find virtually no churches (in what we call Independent Baptist fellowships) that supported a national missionary. Today in 2020, it is hard to find a church that does not.

There have been abuses by unscrupulous national pastors. Some American churches have responded by "throwing out the baby with the bathwater." Still, the majority realize that your nationality, skin color, accent, or culture have nothing to do with sins that disqualify men from serving God. No church would ever dream of dropping all American missionaries' support because one (or some) have rendered themselves unqualified or mishandled funds, so why do we apply that standard to the nationals?

The issue that is more prevalent than all others, which has generated the rapid growth in supporting nationals, has been that of stewardship. But I would submit that stewardship involves more than the support differential between an American missionary and his national counterpart. To me, effectiveness is far more imperative than financial advantages.

Furthermore, just because a man is a national does not automatically mean he will work harder or accomplish more. There are highly effective missionaries serving who, with their gifts, talents, skills, and proper mentoring, are just as effective as a national, or even more so, despite his "foreign-ness."

EXAMINING THE CONUNDRUM

Please reread the conundrum's first question. My answer is a resounding no. Does that answer surprise you? It is not *always* more effective and better stewardship, but I would suggest that it *most often* and *most likely* is.

Let me briefly address the components of the conundrum.

Is It More Effective to Support a National?

It is difficult to imagine that a foreigner could be more effective than a national, but it depends on these two components. If the foreigner demonstrates that his presence there is due to a love for the people rather than just a job, and his national counterpart is spiteful, demanding, and money-hungry, then yes, the foreign missionary could be far more effective. But putting the two men side by side with the same work ethic, burden, compassion, etc., the national will almost always out-produce the foreigner. Not always, but almost always because he has certain advantages.

Keep in mind that the national missionary has an in-depth knowledge of the language the missionary is struggling to master and the culture to which the missionary is unaccustomed. If the missionary sticks and stays for one, two, three, four, five, six, or more four-year terms, he will likely be as effective or even more so than the national. During these decades, the people have grown to love him and realize that he "chooses" to be one of them rather than just passing through. He has demonstrated his love by sharing his support with them, helping them, teaching them, and loving them. But since the vast majority of missionaries do not make it to their second term, they will not know the joy of what could have been—only the struggles of what was.

Another area of ineffectiveness is the lack of understanding of what they (missionaries) are there for. National pastors know how to pastor their people and can be exceptionally proficient, despite a lack of resources like cars, funding, medicines, facilities, pews, PA systems, etc. The missionaries have access to these things, but their boards or mentors have taught that they should not participate in providing such "material" things to the national churches (except, of course, for the one they personally pastor). Instead, they are encouraged to spend their time building their own congregation. So, let's examine the effectiveness of the two. Let's put their shoes on our feet.

Here in America, suppose you have only two fundamental and doctrinally sound churches within 50 miles of your home. They both run about the same in attendance, have their own buildings, and have good pastors. Which one will you and your family join?

Church Number One:

This congregation is pastored by a local man who grew up with you. You have known him for years and observed his dedication and testimony. You know what he used to be and what he has become. His church doesn't have a piano, electric lights, or an AC. The pews were donated by another church that bought new ones, and the floor is just bare concrete with no tile or carpet. The church has a big heart but a small bank account.

However, you can go to him with any problem or concern because he knows your life and culture and can understand you when you speak. Whenever you invite him to your home for a meal, he enjoys whatever you serve and asks for more. Your kids go to school with his kids, your wife shops and fellowships with his wife, and he understands your financial struggles because he makes the same or even less than you do. He has earned your trust and respect through his life, his testimony, and his teaching.

Church Number Two:

This church has a carpeted floor, AC, padded seats, a PA system with guitars, a keyboard, an overhead projector for the singing, and a steeple, making it look like a real church. But as good and kind as the pastor is, he is from another country, let's say Mozambique.

He is a fine man with a lovely family, and from all you can tell, he was a successful pastor in his homeland before he felt a call to come to America. You like him and his family, and you are amazed by his knowledge of Scripture, but you don't get to spend much time with him. He always seems to be busy writing to the churches back in Mozambique that support him, and most of his sermon illustrations have to do with his homeland—not yours. Some you don't even understand. Another problem is he grew up speaking Portuguese and several of his native Bantu dialects. So even though he spent his first two to three years in America taking English classes, he still speaks with a heavy accent that, at times, is difficult for you to grasp. Sometimes he unwittingly makes cultural mistakes that can be a bit embarrassing if visitors are in the service.

That's the downside, but the upside is that he is from a wealthy family (compared to the members). Since he calls himself a "missionary to America" (even though you see him as a foreign pastor in America), and since a group of churches in Mozambique pays his salary, you don't have to pay him. After all, his family seems to be well paid; he has the nicest house in the church and two cars. Rumor has it that his support is more than the combined income of all the church members. If he has any needs or emergencies, his Mozambique supporters send the money to provide for the need. In essence, there is no need for you to tithe or give offerings, except to buy more material things (a different color of carpet, for instance). You do respect him, but you have nothing in common with him. He eats foods imported from his country, and his kids go to an expensive private school. His wife is lovely and sweet, but she only speaks a little English, so you don't really know her well at all.

Here's my question; which of those two churches will you join?

EXPOSING THE CONUNDRUM

Can you see now why missionaries sometimes struggle? You may have missed another point—a point that would alleviate all these difficulties. And what is that? Missionaries are not supposed to be *pastors;* they are supposed to be *church planters* and disciplers of church leaders.

I have never pastored in a foreign land, but I have started at least 12 churches and participated in starting hundreds more. I do this by working with pastors trained by myself, another missionary, or a national leader. They may need help/instruction/motivation to start new churches in their region. Pastors are general practitioners; they need to know how to do nearly everything. Missionaries are specialists; we need to know only two things: church planting and training new pastors (and church planters). We are most successful when we work *with pastors*—not when we try to be one.

Suppose you purchased plane tickets to take a trip. Once everyone was seated, the intercom is activated, and you hear the following: *"Hello, ladies and gentlemen, I'm Captain Bob, and I will be your pilot today. I trained as an Air Force pilot and piloted aircraft like this one for twenty years. So, sit back, relax, and we will be on our way momentarily."*

As you buckle in, you notice the cockpit door open, and you watch Captain Bob walk out and put on an apron. Once again, the intercom is activated, and Captain Bob says, *"Ladies and gentlemen, this is your captain again. I just wanted you to know I have decided to swap responsibilities with our chief flight attendant, Mrs. Jane Smith. I'll be serving your meals and making sure you are completely comfortable. Flight attendant Smith will fly the plane."* How long would it take you to deplane? This is what happens when a missionary gives his time to pastoring rather than church planting.

Several consequences result:

1) Captain Bob's work is left undone because he is the only pilot on the plane.
2) He is not doing what he was trained to do.
3) He takes the job away from someone God called and prepared.
4) Panic, heart attacks, and sprained ankles occur as the passengers all deplane.

Is It Better Stewardship to Support a National?

Supporting a national missionary is certainly cheaper than a foreign missionary. In most developing nations, the ratio is as much as 100 to 1, which means the funds American churches give to support one American missionary; could have supported up to 100 national missionaries.

That was not true in the past because 150 years ago, missionaries worked for a living on the field. They lived like the nationals, ate the same food, their children attended the same school, they walked wherever they went, and health insurance, IRA's, college saving funds, and deputation costs were inconceivable. Missionaries used the same furniture as the locals, plowed the same gardens, and adapted to the same culture. Their most significant difficulty was learning the language. Still, when you are "all in" with no hope or plan of ever going home, the necessity to communicate was a great impetus in learning the language quickly and effectively.

In those days, quitting was difficult. How could you go home and admit that you had missed God's real calling for your life? With little or no financial help that was spasmodic at best, how could you ever hope to raise the funds to go home? Being a missionary was not a career; it was a life choice and a death sentence.

In the first 100 years of British missionary endeavors, the average life span for a missionary was only six years. They shipped their belongings to the field, not in crates but coffins. Many died on the ships on their way to the field. There were no "survey trips" to make sure of your calling or prepare lodgings for your family. There was no deputation or expectation of others to pay your salary. If you were a cobbler in England, you would be a cobbler in Calcutta (William Carey). After all, if the apostle Paul could work for a living while "turning the world upside down," then why couldn't they? That was the thinking then, but as believers back home became more interested in missions, and with their newfound prosperity, gave more to missions, they determined that the methods of missions needed to be changed, and so it developed into what we have today.

When it comes to comparing a missionary with a national, stewardship is not so much in a comparison of *funds* as it is a comparison of *function*. If you support a missionary who is not doing what he was sent to do, then even $1 a month is poor stewardship. And conversely, if a man is doing what he was called and sent to do, then his ministry will grow (as has Final Frontiers), and you may likely find the need to help him do even more by increasing his funding.

And now for the final part of the conundrum.

Is There Still a Legitimate Purpose for The Foreign Missionary?

Yes, there will always be a need for the foreign missionary. But the need has more to do with what he accomplishes than what his nationality is. Supporting churches need to verify the men they support are doing their job, not simply ministering as a foreign pastor but planting new works for and with the nationals. In this way, they can capture their country for Christ.

Over the years, there have been pastors who have listened to our philosophy, tested it, and found that supporting one or more of our national church planters was more effective than many of the foreign missionaries they had been supporting. Not all, but many. They judged effectiveness on results and reporting. Over time, I have seen many churches begin to reduce the number of Americans they supported and increase the number of nationals. As they would drop a missionary or one would retire, etc., they would replace him with a national church planter (missionary).

Several pastors have recently told me that they planned to drop all the missionaries they support and help only nationals. And while you may think that I take pleasure in such a decision, I do not. I understand the frustration pastors have as they deal with men on perpetual deputation; then, after raising all they need, they delay to raise tens of thousands of dollars more for travel and to ship their furniture. In other scenarios, missionaries remain in America though churches have supported them for years. Novice believers wonder why the missionary is still here but are shocked when many others, long on the field, rarely if ever mention a soul saved, a man discipled for ministry, or a church started. Then, there are the letters of resignation from men you have supported for years who now feel led by God to return to America to pastor. Of course, pastors are frustrated and look for a way to ensure that their missions giving is actually reaching the mission field and accomplishing something.

I know I have painted a very gloomy picture, but it is a reality for many pastors here in America. It certainly was for me as a young pastor decades ago.

But still, many excellent missionaries are serving around the world who have built solid, reproducing ministries and who have affected their new home for the cause of Christ. Should such men lose support simply because they are Americans? Should they be dropped because they consume more funding than the nationals? Should they be unsupported because of the failure of others? God forbid.

I am sometimes accused of being "anti-missionary," which is ridiculous since I am a missionary. Jesus said a house divided cannot stand. In my case, they must feel He made an exception. For some reason, because I point out the apparent failures in our missions programs and missionary training, I am assumed to be hateful and insulting. All I am teaching is what the book of Acts teaches. I have not put words in God's mouth; I have only taught what He placed in His Word.

Suppose a pastor complains about other pastors being lazy, not studying for their sermons, too busy with life to help their members, or being overpaid and underworked. In that case, his members cheer him on, but if I say the same about some (but not all) missionaries, being one myself, somehow that makes me the enemy. Well, poor me! However, I will say that the complaints that have come my way rarely ever come from missionaries. That is because these diligent servants of God know that what I say is true. They appreciate that I say what they are not allowed to say. The most common response I have from missionaries is, "It's about time somebody told the churches what is really going on."

Neither do the complaints come from the church members because many are in business. They see what I see and have long wondered why missions is not run as a heavenly business with policies, procedures, accountability, responsibilities, job classifications, etc. They don't hire a man expecting to mentor him for years; they look for men with experience. They don't hire a man from a foreign land with a foreign language to deal with their clients; they hire an American. They give him a job, a title, a responsibility, and a quota. They don't expect a report from him four times a year talking about his wife and kids; they want weekly progress reports. The businessmen in your church wonder why we do God's work in such a sloppy manner. They know that if they ran their businesses the way we run missions, they would soon be out of work.

Let's just be brutally honest. The rapid growth of Christianity today in such places as Brazil, Mexico, the Philippines, and India, is because once upon a time, there were American, British, Dutch, and German missionaries who left all they had to go and give their lives to and for those people. They won them, discipled them, trained them, and enabled them to do what they had been doing. Sure, the nationals have more remarkable results; they should. Shame on them if they don't. But it all started with a foreign missionary who knew what he had come to do, and he did it.

In the end, the missionary's job is to work himself out of a job and move on to another field and start over. This is not a process of failure; it is a process of absolute success. For a genuinely biblical missionary, anything less is a failure.

We can do better in stewardship, so let's do it.

Often, missionaries have characteristics deep inside developed by their family, culture, home church, Bible college, and country. As Americans, for example, we tend to be more aggressive in our efforts. That is a positive. We also tend to be concerned only with ourselves and our ministries rather than helping others with theirs. That is a negative. We also tend to tear down and build bigger barns rather than spread out and plant new fields. We also tend to be highly egotistical and entrepreneurial. We are eager to learn from someone older and just as eager to outdo him rather than to emulate him. Our goal is to be our own boss and the leader of the others around us. We want to teach others what we have no experience doing and lead others where we have not yet gone. We want titles and recognition and accomplishments to gain honor, but we step on the backs of those who trained us. We work hard, but we seem to hardly work, as there is little evidence that we were ever there.

Often when I am with missionaries, I listen to what they have to say, ask questions about various points, and then try to determine what Bible college they attended or even what mission board they are with. It's a little game I play.

- Some are prone to be highly evangelistic with no follow-up. They were taught that success is revealed in numbers—the higher the number, the greater their ministry's validation. Their discipleship is a thirteen-week course designed to develop loyalty in attendance and giving, not studying and understanding God's Word. All their emphasis is on soul winning with no thought of real discipleship. This is because they were never really discipled. They are all zeal with little knowledge. When they perish, it is usually back home as many of these leave the mission field. They grow discouraged because they cannot understand how they can win thousands to Christ, yet only dozens come to church. They are good men who love Christ. Unfortunately, they were inadequately trained as to what their biblical function is. They have not realized that the farmer's job is not just to sow the seed; it is also to water it, nourish it, prune it, and harvest it. The sowing is only the beginning of a future harvest. And the harvest is not the planting or the reaping; it is the gathering. They are just the process that leads to the purpose.

- Some are more studious. They develop fantastic sermons and institute courses for the three men in their institute, but they are all knowledge with no zeal whatsoever. All they do is religiously formal and in the setting of the church facility. They have few converts and will probably never start a church. These men feel they are professionals who feel they have something to teach, but they do not see the urgency to build their student body with converts. The preachers they may produce will be like them—full of knowledge and void of evangelism. They will know how to counsel but have few families to practice on. Typically, they will retire before death but will not be replaced by a trained man because they have not fully trained one. Instead, they will rely on their mission board to send a replacement. After all, that's what they were.

- Some go as tentmakers and align themselves with a national church. While working, they develop relationships with employees, vendors, customers, and suppliers. (Some concentrate on teaching English and, while doing so, win their students and plant a church. Most of their converts are young men and women who are college students or young professionals.) They grow slowly and steadily and produce reproducing house churches that grow into established congregations. Their zeal seems to be more for discipleship than for evangelism, but they have a balanced mixture of both. They are zeal with knowledge. They tend to produce fruit that remains by concentrating on the individual convert's full discipleship and expecting a harvest later from their labors today. When these missionaries perish, no one knows because they have already moved on from one place to another, reproducing themselves in the lives of others. News of their demise sometimes reaches their "fruit" months later.

- Some missionaries know why they are there (to win, disciple, and plant churches) and were appropriately trained in their own culture and gained ministry experience before ever leaving for the field. They, like tentmakers, are a perfect mixture of zeal and knowledge. They tend to develop multiple institutes, knowing it is more effective in training their converts and their converts' converts. As the number of disciples grows and their ministry expands, they don't ship in students to build their school; they start new schools for each region. They tend to be evangelistic in all their efforts but spend enormous amounts of time on future church leaders' discipleship. They do have a discipleship course but also realize that biblical discipleship is an ongoing, lifestyle effort, just as Christ's disciples lived, ate, slept, and worked with Him. They learned from His teachings and His example. Then they repeated that process in their own ministries. They are phenomenal. When they perish, their ministries continue because they designed them that way. Their ministry is not dependent on them, but on the principles they taught their disciples, spiritual discipleship and reproduction.

Eliminating the Conundrum

***Suggestions for Missionaries*:**

- I know you are competing with the nationals' production, but you do have an advantage; many pastors still don't trust nationals, and you can visit the churches that support you. So then, make constant visits, if even by email, Facebook, or Zoom. Take advantage of your advantages.

- Do as Paul told Timothy and prove your value. Don't rely on your title to prove your worth; rely on your labors. This is a biblical principle. God despises sloth in any form, so as a servant of God, His steward, and His ambassador, we should despise it as well.

- Again, obey Paul's instruction to Timothy: "stir up the gift of God that is in you." Realize that if you are called to be a missionary, you have been exalted by God to be the first of the gifts He will give to a people somewhere. All others will follow you. You are not the caboose; you are the engine. Your influence and message will ultimately change a tribe, a nation, or a continent. Be worthy of your calling; don't let it remain paralyzed, stir it up.

If you are of European ancestry, you know the gospel today because, at some time in centuries past, someone who was downline from Paul ventured north to preach to our ancestors and turn them from darkness to light. They had no idea of the repercussions of their missionary venture, and you have no idea of the forest that will come from the seed of a single tree that you plant.

Suggestions for Churches:

- Share with your members the successes of missionaries when you learn about them. Arrange for a Skype or Zoom call so your members can meet them online and learn what they are doing and how they are doing it.

- When you are confronted with a negative situation or feel the need to drop a missionary's support, be upfront with your people as to why and share what you have learned from the experience and any changes that need to be made in your missions program.

- It doesn't matter how much a missionary receives in support, as long as he is worthy of it and uses it for our great King's service. Ensure the men you support are winning souls, discipling converts, training new pastors, and planting new churches. If they are, continue to help them, perhaps even increase their support if it is needed. But if they are not, hold their feet to the fire. Ask them why and demand a response. And if they continue not doing what you are supporting them to do, then drop their support by all means. (Give them an acceptable cutoff time—not to improve since they have already shown their lack of commitment, but so they are not left stranded.)

But you say, "We can't drop a missionary!" Well, why not? You would fire a music pastor who for years didn't prepare for the services. You would fire a youth pastor who for years barely ever taught a class and didn't have youth activities. Why are missionaries so sacred? We have created a welfare mentality in our mission programs that defy any hint of stewardship or accountability. Remember, it is not to me that you will answer for this, but to our Lord.

#17
Why Does Final Frontiers Emphasize Supporting National Church Planters Rather than National Pastors, and Is Doing So Biblical?

Explaining the Conundrum

In Job 12:5, we read, *"He that is ready to slip with his feet is as a lamp despised in the thought of him that is at ease."* Most commentators would agree that the verse refers to the arrogant attitude of those at ease, comfortable, secure, and prosperous toward those whose lives are slipping away from them due to their poverty and circumstances.

When I started Final Frontiers in late 1986 and began to represent national preachers' ministries, this was the most common attitude I experienced from mission leaders and pastors. Being comfortable in their American ministries, funded by their American salaries, and unaware of any other than their own American culture, they discounted the worth and work of nationals who were hungry, living in perpetual poverty, and hindered by their social and political situations. I looked for sympathy but found very little. As time went on and the *cause* I was promoting began to catch on, attitudes changed, and with them, personal involvement.

I soon experienced that those who had once fought me over the concept of supporting national preachers were now supporting them with great zeal but little knowledge. As a result, over time, it became apparent that many nationals were abusing the generosity they were receiving. Once again, the entire concept was being hindered by the sins of a few. Monies that had once flowed generously to aid national preachers were beginning to trickle or were cut off entirely.

Admittedly, I was among the eager supporters in the beginning. I would support any preacher who came to me with a need. Then one day, some of the trusted men I had been helping warned me against the support of others whom they knew were lazy, dishonest, and even of a different but hidden doctrinal belief. Because of this, I had an option. I could "throw out the baby with the bathwater" and stop supporting nationals, or I seek help and advice on how to fix the problem. In doing this, we had to make some requirements in our choice of men to support and develop criteria by which we would give support.

EXAMINING THE CONUNDRUM

To resolve the problem, we came up with a two-part solution: Recommendation and Application. Here is how we handled it.

Recommendation:

1) We determined that we would not consider an application for support unless it came with a referral from a missionary from a fundamental board or from a national preacher with whom we already had a relationship.

2) We determined that the referral must be based on a long-term, personal knowledge of the man and his ministry. In other words, the one recommending the preacher for support should not make the recommendation because he knows about him but because he knows him.

3) We determined that we would not support a preacher unless he was attached to a local accountability group of other preachers—no lone rangers.

4) And since these leaders were always eager to get their own men supported, it led to a temptation to refer men who may not meet all our requirements. To avoid this, we determined that if the man making the recommendation refers us to a preacher who does not fully meet our qualifications, he would permanently lose the right to recommend another man. In other words, we had a "one-strike, and-you're-out" policy.

But all that had only to do with the referral. Then we developed an application and a process to determine if the preacher truly met our requirements.

Application

We developed an application that focused on these components:

1) Is he doctrinally sound?

2) Is he morally pure?

3) Does he have experience in starting new churches?

4) Does he have experience in training other men for ministry?

5) If we agree to support him, will he pledge not to solicit or accept another ministry support?

While these look like five easy questions to answer, each had to be verified with details. For example, if the applicant claimed to have started five churches, he also had to tell us their names and locations. In this way, we could verify whether what he claimed was true or false. These questions allowed us to learn about his family life, his testimony, who trained him for the ministry, what he has accomplished in the past, etc.

Regarding number 5, we asked this to keep a man from getting support from various ministries. We do not want to support them in building an empire, but rather because they have both worth and need. Furthermore, we did not want to pile on support for one while others went with no support at all.

When I decided on this policy, I had no idea how it would affect us in the years to come. On numerous occasions, other ministries copied our program and learned our national leaders' names by reading our Progress Report; then they would contact those directors and ask them to break their fellowship with Final Frontiers and work with them. If we learned that the national accepted their invitation, we would immediately drop their support. In some cases, we pulled out of entire countries because other organizations had targeted our men there, promising them more funding but rarely ever giving it.

This is morally wrong, but it is how the world does business, and unfortunately, many preachers in America and many missionaries from America do not see this method as unbiblical. To them, it is business as usual. To me, it is envy. Their reasoning is evidently, why spend years developing new contacts when I can take one that is already vetted by another ministry?

Beyond our referral and application process is our continuing accountability, but an explanation is unnecessary as it is not relevant to this conundrum.

EXPOSING THE CONUNDRUM

It did not take many years of working with national preachers and absorbing criticisms, sarcasm, and being ridiculed for doing so before we developed a vetting and accountability process that has been copied by dozens if not scores of other ministries. I confess this bothered me initially, but as time passed and pride eroded, I realized that imitation really is the sincerest form of flattery. Rather than fight the competition, we tried to develop it by offering them our training classes and literature. Many of them took my essays and brochures and whited out our name, replacing it with their own. I began to understand why Paul had the attitude that though he might be criticized and abused, at least the gospel was being preached. I realized too that these other ministries live in circles that don't know me, so they will be able to build an army from those contributors that I would never be able to influence. To God be the glory! I like to tell others that we may be the Army, and they the Navy, but we all serve the same Commander-in-Chief.

I once attended a Virginia conference, and my ministry table was next to another ministry that also supported national preachers. After I spoke, we all went to our tables to meet and greet the church members. I noticed the brother at the table beside me was straining to listen to how I would answer questions. When all was over, and we were putting away our materials, he tried to recruit me to come to work for their ministry. He insisted I could be more productive working with them, and besides, Final Frontiers was not giving me a salary, and they would.

What he did not know was that I had trained the man who started his ministry. We thought about hiring him, but we saw some questionable issues during the vetting process, so we rejected him. In the meantime, I had taught him every step of our process, and so he used that knowledge to start his own carbon-copy ministry. As I read their literature, I couldn't help but chuckle when, once again, I saw my writing be plagiarized and used by yet another ministry.

This scenario has occurred time and time again. When I was 35 and 45, it bothered me, but now at 65, I thank God for my ministry's fruit that I don't even know about. Treasures in heaven—that's what it's all about!

Why then have I taken the time and ink discussing these trivial issues? It's so that I can now make my point. And what is that?

When I began this ministry, the idea of supporting national preachers was unheard of, even ridiculed and rejected. In time the value of supporting them became apparent, and the cause grows even today. But in these decades, Final Frontiers made a significant change in our ministry that went unnoticed by most. Frankly, though I expose it now, it will remain virtually unnoticed. In 1986 when we started, as far as we know, we were the first Baptist ministry in America started for the specific purpose of supporting national pastors. Now there are at least 600 similar ministries, or so I have been told. We have helped at least a dozen of them start, as I have already mentioned. But even though we are now only one of the 600, we are still in a group that, again, as far as I know, has no other ministry in it than ours.

How can that be? It is because of one little, huge distinction that we are different from all the others. It is not that we started first or that we have more preachers than the others (and frankly, we have more than most all the others combined); it is because we no longer support national preachers. We don't even support national pastors. We did at the beginning, but for the past 30 years, we have not. Then what pray tell do we support? What makes us different? We support only national church planters.

In the beginning, I wanted to help all of the preachers I could. Very soon, I learned their numbers were too big, and my resources were too small. Eventually, I realized I was helping poor "pastors" of one congregation at the expense of not helping "poor church planters" who produced a larger harvest and had no congregation to rely on for support.

In the early days, some who disagreed with my ministry would say that the pastor should be supported by his own congregation. I agreed 100 percent, but sometimes they have nothing to give. In the 1990s, Nicaragua had a 70 percent unemployment rate. No job = no tithe = nothing for the pastor. Even today in India, the members will bring an egg or a bag of rice or a stalk of vegetables as their tithe. They have no money. When American pastors would insist the national pastors live off the people's tithe, I would remind them that you can eat an egg, but you can't wear an egg. You can't strap it to your feet as a sandal, and you cannot inject it as medicine. I reminded them that the Word tells us to *"do good unto all men, especially those who are of the household of faith."*

I still believe in helping national pastors whose congregations cannot sufficiently help them. And by the way, if you believe that the pastor should be cared for by the congregation, then why are you supporting American "missionaries" who pastor churches? What's good for the goose should be good for the gander.

I also believe in helping national preachers who are not pastors; they are biblical evangelists who use their calling to strengthen the local churches and train the members in evangelism. They need support as well.

So, you may wonder, if I believe in supporting national pastors and preachers, why do we make an issue about *not* supporting them? I believe God's purpose for Final Frontiers is to support national church planters. Most of them are pastors, but we don't support them because they are a pastor, we support them because they reach out from their one congregation to start other churches. They are church planters who happen to be pastors too. And they are, as we require, "actively and consistently involved in church planting and training others for the ministry." The same goes for the evangelists that we support. If they live as American evangelists do, by preaching in churches to believers, we don't support them. But if they are biblical evangelists, winning the lost and helping to plant and build local churches, then we do.

Do you see how changing definitions of biblical terms can affect the eventual annihilation of the true meaning? If we lose the meaning, we lose the purpose.

Our purpose is to help fulfill the Great Commission in our lifetime by supporting those whose efforts will help accomplish that. If they are exhibiting all the components of the Great Commission in their lives, we help them.

When Should You Not Support a National Church Planter?

For us, that is an easy question to answer—not even worthy of the status of being a conundrum. We stop supporting our preachers if:

1) They die.
2) Their doctrine changes.
3) They no longer need help.
4) They start receiving funds from a similar organization.
5) They stop planting churches.

We used to say that to qualify for support, a preacher must have already started at least one church. After all, we were supporting church planters. Over the years, we saw a pattern of a man getting funded, starting a church, and then staying there as a pastor. Usually, he left Bible college and went back to his hometown where his burden lay. We were glad to have helped such a man, but that is not our purpose. So, we changed our policy. To qualify now, a man must have already started at least two churches and have at least one man serving in ministry that he won to Christ, discipled, and trained for the ministry. That's to get support. To keep it, you have to be "actively and consistently involved church panting and training others for the ministry." We monitor that with quarterly reports and the oversight provided by our nearly 1500 national directors, who oversee the work of over 28,000 national church planters.

Now for the Final Part of the Conundrum—Is It Biblical to Support These Men?

I think a better way to ask that question is to ask, "Is it biblical *not* to support national church planters (missionaries)?"

When Paul wrote the common-sense declaration about supporting missionaries *("how shall they preach except they be sent")*, was he referring only to sending Jewish missionaries to the Gentile world? There is no indication of that. In fact, in all his writings, you never one time see Paul asking for Jerusalem to send more Jewish missionaries. Paul understood that the best person to reach the Greek was another Greek. He won and recruited Gentiles to help him reach the Gentiles.

That is a biblical principle. On the other hand, we never read of Paul's discouraging a Jewish missionary from helping; he simply didn't ask for their help.

There is also the verse that tells us to help those who are of the household of faith. Are we to read that differently? Was Paul saying help believers who need your help unless they are pastors or missionaries? No, he didn't say that, and he didn't imply it.

Then in John's third epistle, the apostle rebuked a local pastor for two matters: first for refusing to help the traveling preachers (likely nationals-as they were strangers), and second for forbidding his church members to help them as well. John rebuked him before his entire church by his letter being circulated and further threatened the pastor by saying he would deal with him the next time he was in town.

If we took the time, we could point out numerous examples of national preachers being helped, both in the Old and New Testament. But the truth is, even if the Scriptures were silent, and they are not, it would still be logical to help those who are our brothers in Christ, who preach where we cannot or will not, in languages we don't know, in cultures we don't understand, and in countries where we are forbidden.

Are we to surmise that the world and the "*fulness thereof*" is no longer the property of the Lord? That, for some reason, American money does not fit into the term "*fulness thereof*"? Must we believe, as some used to say, "American money belongs to American missionaries"?

Are we to believe that missionaries have given their lives only so that they can be replaced by more foreign missionaries and not by their own fruit? Or are we to believe it is only acceptable to financially support a man with the same skin color as ours, the same hair color, language, and accent? Did God not make all men from one man? Did He not offer redemption for all men through one Man? Did that same Christ not commission us with His final words to go into all the world, to every country, every race, every tribe, and to preach His glorious gospel in every language, redeeming a Bride for Himself?

So, do I think it is biblically wrong to support a national preacher? Absolutely not. I would say instead that it is wrong not to support them. But then, that's just me.

Eliminating the Conundrum

Suggestions for all:

- *If you cannot trust the nationals with money, then you can't trust them at all.* Many ministries claim they "work with nationals," and I applaud them all. Surprisingly, we don't work with nationals—we work *for* them. They tell us what they need, and we go to work to provide it. But there is a difference between actual support and peripheral help.

I know a church planter in Honduras who is a pastor. His name is Carlos Messan, and he was my wife's pastor in her young adult years before we were married. Churches here gave him a low-interest loan to build his facility and donated a truck to his family. But they refused to support him financially. Why? They believed if you give money to a national, it will ruin him. First of all, we are all nationals, so I guess you can't support missionaries anymore. Second, I'm confused; $50,000+ for a building and $10,000+ for a vehicle won't ruin him, but $25 a month to buy food for his family (and gas for his car) will? That rationale defies logic and reeks of prejudice.

- *If your ministry can't trust the nationals with my money, don't ask me to give for them.* I know of one ministry that supports church planters, but not exclusively. Still, they try. They, like me, like to illustrate how hard the nationals work and what a good job they do and how they are worthy of support, but they refuse to give support directly to the national preacher. They require that the funds go through an American missionary. Evidently, they cannot trust their trusted nationals with cash, but if the funds first touch an American hand in the process, then all is well. If you can't trust your men, then why are you asking us to support them?

- Determine what you want to support with your missions giving and target those who meet those criteria. Here again, I advise givers to make a distinction between giving for missions and giving for ministry. We raise funds to support church planters, but we also raise funds to help them with buildings, equipment, motorcycles, medicine, Bibles, etc. We also support children and feeding centers. But we would never give money designated for church planters to any other cause.

Note:

If you are interested in learning more about supporting a church planter through our ministry, please go to our website for more information (www.FinalFrontiers.world). You can personally select and support a man for $50 a month or, by contributing to our Great Commission Fund with any amount as often as you choose, you can help scores of preachers around the world. In either case, you will receive their quarterly accountability reports. Partner with a national preacher who is a veteran church planter with years of experience training other men in ministry. Or help us fund his feeding center, Bible institute, or Bible distribution efforts. For more information, read conundrum #18.

#18
What Is the Great Commission Fund, and How Is It Better than Direct Support of National Preachers?

Explaining the Conundrum

When I started Final Frontiers in 1986, I knew of no mission organization founded explicitly to support national church planters. Had I found one, I would have eagerly joined it. My intention was not to be a ministry founder or a ministry leader but to be a minister who serves and equips God's other ministers. I had experienced prolonged periods of devastation, having to feed my family from garbage cans, and at that time had worked for years with no salary. To survive, I did odd jobs, delivered newspapers (my route had 5,000 papers), and sold avocados on the street with my brother Ben. (We couldn't afford a city permit, so we were frequently being shut down by the city police.) I never knew if they were after us because of having no permit or if that was an excuse to stop and buy some avocados. At that time, I was the pastor of a small church. I knew God had called me to missions, and my members did too. I was waiting for God to tell me what and where He wanted me. Most missionaries want to be the next Paul. I wanted to be the next Barnabas…and still do.

By the age of twenty-five, I had already seen and been affected by enough ministry scandals to know that I wanted to avoid it at all costs. At age thirty, I learned about an organization that supported the projects of missionaries and national preachers. One of their executives met with me and learned about my interest. He spoke with his team, and they extended an invitation for me to join them. However, something didn't seem right, and as I investigated their ethics by speaking with some, those for whom they had claimed to raise support for never received a dime, so I decided not to work with that ministry. After learning what I had discovered, several on their executive team resigned within a few years, and their board eventually fired the rest. The ministry bounced back and still functions today.

Shortly after starting the ministry, my great friend and assistant pastor, Mike Corsini, gave me a book saying, "Jon, you've got to read this book. This man sounds just like you." The book was titled *The Coming Revolution in World Missions* by K. P. Yohanan. In it, he promoted the same concept of missions that God had laid on my heart, though he was not restricting it to church planters but to all workers for Christ, especially pastors. A few months later, my family was preparing to move back to Georgia from California. Knowing I would pass through Dallas, I called his office, hoping to make an appointment to see him and gain some much-needed counsel. He was out of the country, so I explained what I was about to do and asked if the staff could give me any advice. Unfortunately, the person I spoke with was unwilling to help, leaving me with no mentor to guide me in this "new" type of ministry, whose foundation seemed to be laid on quicksand.

So here I was, an unknown young man of thirty years with no missionary experience, trying to get meetings from men old enough to be my father who were loyal to their established mission boards and resentful of my upsetting the proverbial cart. I had no one to give me advice, and even my college friends wanted nothing to do with me. My dad understood my intention and two of my brothers did as well, but that was about it.

Soon, as I started getting meetings in churches, mission board executives would patronize me saying, "Son, that's a lovely dream you have, but someday you'll wake up." They began to warn pastors not to allow me to present my "heretical" views of missions in their churches. Then they wrote articles in their magazine claiming that what I was doing was "unbiblical" while never giving any references to support their claim.

I didn't need long to realize that though I felt I had stumbled upon something new, there was no doubt that many scores of missionaries had and were sharing their support funds with their own men, but they were doing so in an unofficial manner. One missionary friend with whom I had spent four years in college told me that he supported many of his trained men from his support. I knew his board had a policy against supporting nationals; in fact, they were my chief protagonist. With that knowledge, I asked him if his board knew what he was doing, and he affirmed they did.

"How do you get away with it?"

He told me that the money he raised was his, and they agreed he could do with it as he liked but that he could not officially raise support for others.

I know that some of you are trying to discern how a mission organization could have such a policy. Don't waste your time. It was a philosophy in the past century based on American cultural superiority and bigotry, ignoring ample biblical endorsement and supported by examples of ruin and failure of some that they applied to all nationals. (Today, they no longer endorse their predecessors' unbiblical view.) As I told his board president and several others, I told my missionary friend that if they freed their missionaries to raise support for their Timothies, they would put me out of business. And I would be glad.

At that time, with such prejudice abounding in our pulpits, the idea of a ministry that existed solely to help fund the ministries of others was unheard of. But God blessed us, and our Bible-based philosophy of missions began to be gradually accepted. And whereas in 1986, when finding a church that supported a non-American missionary (a national) was virtually impossible, today, it is virtually impossible to find one that doesn't.

I have disclosed all of this background for one purpose: to reveal that, having no teacher to guide me and no how-to book to instruct me, I had to build our policies and procedures based on trial and error. And to be sure, the Holy Spirit was with me, as I would see time and time again. His leading was repeatedly affirmed as I would implement a policy and later see it in the book of Acts.

Examining the Conundrum

Over the decades, this "new" method of doing missions has been copied and reinvented repeatedly. Now we hope to improve on it one more time.

The "ministry plan" I conceived in 1986 was an adaptation of churches supporting American missionaries by choosing which ones and how much they would give. I merely introduced the option of, rather than only adding another American to their list, they could now support national missionaries as well. Though rebuffed, ridiculed, confronted, doubted, and even scoffed, the results proved that the idea worked, which is why we have always published statistics on the last page of our quarterly Progress Report. It is not to brag but demonstrate that supporting nationals is a viable and perhaps, even a superior alternative.

It was slow going at first because the idea seemed new, though the concept is as old as the book of Acts, and on top of that, people did not yet know me—so how could they trust me? *(The older I get, the less that is a concern. After all, how many missionaries do you know of or support who like me, have been missionaries for 35 years? Statistically, over 90 percent of those who start deputation never make it to their sixth year of service.)* As I crisscrossed America, churches and even families slowly began to support national preachers they had never met and whose language they could not speak. They did this because they believed in my plan, and they believed in me. Now, rather than looking for supporters and convincing them of our methods, they look for us. The word-of-mouth assistance from our supporters is impressive.

As I said, our plan worked, and over time, though I tried to recruit other missionaries to help me, it seemed that most, though fully persuaded of the concept, wanted to start their own ministries using our plan. But as age and experience began to give validity to myself and Final Frontiers, the trust factor grew, and our numbers began to swell. By our twentieth year, we had statistically become one of the five largest missions organization in existence. And by our thirtieth year, though most people still have never heard of us, some say we are now the largest with a network of more than 28,000 preachers overseen by nearly 1500 local, national directors (as of December 2020).

This enormous growth began to produce growing pains. Doing a self-audit of our ministry's results, we realized we had reached a point where we could grow no further, while the world had still not yet been fully evangelized. What was going on, and why?

EXPOSING THE CONUNDRUM

My ministry-plan began to reveal cracks that were beginning to become crevices. Our ministry growth had always depended on finding one sponsor for one preacher at a time. But our ability to expand had become severely handicapped as some preachers, due to their ministry growth, local economy, or family size, needed more sponsors. Whereas before, five sponsors could fund five preachers, in time, those same funds could only support only four, three, or two.

Because each sponsor was tied to an individual preacher, when a sponsor stopped giving, our immediate and urgent need was to find a replacement sponsor so the preacher would not suffer. This resulted in zero net growth in the number of sponsors. And when we had to drop the support of a preacher (usually due to death or no longer having a need), fewer and fewer of the sponsors were willing to take on another in his place. In the early years, probably 90 percent would continue and support another preacher; today that number is closer to 25 percent.

One sponsor dropping affected only one preacher, which we could easily replace. But after growing so large, we could have ten or more drop in one day. People die, they retire, they lose their job or lose interest, a child goes off to Bible college, a friend becomes a missionary, or the church has an urgent need. That means the next ten sponsors we found caused us to break even rather than grow. And we are all about growth. Over the years, we had some churches and even families that supported 50, 100, or more preachers. When one of them would drop support, we had to find enormous numbers of replacement sponsors. It could take a year to find that many, and in the meantime, the preachers are suffering.

One time we lost almost a third of our preachers' support in the space of several years. A church decided they wanted to have their own ministry (like ours), so they dropped their support. A family that gave generously retired. Others lost the breadwinner. I was beginning to get discouraged and constantly wondered what the solution could be. My son Daniel, my son-in-law Michael and I met frequently for brainstorming sessions, hoping to find a solution. During these sessions, we discovered two trends:

First, a *trend of attrition* had become apparent that was not true in our first twenty years. Still, after being well into the new century, for some reason which we cannot ascertain, it seemed that those who were interested in missions became more interested. Those who had only a marginal interest fell away. In recent years, however, we have seen consistent growth in the number of sponsors but a significant increase in the average amount given by existing sponsors. While this is a blessing to be sure, we knew it would not seal the ever-expanding cracks in our program.

Second, we noticed an *economic trend*. Seemingly, the better the economy, the less likely a sponsor is to take on another preacher; the worse the economy, the more willing they are to do so. This seems strangely backward, but it is our reality.

The unwillingness of supporters to take on another preacher in the place of the one who passed away or no longer needed help stunted our ability to grow in the number of preachers we could support because we were continually trying to catch up. We were in effect taking three steps forward and two steps back. Some months it was more like three steps forward and four steps back. For example, about a decade ago, the 120+ preachers we supported in Vietnam wrote us a wonderful letter, thanking us for our twenty years of help and then said that they no longer needed it as their churches had grown and their economy had improved; thus, they asked us to give their support to other preachers in other lands who needed it. When we contacted their sponsors with their message of gratitude and a suggestion to transfer their help to others, about 40 percent chose not to do so; thus, in one day, we lost 120+ preachers and about 50 sponsors. Several months later, the same thing happened with another group of about 40 preachers in Cambodia.

We don't give salaries to these preachers; we give them subsidies because we do not want to remove the national churches' responsibility to take care of their own. However, increasing the number of preachers we can help and thereby the number of souls saved, churches started, and more preachers trained is entirely dependent on the number of sponsorships we acquire and the amount of funding we receive.

But what if it wasn't? What if losing one sponsor did not mean losing a preacher? And what if losing one preacher did not have to result in a 40 to 60 percent chance of losing the sponsor? And while we're at it, what if money grew on trees, and what if milkshakes didn't make you fat? Any of these would make me happy; all of them would probably kill me with glee. But what if I could get two of them—the two that are most important?

I am happy to say that we have found a way to break the link between limiting the number of preachers equaling the number of sponsors. As a result, we are growing again—faster than ever before, and the stats prove it. We discovered this a few years back when Daniel and Michael took over the ministry's administration and tweaked my 30-year-old ministry plan. Results-wise, it blew the roof off our ministry. We decided that rather than announcing it, we would first test the concept for several years to be sure it worked. We did so by supporting a group of new preachers using our old "undesignated preacher fund." In other words, we used funds given to help any preacher in need, rather than being targeted for a specific preacher. The idea worked so well that we took it to the next level.

We began to "pool" all the funds that came in for the preachers, whether regular monthly sponsorships, special offerings, or whatever, dispersing them equally to all the preachers on our support list. In doing this, *we were careful to make sure that all sponsored preachers always received their full designated funds.* At the same time, the surplus would go to benefit massive numbers of unsponsored preachers.

Finally, after several years of testing and getting the kinks out, we officially launched our "Great Commission Fund." Suddenly, anyone and everyone could support a national church planter, whether they want to give $50 monthly as sponsors do or $10 occasionally when they can afford it. We disperse the funds among as many preachers as possible. Some will get a little, some more, depending on their need and local economy, *while assuring that any sponsored preacher will still receive his full designated amount.* And the really good thing is, there is no reason for anyone to stop their support if their preacher dies, etc.; their support goes into a fund to help multiple preachers and not to an individual. (Of course, a sponsor can stop giving at any time.) Time has proven that this method is far more successful and fruitful than the individual sponsorship method. We still allow sponsors to choose a specific preacher to personally support as we always have (traditionally called *Sponsorship*). Still, we encourage them to give to The Great Commission Fund instead (which we call *Partnership*).

Eliminating the Conundrum

How This Affects Those Who Support the Great Commission Fund:

- The Great Commission Fund (GCF) is designed expressly for those who are not so concerned about whom they help as they are about the following:

    1) Helping effectively
    2) How many more church planters they can help

- It allows them to have greater accountability. Rather than receive a two-page accountability report from one preacher every three months (Sponsorship), you receive a multipage report every month or two with photos and ministry details (Partnership) from a random preacher your funds helped (combined with that of others).

- This program alleviates the need for a specific report to a specific sponsor. Each report will be from a different preacher in India or Guatemala, Cambodia, Ukraine, Kenya, or the Middle East, etc. Every person who gives to the Great Commission Fund will receive the same monthly report by email, creating a community of missions-minded people across America who will learn about the same preacher by his incredible testimony. Then each month, you'll learn about other men, ministries, cultures, prayer requests, and opportunities. Imagine sharing this information with your children around your dinner table or at your Bible study. We believe this will not only give you a better understanding of how effectively your funds are being used but will also open your mind and heart to pray more fervently for thousands of God's servants everywhere.

- As for accountability, the Great Commission Fund offers you the opportunity to help more preachers with more results and to receive two to three times more accountability reports. Each report contains photos and explanations of cultural, geographical, legal, and traditional issues that you are not aware of, which they deal with daily. Some of these reports will come directly to you by email, while in each issue of our quarterly Progress Report, we will place others, hoping to encourage more to join with us by supporting the Great Commission Fund.

- It is affordable. Over the years, I have met hundreds of people who wanted to help a church planter but could not afford the sponsorship of $50 a month. Now anyone can join us and help fulfill the Great Commission in our lifetime. Can you imagine the impact we will make together? To participate, please contact us online or send your gift to Final Frontiers, designated for the Great Commission Fund.

How This Will Affect All Our National Church Planters:

- It expands the numbers we can fund. While we continue to send all *sponsored* men their regular support, the balance of funds from the GCF will be sent to the directors, allowing them to help their preachers as needed. Many of the men only need $10, so why give them $50? Others need $75, so why restrict them to only $50?

- The GCF gives flexibility to the amount we give them. A church planter in a city requires more funding than one in the country who can grow some of his food. A man with five children needs less than a single man, etc. The funds are dispersed by the national director in charge on the ground who knows each man's needs. In the past, we found that some young men had two or three sponsors while other men, older and more experienced, had one or none. This didn't make sense and could quickly breed discontent in that local fellowship. With the GCF, this disparity is no longer an issue.

- It also expands other ways to help them. It allows the preachers to target projects and needs that enhance church growth and survival.

Some men only need support for a project or a particular need. They don't need personal support. The GCF allows him to meet that need and help his men without waiting for an unnecessary sponsorship.

Pastor Solomon is one of our directors in India. Upon learning about the Great Commission Fund, he wrote,

> *I agree with your idea to empower the national director. Now I can exercise discretion to channel the resources to the preachers and also to be able to meet some unforeseen expenses in the area of ministry expansion. This will be very fruitful. Yes, brother, we can sometimes not expand and meet with new churches that we planted though they need regular visits. This is only because we do not have funds for petrol. Our typical preachers are finding it hard to do so because the number of churches under them is spreading out as we preach in more villages. In such cases, we need to deploy new workers to sustain the infant churches. Now we will be able to plug this gap. Once again, your plan is very beneficial."*

Solomon was expressing how glad he is to support more of his men who have been waiting for sponsorship for years—and having gasoline to visit the churches, funds to purchase Bibles for the converts, and expand their ministries.

So then, you have the answer to this final conundrum. Now will you join us in supporting more national church planters and enabling them with funds to enhance and expand their works? I hope you will whether by Sponsorship or Partnership.

Closing Words

When I wrote *The Great Omission* in 2010, I was 55 years old. I truly believed that we could fulfill the Great Commission in my lifetime. I was amazed over the following decade to hear so many missionaries, pastors, and laypeople express their similar concerns about the state of the modern missions movement and were pleased that I had been able to give their voices and views some volume and exposure.

Thousands of copies have been sold or donated to interested people, to foreign Bible institutes and Bible colleges in America. Since then, I have been contacted by many young missionaries telling me that reading the book had changed their lives and ministry. Older missionaries expressed gratitude that someone had finally revealed the weaknesses of the modern missionary movement. Several Bible college presidents responded that they would like their missionary students, and all their students, to spend a month or a semester with me on a mission field, attainting firsthand exposure to our methods. I welcome that. *The Great Omission* is already in Spanish, and it is currently being translated into at least three languages in India. The more missionaries we can train globally to be church planters, the sooner we will complete the task given to us.

My burning desire is to mentor young men and ladies worldwide as the apostles Paul and Barnabas did, day by day, on the field and outside of the classroom.

But now it is the end of 2020, and I am 65 years old. I am often asked if I will write a sequel to *The Great Omission*, but that was not the book's purpose. Instead, I wanted to address serious questions that have been asked in emails, in churches, during "mission think tanks," and from those traveling with me on our *Visionary Trips*. I took these tough, debatable questions and tried to formulate answers based on Scripture, logic, and experience. I hope I have succeeded.

If the content of this book has blessed you, I encourage you to keep learning. Visit our website, www.FinalFrontiers.world, and register to receive our email alerts and *The Progress Report*, our free, quarterly magazine. I would also encourage you to join me for a one-week or longer *Visionary Trip*. I host these throughout the summers in Honduras but continuously travel through the year around the world, never traveling alone.

Currently, I am working on a 50-week video class that will be available through our website. Each session will be about 15 minutes long and end with an online test, allowing you to earn a certificate. All we do is part of our ongoing effort to teach this generation and those who follow the scriptural teachings of what I call a "biblical missionary."

To Pastors:

Thank you for all you do to further the cause of Christ and to support missions. You are incredible. I know that I have written many things that some of you have never heard before and never considered. I pray they will help you as a pastor and give you a greater understanding of what missions really is, not what you have been told it is. And that you will be encouraged to make changes in your policies that can affect the world.

For that purpose, I am currently writing a manual for pastors on developing and maintaining a mission's program. I want your church to excel in missions beyond your imagination. I am at your service to talk or to teach if you so desire.

To Those Who Are Missionaries (Foreign and Nationals) and to Those Who Want to Be:

I am one of you, though perhaps an elder brother. I pray you to learn from what I have discovered in God's Word and from what I have experienced in nearly four decades of missionary service. Your task is incredible.

Always remember that God called you and chose you from among all His servants. You are not a missionary; you are a **MISSIONARY**; and as Quick Draw McGraw was famous for saying, "And don't you forget it." (You young guys can Google it.) Never think lowly of the calling God has given you. It is your high calling in and for Christ.

If you feel I can help you, please contact me. As long as I live, I live to serve Christ by serving you.

– Jon Nelms, *Missionary*
jnelms@finalfrontiers.org

About the Author

Jon Nelms

After being called to missions at age eleven, Jon was mentored by several men for the next nineteen years. During that time, he learned soul winning, street preaching, bus ministry, youth ministry, served in various pastoral capacities, and helped plant a church in the NYC area.

In 1986 God led Jon to meet several national preachers in northern Thailand, and he discovered that he could help support them as missionaries to their own people for a fraction of the support he needed. Final Frontiers was born from that discovery.

Thirty-five years later, the ministry has a network of over 28,000 church planters in nearly ninety countries. These men collectively have planted nearly 400,000 house churches (as of 2020). More than fourteen million conversions have been recorded, and the typical Sunday worship attendance for these churches exceeds forty million.

Jon is married to Nolin and has two children, Daniel and Sara, married to Nolvia and Michael. He has six grandchildren, Valentina, Jennifer, Elizabeth, Colin, Sean, and Emma.

ACKNOWLEDGMENTS

LET ME START by recognizing the scores of missionaries, pastors, and national preachers who have stretched my mind by posing the issues discussed in this book. Like me, you have to live with these often unconfronted conundrums, fearing that your solution may cause you the loss of support and even relationships. I have accumulated enough experience and years that such concerns no longer hinder me. Still, I would not have arrived where I am without both your ministry and mental stimulation. So, thank you all for blessing me with your concerns, opinions, and instruction.

I so greatly appreciate the work of the editor, Linda Stubblefield, who has patiently corrected my errors and made my words and thoughts more palatable. As I reviewed her "suggestions" in my draft, I was constantly amazed at how she seemed to grasp better what I was trying to convey than I did. Truthfully, I put some thoughts on the pages, but she wrote the book. I could have done it without her, but you wouldn't have had a clue of what I was trying to say.

Next, my heartiest gratitude goes to Heather Black. No matter what tentative designs I may have for a cover, her suggestion always blows them away. Somehow she takes the thrust and thoughts of the content and makes a cover that at one glance says it all. Heather is the artist of the proverbial picture that is worth a thousand words. Her skill and professionalism amaze me. (www.heatherblack.studio)

Finally, I want to acknowledge you, the reader, who has to labor through the dark and twisted labyrinth of my thoughts. I hope to provide you with the sword you need to slay your conundrums. Thank you for honoring me with your reading and blessing others with a copy.

For additional copies of *Great Comission Conundrums*, visit
www.TheGreatOmission.com

ABOUT
The Great Omission

IN HIS BOOK, *The Great Omission*, Missionary Jon Nelms "tells it like it is" by exposing the failures in missions and the reasons behind them as he leads the reader to logical, biblical, and proven solutions, that, if followed, will allow this to be the first generation to fulfill the Lord's Great Commission since it was assigned some 2,000 years ago. Drawing from personal stories gleaned from his 24 years of missionary work around the world, Jon will stir, motivate, and may even upset you. In doing so, he will challenge your conceptions and lead you to consider God's plans and methods that have been laid aside to perpetuate the unsuccessful, unbiblical methods that have handicapped missionaries for centuries. It is not likely that you can even get past the preface without your concept of missions being both challenged and changed.

For your copy
of *The Great Omission*, visit
www.TheGreatOmission.com

www.ingramcontent.com/pod-product-compliance
Lightning Source LLC
LaVergne TN
LVHW020539100826
845148LV00010B/1529

* 9 7 8 1 7 3 6 9 5 7 4 0 0 *